What Your Colleagues Are

"Lessons and Units for Closer Reading reassures teachers like me to the same degree that it instructs. It is no accident that Nancy uses words like *coherence, connections,* and *synergy* in her opening pages. Through her unit and lesson design, she brings that coherence to us in incremental, practical ways—ways that new and experienced teachers can easily absorb into their teaching practices. Nancy is giving us what we *want:* specific lesson ideas based on a solid framework that uses children's literature, but it is actually what we *need,* too."

—TANNY MCGREGOR, Education Consultant
and Author of *Comprehension Connections*

"In her new book, *Lessons and Units for Closer Reading,* Nancy Boyles offers teachers what they ask for and need the most—practical, useable strategies and examples in the form of actual close reading lessons—32 to be exact—along with 20 videos accessible through QR codes that show how to implement these close reading lessons and related strategies. What a treasure trove of modeling and guidance for teachers! As a former elementary educator myself, how I wish I had had this powerful resource to help me become a better teacher of reading."

—LARRY AINSWORTH, Education Consultant and
Coauthor of *Common Formative Assessments 2.0*

"The Common Core Standards call for students to be able to read texts closely to make meaning and for students to build knowledge systematically (CCSS for ELA, p. 33, 2010). This book provides a vivid picture of instruction that supports this kind of learning. Boyles' text speaks to the teacher who has been grappling with how to develop units and strategically integrate close reading lessons, providing clarity and inspiration. This is a must-have text for educators and will remain a go-to resource in my professional library for many years to come."

—SUNDAY CUMMINS, PhD, Literacy Consultant and
Author of *Close Reading of Informational Texts*

"Now you understand what close reading is, but you need the nitty-gritty. Presto, Nancy Boyles delivers eight stellar units of study. Her lessons are practical; the text-dependent questions for all those marvelous picture books save you a few weeks of arduous planning. But what I admire most of all? The gallery of student work she's gathered, with her commentary about strengths, needs, next steps. It's a rare window into another practitioner's thinking about what constitutes higher-level reading and writing work. Everybody's talking about it, but no one has done such a good job showing it until now."

—LESLIE BLAUMAN, Teacher, Education Consultant, and
Author of *The Common Core Companion: Booster Lessons, Grades 3–5*

"Everywhere you turn, headlines call for students to read with *depth* and *rigor.* But few teachers get the support they need to bring this about for 25+ students each and every school day. Nancy Boyles' new book gives them that 'how-to,' and it's remarkable. She provides eight units of study [plus] a valuable planning guide that shows them how to design their own units with a depth that motivates and engages students. Once teachers ace the planning process, the day-to-day implementation of the units becomes easier. I predict that this book will become teachers' favorite resource for unit design."

—LAURA ROBB, Education Consultant and
Author of *Vocabulary Is Comprehension*

For Lily, my dog, who enriches my life in countless ways

For Ron, my husband—for continuing to love me even though I flunked retirement

LESSONS & UNITS
FOR
Closer
Reading

Ready-to-Go Resources
and Planning Tools Galore

NANCY
BOYLES

FOREWORD BY
TANNY MCGREGOR

resources.corwin.com/boyleslessons

FOR INFORMATION:

Corwin
A SAGE Company
2455 Teller Road
Thousand Oaks, California 91320
(800) 233-9936
www.corwin.com

SAGE Publications Ltd.
1 Oliver's Yard
55 City Road
London EC1Y 1SP
United Kingdom

SAGE Publications India Pvt. Ltd.
B 1/I 1 Mohan Cooperative Industrial Area
Mathura Road, New Delhi 110 044
India

SAGE Publications Asia-Pacific Pte. Ltd.
3 Church Street
#10-04 Samsung Hub
Singapore 049483

Publisher: Lisa Luedeke
Development Editor: Wendy Murray
Editorial Development Manager: Julie Nemer
Editorial Assistant: Emeli Warren
Production Editor: Melanie Birdsall
Copy Editor: Patrice Sutton
Typesetter: C&M Digitals (P) Ltd.
Proofreader: Susan Schon
Cover Designer: Rose Storey
Interior Designer: Scott Van Atta
Director of Marketing Strategy: Maura Sullivan

Copyright © 2015 by Corwin

Note From the Publisher

The authors have provided video and web content throughout the book which is available to you through QR Codes. To read a QR Code, you must have a smartphone or tablet with a camera. We recommend that you download a QR Code reader app that is made specifically for your phone or tablet brand.

QR Codes may provide access to videos and/or websites that are not maintained, sponsored, endorsed, or controlled by Corwin. Your use of these third-party websites will be subject to the terms and conditions posted on such websites. Corwin takes no responsibility and assumes no liability for your use of any third-party website. Corwin does not approve, sponsor, endorse, verify, or certify information available at any third-party video or website.

Printed in the United States of America

A catalog record of this book is available from the Library of Congress.

ISBN: 978-1-4833-7567-0

This book is printed on acid-free paper.

15 16 17 18 19 10 9 8 7 6 5 4 3 2 1

Photo courtesy of Rick Harrington Photography

Contents

THE UNITS AND LESSONS

THE END OF THE STORY: REFLECTING ON STUDENT WORK   293

APPENDICES, VIDEO CLIPS, AND REFLECTION QUESTIONS
On the companion website at resources.corwin.com/boyleslessons

20 exclusive videos are linked to QR codes throughout the book.

For bonus classroom footage and a Q&A with Nancy Boyles, visit the companion website.

To read a QR Code, you must have a smartphone or tablet with a camera. We recommend that you download a QR Code reader app that is made specifically for your phone or tablet brand.

Visit the companion website at
resources.corwin.com/boyleslessons
for appendices, videos, templates, and professional
development and other resources.

Foreword

Tanny McGregor

No doubt about it, I'm a middle-aged teacher. Like most teachers around my age, I often look back at education and think about how things have changed. Take picture books, for example. I remember how in the 1980s finding a great picture book would energize my spirit and serve as the foundation for solid instruction in my classroom. I could cross the curriculum with a picture book. I could integrate the arts, stimulate meaningful conversation, and give my students yet another opportunity to love reading a little bit more. I recall countless conversations with colleagues about books and authors, about units and ideas. In the hallway, the parking lot, and even in the ladies room, we talked about picture books.

It sure seems like things have changed. One of my teaching partners recently said to me wistfully, "Remember when we used to get together and talk about books?" The teachers I know feel so bogged down with mandates, assessments, and increasing workloads that conversations about books seem a luxury, something from a gilded age of teaching and learning that has slipped into the past. Many of the topics that occupy our thought life now seem to drain our energy not charge it. If we are not careful, we might wake up one day to realize our instruction has become about toeing the line rather than teaching the child, and bland, like our lives would become without books.

It does not have to be this way. Even with changing standards and a restless political atmosphere, meaningful instruction can still hold its own . . . and picture books can actually work to unite all of the disparate instructional pieces. Yes, some things have changed. But some things will always stay the same: we need picture books. They can help us make meaning out of the chaos in our lives, and, most important of all, books bring a child into an everlasting relationship with reading.

So it was serendipity that I received the advanced proof for *Lessons and Units for Closer Reading* because Nancy Boyles understands. She knows how so much around us has changed. She recognizes the current state of affairs, but holds on tightly to what matters in the classroom. In this book, Nancy takes what some think of as "new" instructional terms and demands, like rigorous standards, complex text, and close reading, and shows how these practices can live in harmony with beautiful, engaging picture books. She shows us that close, attentive reading of an author and illustrator's meaning is, to quote the Talking Heads, same as it ever was. So this book reassures teachers like me to the same degree that it instructs.

It is no accident that Nancy uses words like *coherence, connections,* and *synergy* in her opening pages. Through her unit and lesson design, she brings that coherence to us in incremental, practical ways— ways that new and experienced teachers can easily absorb into their teaching practices. Nancy is giving us what we *want*: specific lesson ideas based on a solid framework that uses children's literature, but it is actually what we *need*, too. We need to be reminded that the rigor and cognitive demand that some think of as 21st century instruction can meld with the beauty and simplicity of words and pictures . . . in books made for children.

Acknowledgments

I am grateful for the opportunity to again be part of the Corwin family and for the always spot-on support of Corwin Literacy's Three Musketeers—

> Lisa Luedeke, publisher—for her wisdom and capacity to see the Big Picture, and especially for taking on the Nancy Boyles challenge, Round 2

> Wendy Murray, editor—for her focus on clarity, her vision for all a book can be, and her talent to make it happen

> Maura Sullivan, marketing wizard—for her creativity, passion, and enthusiasm for product development and for working her magic so, well . . . magically

I appreciate as well all the help from Emeli Warren, Corwin Editorial Assistant—for the endless hours she spent tracking down permissions from publishers and release forms for students. Thanks for being so organized and efficient! Thanks also to Corwin Production Editor Melanie Birdsall for her patience and perseverance in making sure the layout of *Lessons and Units* was just right! (I'm sure she thought this was her full-time job for a while.)

I want to acknowledge, too, the literacy leaders in whose districts I've spent much time during the last few years, exploring with them and their teachers the complexities of close reading through curriculum development and direct work in classrooms: Learning alongside all of you has made this close reading journey a wonder-filled adventure (with a few laughs along the way): Elaine Parsons and Imma Canelli from New Haven; Patti Darragh, Tracy Wootton, and Sara Querfeld from North Branford; Jen Tapia from East Aurora; Sue Perrone from Meriden; Terry Buckingham from Trumbull; Dena Mortensen from Waterbury; and Laura Miller from RSU 20.

And then there are the teachers who stepped up to teach close reading lessons and provide student work samples for this book: Gina Kotsaftis, Brianne Forcucci, and Kathy Troccolo—Naugatuck; Connecticut; Erin Hoppe and Kate Simons—Greenland, New Hampshire; and Jeanne Savoia—North Haven, Connecticut.

And the authors (including one nine year old) who provided short, nonfiction texts: Bob Crelin; Robert Burleigh; Stephanie Young; and Sierra.

A shout out as well to the students from John Barry School, Meriden, Connecticut, whose beautiful faces smile forth from the photos in this book, courtesy of Rick Harrington Photography.

And finally, immeasurable gratitude to Jennifer Kruge, principal of Salem School in Naugatuck, Connecticut, and her literacy coach Gina Kotsaftis, for all they did to make this book's accompanying videos a reality, and to the Salem teachers who engaged in this work with us: Kathy Troccolo, Kris DiMaio, and Patrick Norris. I had the pleasure of working with the best-ever class of fourth graders whose readiness to learn was apparent from the first minute of the first lesson. BIG thank you to producer Kevin Carlson of Seed Multimedia and his team for making our Hollywood experience so much fun for us all, and to Barb De Hart, Corwin Senior Manager Multimedia Product Development, and Wendy Murray, Editor, for journeying all the way to Connecticut from their individual corners of the universe to oversee this project. What an honor to bring close reading to life through this celebration of technology and the collaboration of so many capable and dedicated colleagues.

Photo courtesy of Rick Harrington Photography

A Guide to Using the Lessons and Units

Welcome to *Lessons and Units for Closer Reading*. As I was drafting it, I nicknamed it "the sequel" because it picks up where my previous book left off. I wrote this book in response to what teachers who had read my previous book begged to have next: close reading lessons. The first book, *Closer Reading, Grades 3–6*, explains the *why*, the *what*, and the *how* of this instructional practice. What else could teachers possibly want or need?

"We want *names*," they told me, "titles of books well suited to close reading."

"We want *lessons*," they said. "We *do* understand what close reading is now, and we're excited about trying it in our classrooms, but our administrators want it in place *yesterday*; we need help. We need a book we can use to get us started."

Ah, I got it: *Use*.

So this is not a book just to *read*. This is a book to use. I hope you will use the thirty-two lessons included, all embedded into eight easy-to-implement units. And be sure to also use the Quick Response (QR) codes that provide access to video clips showing a close reading lesson and follow-up instruction.

In each unit, the close reading lessons connect, and this coherence helps students learn.

Photo courtesy of Rick Harrington Photography

Before we delve into the units, let's take a quick tour of the *whys* and *hows* of their curriculum design so that you may use them effectively—and eventually create units of your own.

The Goal: Providing the Right Kind of Help

In a teacher's world, the bottom line is always *time* and *resources*—not because teachers are unwilling to spend time outside of their school day gathering materials, planning lessons, and collecting and interpreting data but because there simply aren't enough hours to get all of this done *and* get enough sleep to show up the next day with two shoes that actually match. (Yes, I'm speaking from experience here.) So when teachers began to sound the alarm for close reading lessons based on the model I presented in *Closer Reading*, I wanted to help by giving them what they needed—but I also knew the lessons alone weren't quite enough, and here's why.

In our frenzy to implement close reading almost instantaneously, there seems to be randomness happening. I visit many elementary classrooms where teachers pull their class together on a rug and teach a nice close reading lesson around a complex picture book, poem, article, or excerpt from a longer text. But when I ask teachers why they chose that *particular* text, and why *now*, they often are at a loss for words. "Isn't it enough that I found this complex text and taught this virtuoso close reading lesson?" their expression seems to ask.

Learning Pathways, Units, and Anchor Texts

Learning Pathway	Unit Focus	Book 1	Book 2	Book 3	Book 4
Studying a concept	Leadership	*Weslandia* by Paul Fleischman	*Night Flight: Amelia Earhart Crosses the Atlantic* by Robert Burleigh	*Testing the Ice: A True Story About Jackie Robinson* by Sharon Robinson	*Nelson Mandela* by Kadir Nelson
Studying a person	Abraham Lincoln	*Honest Abe* by Edith Kunhardt	*Looking at Lincoln* by Maira Kalman	*Abraham Lincoln Comes Home* by Robert Burleigh	*Abe's Honest Words: The Life of Abraham Lincoln* by Doreen Rappaport
Studying a topic	The Moon	*Faces of the Moon* by Bob Crelin	*Thirteen Moons on Turtle's Back* by Joseph Bruchac	*Moonshot: The Flight of Apollo 11* by Brian Floca	*The Man in the Moon (The Guardians of Childhood)* by William Joyce
Studying a genre	Fairy Tales	*The Princess and the Pizza* by Mary Jane Ausch and Herm Ausch	*The Cowboy and the Black-Eyed Pea* by Tony Johnston	*Extra! Extra!: Fairy-Tale News From Hidden Forest* by Alma Flor Ada	*Once Upon a Cool Motorcycle Dude* by Kevin O'Malley
Studying an author	Robert Burleigh	*Home Run: The Story of Babe Ruth* by Robert Burleigh	*Flight: The Journey of Charles Lindbergh* by Robert Burleigh	*Look Up! Henrietta Leavitt, Pioneering Woman Astronomer* by Robert Burleigh	*Tiger of the Snows: Tenzing Norgay: The Boy Whose Dream Was Everest* by Robert Burleigh
Studying a time in history	Slavery	*Minty: A Story of Young Harriet Tubman* by Alan Schroeder	*Sojourner Truth's Step-Stomp Stride* by Andrea Pinkney	*Now Let Me Fly: The Story of a Slave Family* by Dolores Johnson	*Up the Learning Tree* by Marcia Vaughan
Studying a theme	A (person's) home is special for many reasons	*Let's Go Home: The Wonderful Things About a House* by Cynthia Rylant	*Going Home* by Eve Bunting	*A Thirst for Home* by Christine Ieronimo	*On This Spot: An Expedition Back Through Time* by Susan Goodman
Studying a current issue	The importance of clean water	*A River Ran Wild* by Lynne Cherry	*A Life Like Mine* A DK/Unicef Publication	*One Well: The Story of Water on Earth* by Rochelle Strauss	*The Boy Who Harnessed the Wind* by William Kamkwamba and Bryan Mealer

Well, yes—and no. Plunging into a sophisticated text with the intellectual rigor required for close reading is a worthy start. Teachers recognize such instruction as purposeful and focused. But do their students recognize the purpose? Do they see how the close reading skills they are honing today will work together for some important outcome? If we want to obtain the most benefit from our close reading instruction, we'll need to help students connect the dots.

Teaching for Coherence: Why Moving From Stand-Alone Lessons to Units of Study Matters

Connecting the dots means we'll need to do a few things differently, and I'll explain them each briefly here, but what will be music to teachers' ears is that each of these dot-connecting moves is embedded in all the lessons in this book.

The first thing we need to do is show intermediate grade students how the texts we use to teach them *about* close reading *also* teach them about important themes, topics, and other areas of focus. As we engage our students with these texts, for maximum motivation, we'll also need to show that this content has *coherence*, "a logical, orderly, and aesthetically consistent relationship of parts" (Coherence, n.d.).

Education researchers have long noted that coherence is motivating. Bruner's spiral curriculum (1960, p. 13) recognized the benefits of revisiting a focus area repeatedly through a sequence of instruction that moves systematically toward greater complexity, each new level building on knowledge that preceded it. More recently, Guthrie maintained that students become more motivated with "an ample supply of interesting texts that are relevant to the learning and knowledge goals being studied" (n.d., "Interesting Texts for Instruction" section). And the Common Core's three anchor standards for reading related to "Integration of Knowledge and Ideas" sections also highlight the importance of connecting multiple texts (National Governors Association [NGA] Center for Best Practices and Council of Chief State School Officers [CCSSO], 2014). So how can we achieve this coherence and thus build young students' motivation to read closely? We can do it by building units of study.

For starters, a unit is a "package" of literary and informational texts that all fit together in some way. That fitting together (or coherence) is the key ingredient. The texts might fit together around a concept or theme, a topic, an author, a genre, a current issue, or any other generalization. In this way, we teach with intention, and our students benefit. Why? Because they experience the unfolding of our teaching as a coherent sequence of interactions around texts and ideas. Pursuing units of study is a less haphazard, harried way to teach and learn.

The How-To's of Teaching With Coherence

The texts used for lessons in this book were selected not just because they are compelling stories or rich informational sources but also because each one supports intentional teaching—instruction about an essential idea or understanding that intermediate grade students need to know deeply as they mature academically. Perhaps even more significant is the synergy created by studying several books together. That is why these particular texts have been integrated into units—they each have enough "heft" to merit a few weeks of examination when studied together. Now we just need to decide what kind of "great texts" will best meet our needs.

Picture books have phenomenal depth, and their compactness makes them perfect for teaching. Don't let anyone tell you kids think they're "babyish." Many of the best picture books can't even be appreciated by very young readers.

Photo courtesy of Rick Harrington Photography

Picture Books as Mentor Texts

Above all, let's make sure that our close reading lessons are planned around texts that matter. If we're going to spend all this time on close reading, at the end of the day, students should know not just how close reading works and how to plumb the depths of a text for meaning, but also they should have learned something useful, felt inspired, or perhaps even grown intellectually or emotionally. We should be able to answer the question: close reading for *what*? For this, I turn to picture books.

Bite-Size Complexity. I have a library chock-full of picture books that offer plenty of complexity. As I turn their beautifully illustrated pages, I am amazed by the sophisticated topics they cover and important themes they embrace, the way characters and problems are developed so robustly, the eloquent language, and the varied ways authors present their stories and information. Students meet virtual friends and travel to places that could be as close as their own backyard or as far flung as a distant continent or planet. Picture books offer all the complexities we seek—typically in a mere thirty-two pages.

Visual Support for Background Knowledge. With the support of illustrations and other graphics, these texts build the background knowledge that students often lack when they come to a complex text, especially one related to an informational topic. Open nearly any informational picture book to see what I mean: "Across its frozen seas, tiny algae begin to bloom on the underside of ice" (Dowson, 2011, p. 8). Minus a trip to the Arctic, your students (and perhaps even you) may not readily comprehend this sentence. But if you glance at the picture on page 8 of *North: The Amazing Story of Arctic Migration,* written by Nick Dowson and illustrated by Patrick Benson, you will immediately gain the knowledge you need to understand it. That visualization factor is what makes close reading come alive with picture books.

Small but Mighty Mentor Texts. "But kids can't mark up picture books. I thought close reading required marking up a text?" I sometimes hear this concern from teachers who are initially wary about the use of picture books for close reading. I wholeheartedly support underlining important parts of a text, writing margin notes, coding key passages, and so forth. And, of course, students should have the opportunity to do this regularly as they process complex text. First, though, they need to understand what kinds of passages deserve highlighting. (We've all had the experience of handing students a highlighter and then having a "yellow page" returned to us; wasn't *everything* important?)

Before kids can mark a text meaningfully, they need a better sense of what to mark. Our text-dependent questions (TDQs) and modeling of deep thinking and students' subsequent practice—guided by us—will teach them how to approach a text with the rigor required by close reading.

Offer a Communal Experience of the Text. Because of their brevity relative to a chapter book, picture books provide a chance to read aloud a complete work in the space of a half hour. This isn't just time efficient, it is what creates a strong community of readers. Having a single text for the Initial Close Reading Lesson means all eyes are focused on the same images and words simultaneously. We build community as we build understanding of content and craft. When you return to a text for subsequent close reads is when you'll want additional copies of your picture book so students can apply what they've learned more independently.

Paperbacks for Pairs and Small Groups. If you are like me, you have a stash of favorite picture books in hard cover. These are the ones I want to drive home in a Brink truck at the end of the school year; that's how much I cherish them. But for the follow-up lessons using the featured picture book text, bring on the paperbacks if they are available for your selected titles! And the good news is, it doesn't mean we need a book for each child. Since we want much more student collaboration in this era of new standards, a *few* copies of your book suffice so that students can work in small groups, each group with its own text and pack of sticky notes, so they can now "mark up" the text and track their thinking.

Fair Game for Independent Reading. Remember, too, that close reading should also be part of intermediate grade students' small group instruction and independent reading—where having their own copy of developmentally appropriate texts will be essential for their progress as close readers. Beyond the *why* of using picture books, there's the *how*. I provide additional details about what gets taught in an initial close reading lesson and in the lessons that follow later in this guide, in Steps 6 and 7.

Make Text-to-Text Connections Feasible. Using picture books as mentor texts helps you plan rich units, with built-in pathways for students to compare and contrast one book to another. The key to success in building coherence through units anchored by picture books is the quality of the connections you can make between these wonderful, vibrant texts. We're not just using multiple texts but also exploring meaningful relationships, identifying significant points of comparison, and integrating ideas—all the while, attending to content standards.

Bring About Coherence. Although the Common Core doesn't ask us to identify a greater goal for close reading than simply to unlock complex text, I hope that as teachers we hold ourselves and our students to higher standards—close reading that builds not just skills and strategies but relevance, respect, and responsibility as well. This will not likely happen with sporadic close reading lessons that bounce from here to there, from one topic to another. This will happen with texts and lessons that connect to each other and to children's lives. So here's my new mission: I want to support teachers by providing these connected lessons. I offer eight units to achieve this goal.

The Secret Weapon of This Book's Units: Learning Pathways

The units in this book are unique. They push beyond the traditional notion of a study of a specific theme, such as *overcoming challenges,* or a topic like *animal life in Antarctica,* because they offer students pathways *for learning how to learn*—about topics, about themes, and about other areas of study that students will encounter throughout their academic lives. So, for example, instead of just providing a unit on *fairy tales,* in this book, I show you how to design and deliver units that engage students in the ways of thinking involved in studying *any* genre, of which fairy tales is a subset. Here are the learning pathways covered in this book:

- How to study a concept
- How to study a person
- How to study a topic

- How to study a genre

- How to study an author

- How to study a time in history

- How to study a theme

- How to study a current issue

When we teach by unit, we often say we are teaching *thematically*. Technically, I don't think that is accurate. A genre is not a "theme." An author study is not a "theme." It's relatively easy to recognize these distinctions in some cases, more difficult in others. Three of the most troublesome terms in this regard are *concept, topic,* and *theme*. Here's how I differentiate them.

- I view a *topic* as something fairly concrete that you can name in a word or a short phrase: the Moon, penguins, the rain forest. You can touch something that's a topic, or go there, or at least identify some physical characteristics. Social studies and science text books tend to be organized topically.

- I regard a *concept* as a general category, a bit like a topic because it can be described in a single word or short phrase—but it is more abstract. Some examples might be leadership, friendship, determination, or multiculturalism. You can't put your arms around a concept and hug it. But you can describe it and examine it from different angles.

- I reserve the term *theme*, or *main idea*, to mean something particular about a topic or concept: Determination is important to achieving personal goals; preserving the rain forest means protecting plant and animal life; home is special for many reasons. A theme is never a single word but further defines the territory: not just friendship (which is a concept), *but friends are loyal to each other;* or *you may find friends in unlikely places.*

There are surely more areas of study than the ones included in this book, but these should give intermediate grade students a solid foundation on which to build. The order isn't important. Feel free to teach these units in a sequence that works best for you and your students. Remember, too, that these units have been written for a range of grades. If you are teaching Grade 5 or 6, you may want to modify them to add even more rigor. For third and fourth grades, feel free to reduce the level of challenge if necessary.

Also, think about other units you would like to teach beyond the ones provided in this book. Which ones could be organized by theme? By concept? By historical period? By some other area of study? To appraise the breadth of your unit teaching and to add units for a more robust curriculum, use the chart Teaching Units According to Learning Pathways.

Teaching Units According to Learning Pathways

	Unit Title	Unit Title	Unit Title	Unit Title
How to study a concept				
How to study a person				
How to study a topic				
How to study a genre				
How to study an author				
How to study a time in history				
How to study a theme				
How to study a current issue				

One of my goals for this book is to debunk the myth that close reading is old-style teaching, with kids in rows striving to have the "right" answer about a text. Close reading is about getting *students* to do the thinking—not the teacher.

Photo courtesy of Rick Harrington Photography

How Coherence Leads to Critical Thinking

Okay, we've established that well-chosen learning pathways, ace books, and carefully planned lessons all bring about a coherence of curriculum that, much like a beautifully organized workroom, provides the space in which students can more easily see the tools to use and the patterns of content and ideas we want them to understand. It's like we've done everything we can to set students up for the high-level analytical thinking about texts we want to hear through discussion and read on the page when they write about their learning. But does all this coherence guarantee our students will be deep, critical thinkers? Not quite. In fact, before we can hold them to this standard of deeper thinking, we need to first agree on what it is we're actually looking for in our "critical thinkers."

Seven Criteria for Critical Thinking

To really wrap our arms around the concept of critical thinking, I propose seven criteria that we can examine through our students' discourse about text as well as through their written responses:

1. Are students able to articulate the *problem, question, or issue*, seeing beneath the surface to recognize its cause, not just the symptoms?

2. How *open* are students to examining multiple points of view with fair-mindedness and empathy, even when they don't initially share that point of view?

3. To what extent do students recognize the *key concepts* and big ideas?

4. How thoroughly can students *elaborate* on the key concepts with the most useful details?

5. How relevant and insightful are students' *inferences* based on textual evidence?

6. Do students recognize the *implications* of a situation and predict *consequences*?

7. Are students willing to take a *stand* or take an *action step* that makes a positive difference?

As you read the remainder of this guide, keep your eye on our ultimate goal: critical thinking. And as you implement the units themselves, weave in opportunities to develop critical thinking using the seven criteria as a kind of cheat sheet. For example, find moments within the close reading lessons, in the discussion questions, and in tasks designed for student collaboration to debate multiple sides of an issue and to imagine action steps to resolve a school or community problem.

Critical thinking should play a role in assessment, too. I'll explain more about the role of critical thinking in the context of the two assessments that culminate each unit in planning Step 9 on page 43. Be sure to investigate all of what these assessments have to offer. But I wanted to mention them here because in some ways, it's the assessments that set these units apart from many standards-based units that may be available.

The Ten Planning Steps for Each Unit: Tips for Success

Ideally, unit planning is done with colleagues, each of whom brings different strengths to the table—for the benefit of students.

Before you move forward with teaching one of the units provided in this book, or with creating your own units, you need to give yourself a good stretch of think time or, better yet, meet with your colleagues to talk through the steps together. Doing so will help you plan and teach your units as meaningfully as possible.

These steps work in a couple of ways: first, to give you clearer insight into the *why* and *how* of each unit and lesson component in this book so that your close reading instruction really does lead to the kind of critical thinking we've deemed essential for our students. And second, so you can apply the same ten steps as you plan your own units and lessons.

The thought of designing your own units and close reading lessons, especially in light of the Common Core, nearly paralyzes some teachers with fear; they're afraid to even start. Breathe.

This is not nearly as daunting as it first appears. I've worked with numerous districts on developing a close reading curriculum, and this is what they come to recognize:

- **The real work of close reading happens at the lesson level.** You need an understanding of the architecture of a close reading lesson first. With thirty-two lessons here to draw upon as examples and a brief summary of the principles undergirding instructional scaffolding for close reading in the steps below, that should get you off and running. For deeper understanding of this process and more resources, see my book *Closer Reading, Grades 3–6.*

- **If you can create a good close reading lesson, it is not difficult to use it to design a worthy week of study**, returning to your anchor text for more thorough analysis and more explicit skill building. If you can develop a week of study, you can quite easily use the pattern you've devised to design a month of study—a unit.

What follows now is an explanation of each step you'll do when you implement the ready-made units in this book, and you can use this same sequence when planning your own units from scratch. On the next page, you'll find a visual tour that describes these ten steps and shows thumbnails of the actual planning components.

When you proceed to the steps themselves, be sure to pause at the end of each one to reflect on the questions starting on page 55 and available at **resources.corwin.com/boyleslessons.** The Think About This Step in the Process . . . questions contain points to consider about principles and practices related to the implementation of that step in the provided units and close reading lessons. The How Might You Apply This Step as You Plan Your Own Unit? questions help you apply the thinking for this step as you plan your own units and lessons.

A Visual Tour of the Units

Follow These Same Ten Steps for Your Own Unit Planning

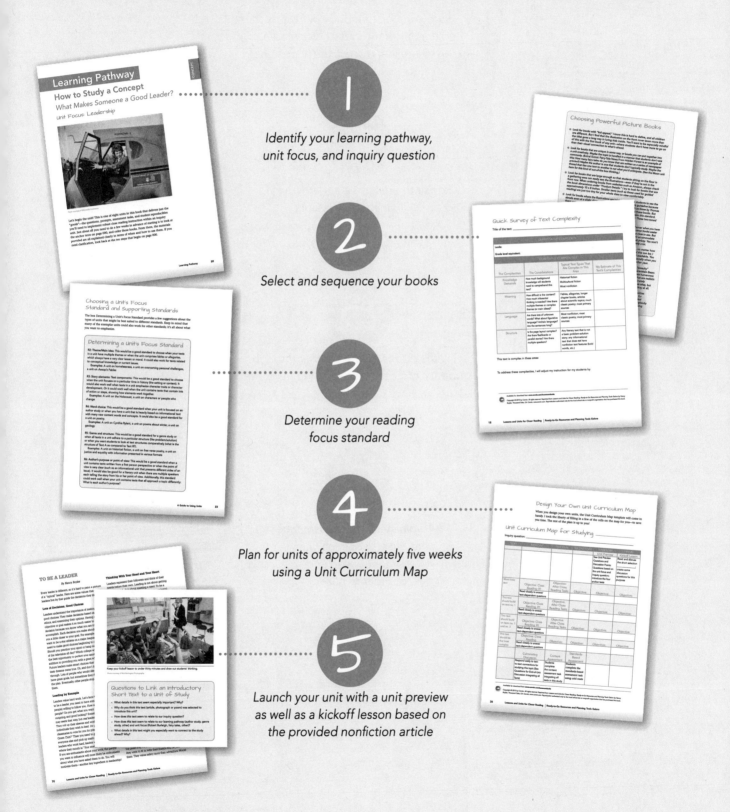

1 Identify your learning pathway, unit focus, and inquiry question

2 Select and sequence your books

3 Determine your reading focus standard

4 Plan for units of approximately five weeks using a Unit Curriculum Map

5 Launch your unit with a unit preview as well as a kickoff lesson based on the provided nonfiction article

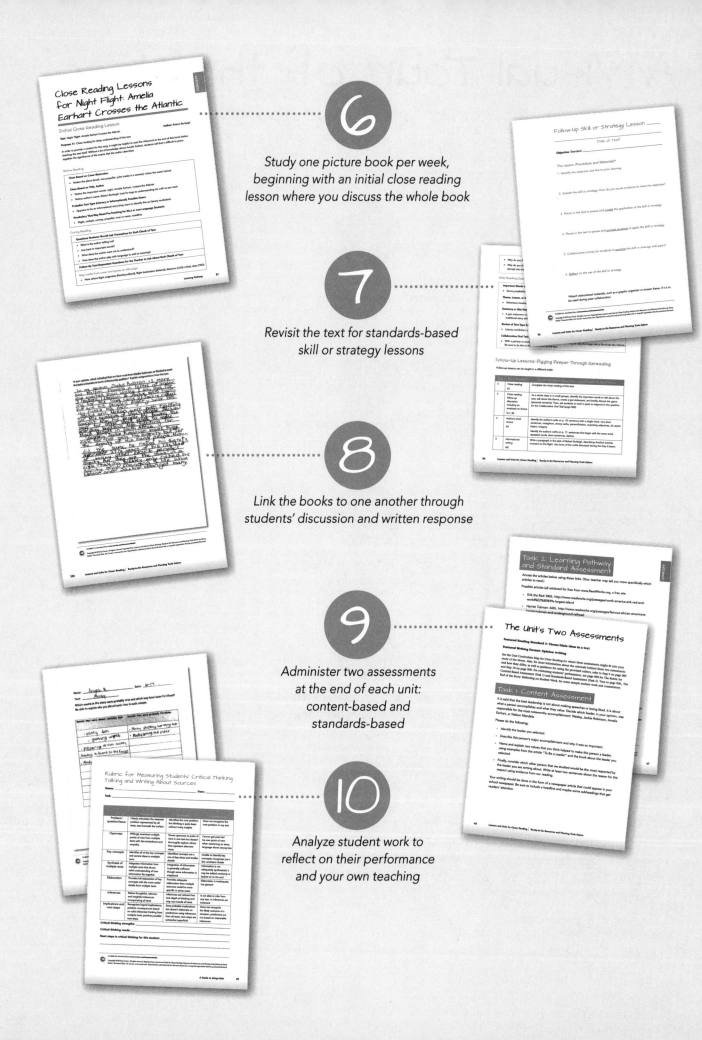

6

Study one picture book per week, beginning with an initial close reading lesson where you discuss the whole book

7

Revisit the text for standards-based skill or strategy lessons

8

Link the books to one another through students' discussion and written response

9

Administer two assessments at the end of each unit: content-based and standards-based

10

Analyze student work to reflect on their performance and your own teaching

Step 1

Identify Your Learning Pathway, Unit Focus, and Inquiry Question

Begin With a Learning Pathway and Unit Focus

First, what will your students study? In this book, I have called these areas of study "learning pathways"—because that is exactly what they are: different roads for students to travel on the way to a broader understanding of the people, places, and events that shape their lives. But to make their learning meaningful, students will need a *focus* for their learning pathway. In this book, the specific unit focus for each learning pathway is

Learning Pathway	Unit Focus
How to study a concept	Leadership
How to study a person	Abraham Lincoln
How to study a topic	The Moon
How to study a genre	Fairy tales
How to study an author	Robert Burleigh
How to study a time in history	Slavery
How to study a theme	Home is special for many reasons
How to study a current issue	Clean water

Naming our unit focus captures the territory, but many children won't find anything inherently captivating in a lone noun, or even in the brief phrase that names the unit study—which is why I like to turn a unit focus into an inquiry question.

Convert Your Unit Focus Into an Inquiry Question

Questions are dynamic. They jump up off the page and grab students' attention, begging for an answer supported by evidence. A question such as, How do you prefer to see the Moon—as an astronomer, an astronaut, a Native American, or a storyteller?, is motivational for a couple of reasons. First, it presents students with a choice. Second, they're intrigued by the novelty. "I never thought about seeing the moon in all these different ways," one fourth grader commented.

In this book, each unit focus has been further refined, so students will answer these inquiry questions:

- How to study a concept: What makes someone a good leader?

- How to study a person: Who was Abraham Lincoln: Boy, husband, father, president?

- How to study a topic: How do *you* prefer to see the moon—as an astronomer, an astronaut, a Native American, or a storyteller?

- How to study a genre: How many ways can you tell a fairy tale?

- How to study an author: How does Robert Burleigh write such interesting informational books?

- How to study a time in history: What choices would *you* make if you were a slave child?

- How to study a theme: What makes home so special?

- How to study a current issue: What's the big deal about clean water?

Consider the Two Assessment Tasks

You will probably find that choosing your unit focus and even converting it to an inquiry question is pretty easy. One point to keep in mind is that you want to cover many learning pathways throughout the year: studying an author, studying a genre, studying a concept—and more. Also, keep in mind that your inquiry question will ultimately play a big part in students' assessment at the end of the unit (see pages 43 and 50, Steps 9 and 10, for more discussion about assessment). Hence, you don't want it to be too broad because that would make it difficult for students to answer in a meaningful way, or too narrow because your unit will cover several weeks and you need sufficient substance.

Consider How-to-Study Questions

How do you study a person, a time in history, an author, a genre, or any other pathway to learning? These are the obvious, up-front questions about each pathway. But more specific questions emerge as you probe the depths of each pathway itself. These specific questions are useful to pose at the beginning of your unit to jump-start students' thinking about *why* they are studying a particular person, concept, time in history, and so on and to help them be metacognitive about their learning. Then, revisit these questions periodically throughout your unit to help students organize their thinking—as scientists, historians, philosophers, and researchers. These questions will not be charted here as they are presented in the introduction to each unit for each unique pathway.

Go to page 55 and the companion website, **resources.corwin.com/ boyleslessons,** for a list of questions that help you think about Step 1 and help you apply this step when planning your own unit.

Step 2

Select and Sequence Your Books

Match Your Books to Your Inquiry Question

Once you have your inquiry question, you can move on to book selection. This may be the most important—and time consuming—part of your entire planning process. I know it looks easy. With so many great picture books available, what could be so hard? Your first challenge is to make sure that every book you choose is a good match for your unit's inquiry question: If the book is about a leader, does it clearly point to that person's leadership characteristics? If the text is about the Moon, does it address one of the four Moon perspectives identified in the inquiry question?

Another key consideration, Common Core aside, is the importance of finding books your kids will *enjoy*. Unless the book will hold their interest, you'll be fighting an uphill battle from the first page forward. The trick here is that beyond the heartwarming story or explanation of fascinating facts, a book also needs to meet some less overt criteria in order to work well: What about its physical attributes? Its accessibility to your population of students? Its authenticity regarding the way it depicts characters and problems? And of course, what about its complexity?

The whole area of complexity is a sticky wicket with all the Common Core asks us to consider. I use the prescribed grade level Lexile bands cautiously, not as a hard-and-fast disqualifier as some Common Core advocates would advise. Remember that Lexile is just a readability number based on sentence length and word frequency. It does not account for any of the critical qualitative complexities that impact comprehension so profoundly: knowledge demands, meaning, language, and structure. I always check the Lexile when selecting texts (or another quantitative measure, such as Flesch-Kincaid, if Lexile isn't available). But when comprehension is at stake, as it always is for close reading, it's the *meaning* in particular, as influenced by the other qualitative complexities, that is the most critical. To aid you in your book selection process, see Choosing Powerful Picture Books (page 20) and the Quick Survey of Text Complexity (page 18).

I analyzed all of the picture books used for lessons in this book according to these criteria. At the end of each book description in the Introduction to the Unit, I identify the notable complexity or complexities for each book. You will see that a book is not complex in all areas. You will also see that different books demonstrate different complexities.

Quick Survey of Text Complexity

Title of the text: _____

QUANTITATIVE COMPLEXITY			
Lexile:			
Grade level equivalent:			
QUALITATIVE COMPLEXITIES			
The Complexities	The Considerations	Typical Text Types That Are Complex in This Area	My Estimate of This Text's Complexities
Knowledge Demands	How much background knowledge will students need to comprehend this text?	Historical fiction Multicultural fiction Most nonfiction	
Meaning	How difficult is the content? How much inferential thinking is needed? Are there multiple themes or complex themes (or main ideas)?	Fables, allegories, longer chapter books, articles about scientific topics; much classic poetry; most primary sources	
Language	Are there lots of unknown words? What about figurative language? Archaic language? Are the sentences long?	Most nonfiction; most classic poetry; most primary sources	
Structure	Is the page layout complex? Are there flashbacks or parallel stories? Are there multiple speakers?	Any literary text that is not a basic problem-solution story; any informational text that does *not* have nonfiction text features (bold words, etc.)	

This text is complex in these areas:

To address these complexities, I will adjust my instruction for my students by:

Sequence Your Books

When you have assembled your books, you will next want to think about the order in which you will teach them. Begin with what's most basic, the least complex—using more than a text's Lexile as your guide. This will allow you to build understanding of the unit focus, the learning pathway, and the inquiry question. Then move on to deeper understanding of the focus itself.

For example, in the unit about Abraham Lincoln, I started with *Honest Abe*, a biography. It contains a lot of information, but it is straightforward and provides a nice overview of Lincoln from birth to grave and the highlights in between.

Then I move to *Looking at Lincoln.* This would not have been a good initial text because it's not really sequential, just snippets that add dimension to Lincoln as both a hero and a human being. There's the added complexity here of two different points of view, the "official" documentation that the narrator (a little girl) researches in books and her own private musings on the information she finds. I originally thought I'd use *Abraham Lincoln Comes Home* as the final text because it's about the funeral train that carries his body back to Illinois. Why wouldn't this be last in a study of Lincoln? However, I took a closer look at *Abe's Honest Words* and realized this should be the grand finale. It embeds quotes from Lincoln's speeches with all of the complexities we expect from primary sources: archaic language, deep themes, and reliance on context. Students would best comprehend this text with all of the other texts behind them. Bottom line: Can you answer the question, Why have I chosen this particular order for these particular texts?

Go to page 55 and the companion website, **resources.corwin.com/ boyleslessons,** for a list of questions that help you think about Step 2 and help you apply this step when planning your own unit.

Choosing Powerful Picture Books

● *Look for books with "kid appeal." I know this is hard to define, and all children are different. But I find that the illustration on the front cover (even more than the title) goes a long way in luring kids inside. You'll want to be especially mindful of this with the first book of any unit—where students don't have more to go on than their visual connection to what's ahead.*

● *Look for books that are unique in some way, or books you can put together into a unit creatively. Maybe the topic is handled in a manner that students don't see commonly. (Extra! Extra!: Fairy-Tale News From Hidden Forest is an example of this: How many fairy tales do you know that are written as a series of newspaper articles?) Maybe the author is one that students don't typically study. Maybe the thread that ties one text to another is not what you'd anticipate. (See the Moon unit beginning on page 119 for this kind of out-of-the box thinking.)*

● *Look for books that are large enough so that students sitting on the floor in a gathering area can easily see the illustrations—even if they're not in the front row. When ordering books from websites such as Amazon, always check the book dimensions under "Product Details." I try to look for books that are approximately 10 x 8 inches. Smaller texts (such as those used for guided reading) are just too tiny for your whole class to view comfortably.*

● *Look for books where the illustrations are bright enough for students to see the details even at a slight distance. It's hard to always follow this guideline because there are some amazing illustrations that are quite dark (such as those by Thomas Locker) that are definitely worthy of close study. And I do use these books. But somber-toned illustrations have to be really great for me to relax this standard. Don't rule out illustrations that are just black-and-white either. These two-toned images have their own special allure for close study.*

● *Look for books that are soft cover (paperback) rather than hard cover when you have a choice. This is mostly an issue of economics. In fact, I find hard cover books easier to teach with; they're more durable when holding them up for the class to see. But if your plan is to acquire multiple copies (which you'll want to do to accommodate students' collaborative work), purchasing hard cover copies will get pricey. You won't need a copy for every child in the class, but five or six copies will help a lot.*

● *Look for books you can actually find. If the book is out of print, no matter how much you love it, don't plan a unit around it. I know how painful this can be; I practically cry when a book I've cherished for years is no longer available. You can try borrowing books from libraries, but that gets tricky, especially when you need multiple copies and you want to teach the same unit year after year.*

● *Look for books that represent a topic authentically. I'm not a fan of "preachy" books constructed for the sole purpose of teaching a lesson. (The Berenstain Bears books are an example of this.) I like texts with robust characters whose humanness is apparent in both their strengths and weaknesses. I like problems that are realistic and endings that are sometimes happy, and sometimes not—but ultimately show the need for compassion and empathy. Cartoonish characters are okay, but caricatures that depict races and cultures in stereotypic ways are not okay at all.*

● *Look for books that over time cover a full range of qualitative complexities as defined by the Common Core: knowledge demands (requirements for background knowledge); meaning; language; and structure. For detailed information on this, see my book Closer Reading, which discusses complexity in greater depth. For a quick reference, use the Quick Survey of Text Complexity on page 18.*

Step 3

Determine Your Reading Focus Standard for the Unit

Adopt a Less-Is-More Approach

Based on my work with district curriculum writing teams, I'd say that aligning standards to curriculum is a major source of confusion. If I arrive on the scene in the middle of this process rather than at the beginning, here's what I almost always see: laundry lists of unit standards—often pages and pages of standards. Sometimes, curriculum teams hand me the units they're developing and proudly announce, "Look, we got almost every Common Core Standard into this unit!"

I do not receive this news with the joy they're anticipating because this is essentially a "do over." Here's why: If you are saying that a particular standard falls within your unit, *it should be directly reflected in your unit assessment.* That's what makes it a *standard*; we're going to measure whether students have achieved it and how well they've achieved it. Teachers can see right away that there's no way they could ever possibly hold students accountable to all of the standards they've designated within the space of their four or five-week units when they list so many standards. Yes, all of the standards do need to be covered intentionally, but covered over the whole year, not within a single unit.

I advise teachers to choose *one main comprehension focus standard per unit.* Ideally, over the entire year, you will "hit" each of the College and Career Readiness Anchor Reading (CCRA R) Standards 2–9 at least once. (Remember that Standards 1 and 10, finding evidence in complex text, will always be present as our "bookend" standards, so we don't need to name them as a focus.) It could also be that you don't list Standards 7–9 as your focus; instead, you might want to include these as *supporting* standards because they may follow another more primary standard in your unit.

Look Ahead at How Standards Will Play Out Over a Week of Study

As an example, a unit's focus standard might be CCRA R6: Author's purpose or point of view. That means that for every book in the unit, there will be a lesson that features purpose or point of view. A possible supporting standard could be CCRA R8: Critiquing text. That means that most or all books will follow the *author's purpose/point of view* lesson with a lesson on possible bias or inclusion of sufficient evidence to support a claim somewhere within the week of study. I tell teachers that if a particular follow-up standard is present for all or most of the books in a unit, and *if* it will be assessed, that standard can be listed as a supporting standard. Bottom line: Your reading units should specify one—or at most two—standards as your focus standards.

Note the Standards Abbreviations

To simplify the identification of standards for the close reading follow-up lessons in this book, rather than repeating the CCRA R prefix every time, I just refer to the standard as

"R" for *Reading*

"W" designates *Writing* where that applies

"SL" stands for *Speaking and Listening*

The focus standard for each unit included in this book is

- Leadership: R2: Theme/Main idea
- Abraham Lincoln: R3: Story elements: How events connect to each other
- The Moon: R6: Author's purpose or point of view; Supporting standard: R7: Nontraditional: Text forms
- Fairy tales: R5: Genre and structure
- Author: R4: Word choice
- Slavery: R3: Story elements: The interaction between setting and character
- Home: R2; Theme; Supporting standard: R9: Text-to-text connections
- Clean Water: R8: Critiquing text

You can see from the above list that each of the CCRA R standards is represented at least once throughout the eight units—so altogether, they comprise a full year of study based on the five-week duration of the units.

NOTE: CCRA R1: Close reading: Finding evidence, is applied in all units.

Look at the unit's Unit Curriculum Map for Close Reading (see page 68 for an example). To see when a standard is a focus standard (versus when it is being tapped as a supporting standard) notice that the *focus standard* is represented in a lesson *every week of the study*. Then, there is also a lesson for a *supporting standard* included every week, or nearly every week. You will also see that there are many other standards also represented within the Unit Curriculum Map. These "supporting role" standards will be addressed thoughtfully in close reading follow-up lessons, and may be monitored through formative tasks, but will probably not play a prominent role in the end-of-unit summative assessment.

Choosing a Unit's Focus Standard and Supporting Standards

The box Determining a Unit's Focus Standard provides a few suggestions about the types of units that might be best suited to different standards. Keep in mind that many of the exemplar units could also work for other standards; it's all about what you want to emphasize.

Determining a Unit's Focus Standard

R2: Theme/Main idea: This would be a good standard to choose when your texts in a unit have multiple themes or when the unit comprises fables or allegories, which always have a very clear lesson or moral. It could also work for texts related to conceptual knowledge or current issues.

Examples: A unit on homelessness, a unit on overcoming personal challenges, a unit on *Aesop's Fables*

R3: Story elements: Text components: This would be a good standard to choose when the unit focuses on a particular time in history (the setting or context). It would also work well when texts in a unit emphasize character traits or character development. Or it could work well when the unit contains texts that include lots of action or steps, showing how elements work together.

Examples: A unit on the Holocaust, a unit on characters or people who change

R4: Word choice: This would be a good standard when your unit is focused on an author study or when you have a unit that is heavily based on informational text with many new content words and concepts. It could also be a good standard for a unit on poetry.

Examples: A unit on Cynthia Rylant, a unit on poems about winter, a unit on geology

R5: Genre and structure: This would be a good standard for a genre study or when all texts in a unit adhere to a particular structure (like problem/solution) or when you want students to look at text structures comparatively (what is the structure of Text A as compared to Text B?).

Examples: A unit on historical fiction, a unit on free verse poetry, a unit on justice and equality with information presented in various formats

R6: Author's purpose or point of view: This would be a good standard when a unit contains texts written from a first person perspective or when the point of view is very clear (such as an informational unit that presents different sides of an issue). It would also be good for a literary unit when there are multiple speakers each telling the story from his or her point of view. Additionally, this standard could work well when your unit contains texts that all approach a topic differently: What is each author's purpose?

Examples: A unit on autobiography or memoir, or a unit on a controversial topic, such as, Should there be presidential term limits?

R7: Nontraditional: Text formats: This could be a focus standard when the unit revolves around an area of study that draws on primary sources, such as photographs, interviews, video or audio clips, and art prints. It could also be a supporting standard if there are a variety of text types that support the main texts in a unit.

Examples: A unit on looking at civil rights through photographs, poetry, video clips, and interviews; A unit on the study of an illustrator's craft, such as E. B. Lewis's or Kadir Nelson's

R8: Critiquing text: This standard, designated by the Common Core only for informational text, could be a focus standard if the area of study is something related to bias or argumentation. It is an excellent supporting standard for a unit that focuses first on Standard 6: Author's purpose or point of view. Once the point of view has been established, critique its fairness to all sides of an issue, evidence for a claim, or information needed to add clarity.

Examples: A unit on current issues where there are pros and cons—like, Are video games bad for kids? Should there be zoos? Should kids be permitted to eat sweets in school?

R9: Text-to-text connections: This would be a good focus standard if the unit examined multiple texts on a given subject or texts that addressed the same theme in different ways. It could be a valuable supporting standard for just about any unit that compares a secondary text to an anchor text.

Examples: A unit on bullying that includes both informational and literary texts, and a unit on George Washington with texts related to different parts of his life or different views on his accomplishments

Go to page 55 and the companion website, resources.corwin.com/ boyleslessons, for a list of questions that help you think about Step 3 and help you apply this step when planning your own unit.

Plan for Units of Approximately Five Weeks Using a Unit Curriculum Map

Plot Your Plan Week-by-Week

After you've chosen your anchor texts, sequenced them, and identified your focus standard, you're ready to move on to mapping your unit. This consists of plotting week-by-week and day by day, what you will teach in your unit. What this requires above all is that you have read your texts thoroughly enough to know how you will use them when you return for additional lessons beyond your Initial Close Reading Lesson. One of those return visits will address your focus standard. But what will the rest of them focus on? There are limitless options from which to choose: lessons for comprehension skills and strategies, for fluency, for writing, for whatever complexity the text offers, and whatever your students need. My book *Closer Reading* identifies hundreds of focus points for follow-up lessons in Chapter 8.

Use the Unit Curriculum Maps Flexibly

In the introduction of each unit you will find its curriculum map (for example, see the Unit Curriculum Map for Close Reading on page 68). These units are approximately five weeks in length. Notice in particular the word *approximately*. If there's one thing we learn early on as teachers, it is that our entire classroom world revolves around "approximately." You will see that the curriculum map for each unit specifies five days each week for teaching the anchor texts, with two days at the beginning of the first week to introduce the unit, and three days at the end of the month to wrap things up and assess.

As you map out your unit, think of it in three parts:

1. **Initiation (Part of week 1)**: Use the Unit Preview Questions and Discussion Points for Studying a [Concept or other focus] including the inquiry question and learning pathway questions to engage students in what they might already know and introduce the books.

2. **Instruction based on the anchor texts (Weeks 2–5)**: Teach the Initial Close Reading Lesson each week and deliver explicit follow-up standards-based lessons for strategies and skills.

3. **Culmination (Part of week 6)**: Encourage students to synthesize the meaning from all texts orally and in writing through end-of-unit discussion questions and the two assessments.

Go to page 56 and the companion website, **resources.corwin.com/ boyleslessons,** for a list of questions that help you think about Step 4 and help you apply this step when planning your own unit.

Design Your Own Unit Curriculum Map

When you design your own units, the Unit Curriculum Map template will come in handy. I took the liberty of filling in a few of the cells on the map for you—to save you time. The rest of the plan is up to you!

Unit Curriculum Map for Studying _____

Inquiry question: _____

TEXT	MONDAY	TUESDAY	WEDNESDAY	THURSDAY	FRIDAY
				Unit Preview	Kickoff Lesson
				See Unit Preview Questions and Discussion Points: Questions based on the unit focus and inquiry question; introduce the four anchor texts	Read and discuss the short selection _____; create some discussion questions for this purpose
Most basic text	Objective: R1 Close Reading	Objective: After Close Reading Tasks	Objective:	Objective:	Objective:
	Read closely to answer text-dependent questions				
This text should build on text no. 1	Objective: R1 Close Reading	Objective: After Close Reading Tasks	Objective:	Objective:	Objective:
	Read closely to answer text-dependent questions				
This text should build on texts no. 1 and no. 2	Objective: R1 Close Reading	Objective: After Close Reading Tasks	Objective:	Objective:	Objective:
	Read closely to answer text-dependent questions				
This text should be the most complex	Objective: R1 Close Reading	Objective:	Objective:	Objective:	Objective:
	Read closely to answer text-dependent questions				
	Culminating Discussion	Content Assessment	Standards-Based Assessment		
	Respond orally to text-to-text connections for studying this topic (See Questions for End-of-Unit Discussion Integrating All Texts)	Students complete the content assessment task integrating all texts in this study	Students complete the standards-based assessment task using cold reads		

Step 5

Launch Your Unit With a Unit Preview and a Kickoff Lesson Based on the Nonfiction Article Provided

Get Your Unit Preview Ready

The preview, which is part of the initiation phase, could begin on the first day of the unit by discussing what it means to study this learning pathway: a person, topic, time in history, or whatever the pathway will be. (Questions for all pathways are included in each unit, so no additional charts are provided here.) You could also identify and post the inquiry question and have a brief discussion around this question that you hope to be able to answer by the end of the unit. Introduce the four books that are the unit's anchor texts, too. Don't tell too much about these wonderful books because you want the content to unfold through the reading of the text itself. But you might want to at least hold up the front cover and show an illustration or two to pique everyone's interest. See the box Unit Preview Questions and Discussion Points for Studying a _____ when you are planning your own unit.

Teach the Kickoff Lesson

The following day, also by way of initiating your unit, teach the kickoff lesson based on the included nonfiction article. This article is designed to be read by the students themselves and is intended to stimulate thinking with key ideas that students can use as touchstones as they explore the picture books designated for the unit. While not technically a "close reading lesson" (because you won't proceed through the text line by line), these brief texts are definitely discussion worthy with opportunities for divergent thinking. Discussion questions are included for the article to get kids thinking about some of the concepts they will encounter and to help set a purpose for the unit. The length of this lesson will depend on how much time you want to spend on the article and questions. If you want to spend more than thirty minutes, it might be best to teach the lesson over two days.

When you design your own units, your kickoff short text doesn't always need to be a nonfiction piece. You could also consider a poem, photograph, or other short text to get students' minds percolating with some early thinking about the study ahead. A couple of my go-to sources for short text for which you don't need copyright permission are Readworks (www.readworks.org) and Newsela (www .newsela.com). For possible generic questions to ask when initiating your own unit with the discussion of a short text, see the box Questions to Link an Introductory Short Text to a Unit of Study. For maximum benefit, customize the questions to match the books in *your* unit.

Unit Preview Questions and Discussion Points

for studying a _____

- *Introduce the learning pathway (for example, studying an author, studying a genre, or some other focus). Discuss what it means to study this particular pathway. (There are unit preview questions and discussion points provided in each unit for the focus area, though you may want to select just some of these questions for study at your grade level.)*

- *Now talk specifically about this learning pathway. For example, if you're studying an author, ask students to name a few authors. If it's a concept or theme, ask students to name a few concepts or themes (like friends are loyal to each other, or perseverance helps people achieve their goals).*

- Introduce the unit focus for this pathway and the inquiry question: *For example, for the genre pathway, explain that the unit focus will be fairy tales and the inquiry question will be, How many ways can you tell a fairy tale?* Ask students for any early thoughts: What could this mean? What could be some examples? Why might it be important to our success as students to find an answer to this question? Where might we find an answer to this question?

- *Introduce the four anchor texts selected for close reading. Show the cover and perhaps an illustration inside to pique students' interest. Do not explain the full story.*

Keep your kickoff lesson to under thirty minutes and draw out students' thinking.

Photo courtesy of Rick Harrington Photography

Questions to Link an Introductory Short Text to a Unit of Study

- What details in this text seem especially important? Why?

- Why do you think this text (article, photograph, or poem) was selected to introduce this unit?

- How does this text seem to relate to our inquiry question?

- How does this text seem to relate to our learning pathway (author study, genre study, other) and unit focus (Robert Burleigh, fairy tales, other)?

- What details in this text might you especially want to connect to the study ahead? Why?

Go to page 56 and the companion website, **resources.corwin.com/ boyleslessons,** for a list of questions that help you think about Step 5 and help you apply this step when planning your own unit.

Study One Picture Book Per Week, Beginning With an Initial Close Reading Lesson Where You Discuss the Entire Book

Video 1

Interview

An interview with Nancy Boyles about why close reading matters.

resources.corwin .com/boyleslessons

Consider These Scaffolding Ideas and Tips for a Successful First Day

After you've previewed the unit and taught the lesson with the nonfiction article, you're ready to embark on the study of the four anchor texts. Plan to spend a week on each text. This Initial Close Reading Lesson is intended to take about thirty minutes. The goal for the first day with each book is to construct meaning with as much depth as you can reasonably achieve. Maintain high expectations because that's what propels thinking forward. But also recognize that you'll be returning to the text to address its significant complexities—so you don't have to accomplish *everything* on your first day of study. On this first day, you are in essence modeling for your students *how* one digs into a text to understand it, and you are inviting them to do so too, based on the text-dependent questions you ask and the questions *they* ask to pursue meaning more independently.

If more than thirty minutes is needed to finish the book, it would be better to find a good stopping point and complete the reading the following day. A word of caution here: One of the issues I observe with many teachers new to the teaching of close reading is that it takes them *forever* to read the book with their students. You need to pick up the pace. When you drag out this process, even the kids who are not typically wiggly turn into wigglers. Check the clock. Know that you have thirty minutes to get this job done. Go!

Video 2

Before Reading: Preview

Watch Nancy and colleagues introduce the Anchor Text and preview the Before Reading phase of a close reading lesson.

resources.corwin .com/boyleslessons

Everything you need for scaffolding students before, during, and after reading is supplied for the Initial Close Reading Lesson each week. My book *Closer Reading* explains each of these instructional components in great depth, including the shifts we should consider before, during, and after close reading in light of the Common Core; check out Chapters 4, 5, and 6 in that book for a thorough description of exactly what your scaffolding should entail. Here, in the chart Close Reading Lesson Components, Links to Video, and Hot Tips for Close Reading Success, I provide an abbreviated version with the important tweaks for each area of the close reading process. When you teach the lessons, you will see that they adhere to the principles below. However, at a glance you may question these adjustments. The purpose of this chart is to explain the intention of each of these shifts.

To view a close reading lesson in its entirety, and access additional videos, go to resources.corwin.com/boyleslessons
To read a QR Code, you must have a smartphone or tablet with a camera. We recommend that you download a QR Code reader app that is made specifically for your phone or tablet brand.

Close Reading Lesson Components, Links to Video, and Hot Tips for Close Reading Success

Before Reading Lesson Components

Lesson Component	Hot Tip
Clues based on cover illustration, the title, and the author	Do not, in general, use these text elements to make predictions, elicit personal connections, or launch a picture walk—which often distract readers from the text itself and the intent of the author. Instead, shorten this part of the lesson by minimizing teacher input. Get students to be careful *observers* of the details in the cover illustration and in the title. Plan to revisit these observations as you read as the intent of what's on the cover becomes clear.
Probable text type (Literary or informational); possible genre	Do heighten students' awareness of the type of text they are about to read. This prepares them to locate relevant text-based evidence.
Vocabulary that may need pre-teaching for English language learners (ELLs) or low language students	Although in general frontloading vocabulary is not a good idea when we want typical learners to retrieve meaning from context, it may be a very good idea for students with weak vocabulary or language skills. Consider collaborating with your ELL teacher, reading specialist, or special education teacher to differentiate instruction for students who truly need this extra support.

During Reading Lesson Components

Lesson Component	Hot Tip
Text-dependent questions for each chunk of text	Remember that your text-dependent questions should cover a full range of standards; be careful not to neglect Reading Standards 4, 5, and 6. Also, when you ask a Standard 1 question about basic evidence, try to ask a follow-up question that will take students' thinking deeper into the text.
Questions students should ask themselves for each chunk of text: • What is the author telling me? • What are the hard or important words? • What does the author want me to understand? • How does the author play with language to add to meaning?	With so much emphasis on text-dependent questions during close reading, it's easy to forget that our real goal is to develop our students' *independent* close reading. The four generic questions in the box to the left will help you achieve this goal. Before asking your specific text-based questions, give students a chance to respond to the text based on these questions, which are generic and can work for any text.

Video 3

Before Reading: Lesson

Watch Nancy teach the Before Reading part of the initial close reading lesson to fourth graders.

resources.corwin.com/boyleslessons

Video 4

Before Reading: Debrief

Watch Nancy and colleagues debrief the Before Reading part of the lesson.

resources.corwin.com/boyleslessons

Video 5

During Reading: Preview

Watch Nancy and colleagues preview the During Reading portion of an initial close reading lesson.

resources.corwin.com/boyleslessons

Video 6

During Reading: Lesson

Watch Nancy demonstrate attention to different standards through text-dependent questions during reading.

resources.corwin.com/boyleslessons

Video 7

During Reading: Debrief

Watch Nancy and colleagues debrief the During Reading portion of the lesson.

resources.corwin.com/boyleslessons

Video 8

After Reading: Preview

Watch Nancy and colleagues preview the After Reading goals of an initial close reading lesson.

resources.corwin.com/boyleslessons

After Reading Lesson Components*

Lesson Component	Hot Tip
Reading follow-up tasks: • Determine important words to talk about the text • Identify theme or central idea • Summarize the text or provide a gist statement • Review the genre	Before students can engage in more analytic thinking about text (like determining an author's purpose, critiquing a text, or making comparisons between texts), we need to know if they have constructed basic meaning. The tasks in the box to the left will provide insights into students' level of initial understanding. These should all be addressed (when appropriate) at the conclusion of the close reading of any text.
Collaborative oral tasks	While some whole-class conversations related to the tasks above might be in order, it is important to move away from teacher-driven discourse and immediate written response and instead allow students to work more independently in partnerships or small groups to discuss various aspects of the text—with their teacher checking in as needed.

*Due to time limitations, it is likely that the After Reading components of a close reading lesson will need to occur the day after the Initial Close Reading Lesson has been completed.

Tips for Posing Text-Dependent Questions for Close Reading

The close reading lessons in this book contain all of the text-dependent questions you'll need for the picture book lessons in each unit. In fact, you may look at these lessons and think to yourself, "There are too many questions here." It is fine to ask fewer questions as long as you're covering the full range of standards. It could be, too, that you'll want to ask some *different* questions, taking your students' lead as they probe various aspects of a text. Take a word of caution: Try to follow Standard 1 questions that monitor students' observation of basic textual evidence with questions that delve into other standards and, hence, deeper into a text's meaning. For suggested standards-aligned questions that could be applied to any book, see pages 86–91 in my *Closer Reading* book, which supplies charts of questions for both literary and informational text. For an absolute treasure trove of questions for *every* Common Core standard see *The Common Core Companion: The Standards Decoded: What They Say, What They Mean, How to Teach Them* for Grades K–2, 3–5, or 6–8—whichever grade span would work best for you.

Tips for Moving Students to Independence in Close Reading

With so many text-dependent questions identified for each chunk of text in all of the close reading lessons, it's easy to forget that the goal is actually to move away from *your* questions to questions that students pose in their own minds to understand the text more deeply on their own. While we could never expect kids to come up with all of the specific queries we pose, they can quite easily learn four basic prompts that address multiple facets of a text (previously mentioned in the During Reading Lesson Components):

- What is the author telling me? (This monitors their observation of on-the-page details.)

- Any hard or important words? (This alerts them to key vocabulary.)

- What does the author want me to understand? (This probes their recognition of inferences: What is the author *showing* rather than *telling*?)

- How does the author play with language to add to meaning? (This focuses on the crafted elements within the text.)

Dare to be bold here in your expectations for student independence. After just a few sessions where you do most of the question-asking yourself, share these four generic questions with students and tell them you will pause your reading frequently so they can apply these questions to individual text chunks. I begin with the first two questions that check for literal understanding and word meaning. You may need to ask some follow-up questions to push thinking beyond these concrete text elements. But you will be surprised by how readily students catch on to this next step in pursuing meaning on their own. Then, take on the challenge of inferential thinking. More modeling of good craft-based questions will be necessary before students can handle this final question themselves; noticing an author's craft in a text is not something with which intermediate grade students have had much experience. Embrace this goal with vigor because *nothing* will be more important to your students in close reading than their capacity to pursue meaning independently! For a resource to support this independence, see the poster and bookmark that pose these questions on pages 120 and 122 of my book *Closer Reading* and on www.corwin.com/closerreading.

Go to page 56 and the companion website, **resources.corwin.com/boyleslessons,** for a list of questions that help you think about Step 6 and help you apply this step when planning your own unit.

Video 9

After Reading: Lesson

Watch Nancy address the four After Reading tasks with students.

resources.corwin.com/boyleslessons

Video 10

After Reading: Debrief

Watch Nancy and colleagues debrief the After Reading tasks with a focus on construction of meaning.

resources.corwin.com/boyleslessons

Video 11

Moving to Independence: Preview

Watch Nancy and colleagues preview moving to independence in close reading and conferring with students.

resources.corwin.com/boyleslessons

Video 12

Moving to Independence: Lesson

Watch Nancy teach a small group lesson and confer with students about the four "good reader" questions.

resources.corwin.com/boyleslessons

Revisit the Text for Follow-Up Standards-Based Skill or Strategy Lessons

Now Shift Away From Teacher-Led Instruction

The Initial Close Reading Lesson as described above and demonstrated through the lessons in this book is followed by Follow-Up Lessons. *These lessons focus on a standards-based skill or a strategy.* The lessons may begin with teacher-led, whole-class conversations, but they should also include or be included in small group or partner-guided practice or in independent work. The focus now will be on a standards-based skill or a comprehension strategy, giving students the opportunity to dig more deeply into content and craft through rereading.

For students to be proficient readers, they need ample opportunities to think, talk, and write about texts.

Photo courtesy of Rick Harrington Photography

When you do return to the text on Days 2–5, think about what makes sense for your text and for your kids! On Day 2, you will most likely engage students in the tasks that compose the After Reading portion of your initial lesson as specified on the lesson plan. Beyond these weekly routines, what complexities of this text warrant special attention? What do your formative assessments tell you about what your students need? This is where we will build skills and strategies explicitly, gradually releasing responsibility to student independence. In this book, I did not write out each of these lessons as the number of added pages would have been prohibitive. But to guide you, I did try to give enough information, both on the Unit Curriculum Map and in the description of the lesson on a chart at the end of the Initial Close Reading Lesson plan.

Remember that any *explicit* lesson should fit into this instructional framework:

- **Brief Explanation of the Skill or Strategy.** The steps needed in applying it and how to know when you've achieved success

- **Modeling.** One or two places in the text where you show students how *you* apply this skill or strategic thinking

- **Prompted Practice.** A few places where you pause to prompt students to use the skill or strategy and monitor how they are applying it

- **Guided Practice.** Opportunity for students to work collaboratively with less direct teacher support to try out the skill or strategy

This instructional framework adheres to the gradual release of responsibility model (Pearson & Gallagher, 1983) that I discuss at great length in my *Closer Reading* book. Notice from the four steps above that in any given lesson, the final (fifth) stage of this model (student independence) is sometimes not present—yet. Student independence is always our ultimate instructional goal, and with enough lessons through enough units, it is imperative that we get our students to this point. Getting students to independence is what it will take to see high performance levels for students on any summative assessment. For teachers who want to be more systematic about instructional procedures for their follow-up lessons than that allowed by the short descriptions in the unit or weekly plan, I supply below a planning template for a Follow-Up Skill or Strategy Lesson. An example of this planning form filled out for a follow-up lesson on *understanding a character's influence* is also provided: Follow-Up Lesson for *The Raft* by Jim LaMarche (2002).

Design your own task sheets for follow-up lessons—or check out the dozens of templates I've provided at **resources.corwin.com/boyleslessons**), in Appendix 1 of *Closer Reading* (available), as well as in my book *That's a Great Answer*, second edition, 2012).

Video 13

Moving to Independence: Debrief

Watch Nancy and colleagues debrief about moving students to independence.

resources.corwin .com/boyleslessons

Video 14

Follow-Up Lesson: Preview

Watch Nancy and colleagues preview the follow-up lesson focusing on understanding theme.

resources.corwin .com/boyleslessons

Video 15

Follow-Up Lesson: Lesson

Watch Nancy lead a follow-up lesson with a text, deepening students' understanding of theme.

resources.corwin .com/boyleslessons

Follow-Up Skill or Strategy Lesson _____

_____

(Title of Text)

Objective: Standard __:_____

The Lesson (Procedure and Materials)*

1. *Identify the objective and link to prior learning*

2. *Explain the skill or strategy: How do you locate evidence to meet the objective?*

3. *Places in the text to pause and <u>model</u> the application of the skill or strategy*

4. *Places in the text to pause and <u>prompt students</u> to apply the skill or strategy*

5. *Collaborative activity for students to <u>practice</u> the skill or strategy with peers**

6. *<u>Reflec</u>t on the use of the skill or strategy*

*Attach instructional materials, such as a graphic organizer or answer frame, if it is to be used during peer collaboration.

Follow-Up Lesson for *The Raft*

(Exemplar Lesson)

Objective: Standard 3: Find evidence in the text that shows how Grandma influenced Nicky. What do her words, actions, and interactions say about her as a person?

*The Lesson (Procedure and Materials)**

1. Identify the objective and link to prior learning

- Explain that today's objective is to develop a deeper understanding of Grandma, to figure out how she influenced Nicky in such a significant way
- Review story quickly, especially how Nicky changed from the beginning to the end

2. Explain the skill or strategy: How do you locate evidence to meet the objective?

- Thinking about what influence means (you are really looking for how a character changes)
- Noticing places in the text where Grandma is making a difference to Nicky: How does she do this?
- Thinking about what Grandma does, what she says, and how she acts with Nicky

3. Places in the text to pause and <u>model</u> the application of the skill or strategy

- **Model: p. 1:** I'm noticing what Dad says about Grandma: "Well, she's not your normal kind of grandma, I guess." (This shows us we know something unusual is coming; we're not sure what)
- **Model: p. 3:** I'm noticing Grandma's words: "We can't stand here all summer," said Grandma. (Grandma seems a little rough, not too sensitive)

4. Places in the text to pause and prompt students to apply the skill or strategy

- **Prompt: p. 5:** I'm noticing Grandma's words: "If you're going to do that, you better wash up." (Grandma is a "no nonsense" kind of person)
- **Prompt: p. 5:** Do you notice anything else that Grandma is saying on this page that helps us understand her? (Grandma's words: "Been carving that old fellow for years"; Grandma likes nature; she likes to carve)

*5. Collaborative activity for students to <u>practice</u> the skill or strategy with peers**

- Ask students to work in small collaborative groups using a copy of the text to find additional evidence and think about what the evidence shows. They can use the template Describe a Character or Person (see next form; ten to twelve minutes exercise)

6. <u>Reflect</u> on the use of the skill or strategy

- Return to the whole group. Ask students to share their evidence and what they think it shows about Grandma and how she influenced Nicky so significantly.
- What was easy about applying this strategy? What was hard?
- How can you apply this strategy in your own reading?

*Attach instructional materials, such as a graphic organizer or answer frame, if it is to be used during peer collaboration.

Describe a Character or Person

My group: _____

_____

Character/Person: _____   **Text:** _____

Thoughts	Words	Actions	Interactions

Based on his/her thoughts, words, actions, and interactions, how would you describe Grandma? Explain why you think she was able to influence Nicky so significantly.

Strategies for Keeping Follow-Up Instruction Kid Centered

I encourage you to adapt the formats of these lessons based on your students' needs, aiming for as much student-directed learning as possible. The Initial Close Reading Lesson each week, with its text-dependent questions, will often be heavily guided by you, the teacher. As explained, you can reduce this teacher focus even in your initial lesson as students take on more of the work themselves with the Four Questions for Independent Close Reading, noted on the planning template and also available on a poster and bookmark in *Closer Reading* and at www.corwin.com/closerreading. Still, this initial lesson is usually a whole-class experience with the teacher front and center. Beyond the first day of the week, try to minimize the "sit and get" mindset. A mini lesson of ten to fifteen minutes or a brief discussion with the whole class is fine. But then get kids moving. Set them to work in small groups or partnerships, where they, not you, lead the learning.

Your most important role beyond Day 1 of the lesson sequence is to circulate and monitor. The key is to make sure students are doing the rereading and thinking work, not you! As you circulate, you want to hear rich discussion that taps the skills or strategies you have decided to practice. The number of times you revisit a text to dig deeper will vary based on your particular circumstances. If you can return to the text three times beyond the Initial Close Reading Lesson and the follow-up to close reading, the plan I've laid out for each week will work well. If you have less time, you'll need to be selective about the focus points you choose. Think about what your data tell you about *your* students' needs. Think too about the components of a text that are the most challenging and worthy of a second look. This will be especially important for English learners and students reading below grade level if we aspire to close that ornery achievement gap.

Go to page 57 and the companion website, **resources.corwin.com/boyleslessons,** for a list of questions that help you think about Step 7 and help you apply this step when planning your own unit.

Video 16

Follow-Up Lesson: Debrief

Watch Nancy and colleagues debrief and identify key takeaways from the follow-up theme lesson.

resources.corwin.com/boyleslessons

Video 17

Small Group Strategy Lesson: Preview

Watch Nancy and colleagues preview a small group strategy lesson on visualizing.

resources.corwin.com/boyleslessons

Video 18

Small Group Strategy Lesson: Lesson

Watch Gina demonstrate a small group strategy lesson on visualizing.

resources.corwin.com/boyleslessons

Step 8

Link the Books Through Discussion and Written Response

Remember that this week's text can become the source of next week's text-to-text connection. Across the length of the unit, maximize the unit's potential by linking the texts to one another, to a host of comprehension standards, to listening and speaking through discussion, and to multiple modes of writing. We want to teach these units not just as the study of four wonderful books but also as four wonderful books that are stronger because they all work together in some significant way. To make these connections come alive, choose important points of comparison. Consider these options:

- **Theme.** Texts that have similar themes
- **Character values or actions.** Characters that respond to situations in similar or different ways
- **Text structure.** Two texts that may have the same message though one may be (for example) a poem, and another may be an informational piece
- **Genre.** Two texts with the same genre that may be compared
- **Topic.** Two texts on the same topic where the authors present information in different ways or offer conflicting information

For additional guidance, in each Introduction to the Unit, I provide Questions for End-of-Unit Discussion Integrating All Texts. I offer more generic questions that can be used to extend learning in any unit you create in the chart below: These questions are easily differentiated. You will note that under each standard I have designated one question especially appropriate for low language students or ELLs with an asterisk (*). While these questions may not be all that easy for these students, they will elicit the evidence you need to determine whether your ELLS and low language kids are getting "the basics" for the application of each standard. A question particularly suited to advanced readers is noted with a hashtag (#). These are typically questions that require more abstract thinking and insights as well as evidence.

Go to page 57 and the companion website, **resources.corwin.com/ boyleslessons,** for a list of questions that help you think about Step 8 and help you apply this step when planning your own unit.

Discussion Questions for Text-to-Text Connections

CCRA Standard for Reading	Text-Dependent Questions for Connecting Texts
Standard 1 Close reading: Finding evidence	• In your opinion, which text presents facts, numbers, or statistics that are the most surprising or interesting? Explain your reasoning with textual evidence. • Which text in this study provides the strongest visual images for you? What do you visualize?* • Which text in this study raises the most questions for you? What are the questions?# • After reading all of these texts, do you have any unanswered questions? What are your questions?
Standard 2 Theme/Main idea	• Do the texts in this study seem to have the same or different main ideas or themes? Explain using textual evidence.* • What kind of research do you think the author of each text needed to do in order to write this [book/article/other format]? • How can you apply the central idea(s) in these texts to a current problem or issue today?#
Standard 3 Story elements	• Which characters seemed the most similar? The most different?* • Do the facts in these sources support each other or contradict each other? Explain using details from each text. • Which text that you read shows the strongest connection between elements, or parts (like setting and problem or characters/people and central idea)? Explain your thinking with textual evidence.#
Standard 4 Word choice	• Which text had the most positive tone (or seemed the most biased, or generated the strongest feeling)? What words in each text lead you to this conclusion? • Looking at all of your texts together, choose ___ words that you consider the *most* important to understanding this topic. Why is each word important?* • Which author is the most persuasive? How does the author's word choice help to persuade you?#
Standard 5 Genre and structure	• Authors organize information in different ways. For the texts you read in this text study, which structure seemed the most helpful to you? Why?* • Do these texts represent different genres or the same genre? What genre(s) are represented?# • Think about the way each author presented his or her information on this topic. Which format would be best for a young child? An older child? Explain.
Standard 6 Author's purpose or point of view	• Do these authors/characters/narrators seem to have the same point of view? Different point of view? What textual evidence supports this?* • Do these texts all seem to have the same purpose or a different purpose? Explain your thinking.# • After reading all of these texts, I agree most strongly with [author] because _____.

(Continued)

(Continued)

CCRA Standard for Reading	Text-Dependent Questions for Connecting Texts
Standard 7 Nontraditional: Text forms	• In addition to the [article/story/other] that you read, you also viewed a [photo/video/website, or other]. How did this nonprint source add to or change your understanding or feelings about this topic? Explain using textual evidence.* • If you viewed a live performance of content related to this topic, how did it add to your understanding or feelings about the topic? To which text did it seem to have the strongest connection? Explain. • Which [graphics/illustrations/photographs/other] were the most effective? Why?#
Standard 8 Critiquing text	• Is the author of each text being fair to both/all sides of the topic? Explain your thinking with textual evidence.# • Do you trust all of the sources you read? Look at the publication date. Look at the name of the author. Is this person considered to be an expert? • Is there any information in any of these texts that you question or think might not be correct? Explain. • Could any of these authors have explained something more clearly? What?*
Standard 9 Text-to-text connections	• If you were writing a report on ____. Where would you add the information from [text 2] to [text 1]? Why?* • These texts all support a similar central idea. Identify the central idea. What is the same/different about the way each author develops this central idea?# • All in all, which text in this study seems the strongest in terms of [message/character development, important facts, or other]? • Find another text that would add to your understanding of this topic. Why did you choose this particular text? • Which text seemed the most personally relevant to you? Why?

(*) A question especially appropriate for low language students or ELLs

(#) A question particularly suited to advanced readers

Step 9

Administer Two Assessment Tasks at the End of Each Unit (Content-Based and Standards-Based)

Use These Assessment Basics

At the beginning of each unit (see the first one on page 66), you'll see the two assessment tasks. I put them early in the unit resources, so it would be clear from the start what the end goal is. Both assessments will address the unit's featured standard but in different ways. A writing format for the assessment (narrative, informative/explanatory, or opinion/argument) is also specified. Note that the unit is not designed to *teach* writing. But students should have recurring opportunities to *apply* different writing formats through their literacy curriculum; these units provide some of those opportunities for different kinds of writing.

You will see on the Unit Curriculum Map for Close Reading that two days during the final week of the unit have been designated for administering these assessments. A rough estimate of the time required for students to complete each task would be an hour—though that will depend heavily on your students and your schedule. Many of the assessment tasks include multiple parts. All of the standards-based tasks require some reading and several also involve watching

When students write about their reading, it gives you a window into what they understand—and also what they haven't quite grasped yet.

brief video clips. For the content-based assessments, it would be helpful to have multiple copies of the text available, though you won't need one for every student. Given the range of grades specified for these lessons, it is likely that some tasks, as they are written, may be too rigorous for your students or not rigorous enough. Of course, you should modify them as you see fit.

Content-Based and Standards-Based

The assessment of content knowledge incorporates the featured standard, but it does so within the context of the *content* students have studied in *this* unit, remembering that the way we build complexity, coherence, and critical thinking over time is through the pursuit of rigorous textual knowledge. Each of these units offers a wealth of opportunities for acquiring new knowledge about subjects that are not just important but relevant and useful too. We want to make sure students really tune in to these rich texts, and we will do so by asking questions that may relate to the learning pathway, the inquiry question, questions integrating multiple texts, or other questions that encourage students to think critically about the unit texts.

There should also be a second assessment that examines whether students have become more competent with the featured standard with texts they have not studied previously. For this, we will need to provide them with questions similar to those of the first task—but with texts that are unfamiliar. If they can respond sufficiently to these questions *on their own*, no instruction provided, we can feel more confident that they will perform well down the line on a summative, high-stakes assessment. For the standards-based assessment, online sources have been suggested. Some of these are downloadable print passages; others are brief video clips with the YouTube or other retrieval sites specified.

Although I tried to identify sources for the standards-based assessments that are available without copyright restrictions and would remain viable for the long haul, there are unfortunately no guarantees in our techno-world that what's here today will still be around when we need it. I trust that you will recognize the intent of the standards-based assessment for a unit after examining the content task and that you will somehow locate your own suitable passages and media texts for this second assessment if necessary.

Evaluate Performance With a Rubric

A generic rubric, Rubric for Content-Based Assessment (Task 1) and Standards-Based Assessment (Task 2) is supplied next. While this rubric and the assessment criteria would be useful in just about any intermediate classroom, whether or not your state is aligned to the Common Core, note that the three assessment criteria and specifications for each level of performance are a synthesis of the criteria used by Partnership for Assessment of Readiness for College and Careers (PARCC) and Smarter Balanced Assessment Consortium (SBAC). If your district or state requires more specific adherence to either of these assessment consortia, you can find those rubrics on the web:

- PARCC: www.parcconline.org/
- SBAC: http://www.smarterbalanced.org/smarter-balanced-assessments/

Rubric for Content-Based Assessment (Task 1) and Standards-Based Assessment (Task 2)

Student: _____   **Date:** _____

Unit: _____

	Task 1	Task 2	Task 1	Task 2	Task 1	Task 2	Task 1	Task 2
Content: Comprehension of key ideas and details and insights (including evidence and elaboration)								
The thinking process (organization, coherence, clarity)								
Knowledge of written language and conventions, including craft								

Evaluation of Content

1. Inaccurate

2. Accurate but too general with insufficient text evidence

3. Accurate with sufficient text evidence

4. Accurate with sufficient text evidence and important insights

Evaluation of the Thinking Process

1. Poorly organized with little to no evidence of logical thought, coherence, transitions, or clarity

2. The thinking is generally logical though there may be some evidence of circular reasoning, redundancy, or omission of a clear purpose

3. The thinking is logical and mostly clear, though lack of a unique voice makes the purpose more general than specific

4. The thinking is logical and clear with a unique voice that is compelling

Evaluation of Written Language: Conventions and Craft

1. Many written language issues that make the piece difficult to read including numerous spelling, punctuation, and grammar errors; awkward sentence structure; little use of relevant vocabulary

2. Writing is readable but not especially fluent with problems such as inconsistent spelling, punctuation, and grammar; some lack of clarity in sentence structure; some imprecise words

3. Generally appropriate written language proficiency for grade level: spelling, grammar, and punctuation that do not interfere with fluency; grade appropriate sentence structure; use of key words from the text

4. Meets all criteria for the grade level and additionally demonstrates particularly strong craft, such as precise word choice, figurative language, and varied sentence construction

---

Interpretation of Rubric Data

Name: _____

Student's strengths for the content assessment:

Student's needs for the content assessment:

Student's strengths for the standards-based assessment:

Student's needs for the standards-based assessment:

Next instructional steps for this student:

1. _____

2. _____

3. _____

Thinking Beyond Standards

As you evaluate your students, try to think beyond national or state standards. Think about students' capacity to think critically as responsible, compassionate citizens. If we're serious about our intent to prepare the children we teach today for college and career tomorrow, we need to make sure they're on track for measures of their success that reach beyond test scores. Do students demonstrate a thoughtful understanding of problems and issues? Are they open to multiple points of view, thoroughly comprehending key concepts? Do they have the capacity to synthesize and elaborate on central ideas and the ability to generate insightful inferences?

What's the ultimate measure of our students' achievement? If they care about knowledge, enjoy conversing about ideas, and are respectful of one another, that's the kind of academic success that counts.

Photo courtesy of Rick Harrington Photography

These are the same questions we posed earlier in this guide as the ultimate measure of our success as teachers of close reading. The rubric on the next page shows what these criteria might look like at three different levels of performance. This rubric can be applied to all of the sources students read, not just the picture books in these units: your novels or chapter books, informational articles, poetry, and primary source documents. What do *all* of your complex texts reveal about the way your students understand and respond to their world?

Go to page 57 and the companion website, **resources.corwin.com/ boyleslessons,** for a list of questions that help you think about Step 9 and help you apply this step when planning your own unit.

Rubric for Measuring Students' Critical Thinking: Talking and Writing About Sources

Name: _____ **Date:** _____

Task: _____

	2 Exemplary	1 Satisfactory	0 Unsatisfactory
Problem/question/issue	Clearly articulates the essential problem represented by all texts; sees beneath the surface	Identifies the core problem, but thinking is quite basic without many insights	Does not recognize the core problem in any text
Openness	Willingly examines multiple points of view from multiple texts with fair-mindedness and empathy	Shows openness to point of view in one text but doesn't thoroughly explore others that represent alternate views	Cannot get past her/his own point of view when examining an issue; language shows strong bias
Key concepts	Identifies all of the key concepts and central ideas in multiple texts	Identified concepts are a mix of key ideas and smaller details	Unable to identify key concepts; recognizes just a few unrelated details
Synthesis of multiple texts	Integrates information from multiple texts that shows solid understanding of how information fits together	Integration of information is generally sufficient though some information is misplaced	Information is not adequately synthesized; it may be added randomly or tacked on to the end
Elaboration	Provides full elaboration of key concepts with the most useful details from multiple texts	Provides adequate elaboration from multiple texts but could be more specific in some cases	Elaboration is inadequate; too general
Inferences	Makes thoughtful, relevant, and insightful inferences incorporating all texts	Inferences are relevant but lack depth of thinking and may not include all texts	Is not able to infer from any text, or inferences are irrelevant
Implications and next steps	Recognizes logical implications; predicts consequences based on solid inferential thinking from multiple texts; predicts possible next steps	Sees probable implications but doesn't elaborate on predictions using inferences from all texts; next steps are somewhat superficial	Does not recognize the likely outcome of a situation; predictions are not based on reasonable inferences

Critical thinking strengths: _____

Critical thinking needs: _____

Next steps in critical thinking for this student: _____

_____

Step 10

Analyze Student Work

Consider Why We Need to Reflect Systematically on Student Work

Our assessment of students should not end with filling out a rubric, even if the rubric is a very good one and captures the essence of a student's capacity to think critically. We need to look systematically at the work that earned the designation of *exemplary, satisfactory,* or *unsatisfactory* across these criteria (or any criteria we're using to assess a piece of student work)—for individual students and across all of our students. We need to ask ourselves *why* and *what's next?*

Conferring one-on-one with students is *always* time well spent.

Photo courtesy of Rick Harrington Photography

See the last section of this book, The End of the Story: Reflecting on Student Work, on page 293 to examine work samples by students who have engaged in tasks associated with unit lessons. While these are not all *assessment* tasks, remember that all instruction should be diagnostic. Students' responses on tasks from today's lesson "inform" the decisions we make about what we teach next—hence their regard as "formative assessments."

A Strategy for Looking at Student Work

You can make this process of looking at student work incredibly elaborate or simple. I choose simple. For individual students, I begin with where they're succeeding and then look at what they're on the verge of understanding. Recognizing this "just right" place where a brand new aha moment is a breath away is exactly where you want to intervene, the next instructional step.

Recognize that there's a marked difference between being *on the verge of understanding* something and *not yet ready to embrace a particular learning point.* This distinction is not always easy to spot in comprehension because there is no nice, neat progression of comprehension skills. Still, we can make smart choices about what to teach next based on the careful examination of almost any rubric.

The rubric for critical thinking above is a good example of what I mean. Unless students can identify the problem or issue, they will not be able to recognize the key concepts associated with that issue. If they can't accurately name the big concepts, they will not be able to elaborate on them or make insightful inferences. Without those inferences, it is nearly impossible to see the implications or next steps.

With your students who miss the mark for inferences and implications, trace the problem back to its roots: Where does the thinking break down? *This* is your next instructional step, your point of intervention. And this is how we arrive at differentiation—because different kids need different "next steps."

One more thing (I'm on a roll here) came to mind: We are all so tuned in to differentiation that supports our lowest performing learners, doing our Herculean best to bring them up to grade level expectations, that we sometimes don't think enough about our high performers. Because these students already meet or exceed grade level standards, we don't worry too much about what's next for them. But we should; every child in our class has a right to expect a year's worth of academic progress each school year.

Don't settle for "good enough" with these exceptionally capable students. Hold them accountable to the highest level of performance. On our critical thinking rubric, they will probably be the kids who are already good at knowing the problem and citing evidence. Pay attention to how they *use* this knowledge: their inferences, insights, and recognition of implications. Also, check the consistency with which they apply their thinking. On the critical thinking rubric scale, consistency will typically yield scores of "2," while inconsistency will earn some rankings of "1." A next learning step for high achievers (or any student) can also be identified by what specific criteria are not being applied consistently.

As a veteran teacher, I keep a lot of this thinking in my head, but a template will serve you well if you are just beginning to analyze student work in this way. It also serves as a simple format for conferring with students. To get started, see the feedback form: Reflecting on Reading Responses for Individual Students. Based on the four response boxes per page, you can see that I try to streamline this process as much as possible.

Video 19

Small Group Strategy Lesson: Debrief

Watch Nancy and colleagues debrief and identify key takeaways from the strategy lesson.

resources.corwin .com/boyleslessons

Reflecting on Reading
Responses for Individual Students

Student's name: _____

Task: _____

Key criteria: _____

_____

Successes: _____

_____

On the verge of understanding: _____

_____

Next instructional point: _____

_____

Student's name: _____

Task: _____

Key criteria: _____

_____

Successes: _____

_____

On the verge of understanding: _____

_____

Next instructional point: _____

_____

Student's name: _____

Task: _____

Key criteria: _____

_____

Successes: _____

_____

On the verge of understanding: _____

_____

Next instructional point: _____

_____

Student's name: _____

Task: _____

Key criteria: _____

_____

Successes: _____

_____

On the verge of understanding: _____

_____

Next instructional point: _____

_____

Looking for Trends in Performance

We also need to look for *trends* in student performance: As a class or a group, what are our students doing well? What is not going so well? How should we proceed with our high achievers? With our low achievers? What will we need to teach or reteach to the whole class? To small groups? To individual students? The answers to these questions will inform our teaching, the way we implement close reading in the future.

Reflecting on Class Performance for a Close Reading Follow-Up Task provides a template for looking at student work for the trends we find as we examine a class or group set of written (or oral) responses to reading. Appraise your students' work honestly to obtain the maximum benefit as you adjust your close reading instruction moving forward.

Recognizing where our teaching is strong, where it could be stronger, and what our next instructional steps will be are hallmarks of reflective teachers who understand the significance of each carefully planned step that led students to a particular level of performance. The ten planning steps outlined here are designed for the optimal teaching of close reading. The units and lessons that follow provide the tools you need to put this plan into action. For even greater impact, kick up the action by designing your own units—with a few colleagues planning together for your grade level or with a committee planning for your whole district. Watch those learning pathways become avenues for student success as close readers become deep, critical thinkers.

Go to page 57 and the companion website, **resources.corwin.com/boyleslessons,** for a list of questions that help you think about Step 10 and help you apply this step when planning your own unit.

Video 20

Curriculum Development

Watch Nancy discuss with teachers the process of curriculum development.

resources.corwin .com/boyleslessons

Reflecting on Class Performance for a Close Reading Follow-Up Task

Text: _____

Task: _____

Teacher: _____ **Grade:** _____

What did you see from students who performed well on this task? (Try to be specific: What made their responses strong?)

What would be a next step for students who did well on this task? (This could relate to both reading and writing)

What did you see from students who did not perform well on this task? (Try to be specific: In what ways were their responses weak? What were you hoping to see that you did not see?)

What would be a next step for students who did not do well on this task? (This could relate to both reading and writing)

Reflection Questions for the Ten Steps of Unit Planning and Teaching

	Think About This Step in the Process . . .	How Might You Apply This Step as You Plan Your Own Unit?
Step 1	<ul><li>How might teaching students about different pathways be valuable?</li><li>What do you see as the value of converting a unit focus into an inquiry question?</li></ul>	<ul><li>Identify a learning pathway that would be a useful area of study or fun for your students—and then decide on a unit focus. (For example, you might choose studying a genre as your pathway and then mysteries as your unit focus.)</li><li>Now turn your unit focus into an inquiry question. (For example, are these mysteries fact or fiction: The Loch Ness Monster, Big Foot, Yeti?)</li></ul>
Step 2	<ul><li>What qualities in a text do your students seem to value most?</li><li>What particular challenges do your students present that you will want to consider when choosing texts for a unit of study?</li></ul>	<ul><li>Using your unit focus (such as mysteries: fact or fiction), locate and assemble a selection of texts that would be appropriate for your students. These sources could be picture books or other relevant texts. List books here.</li><li>Analyze the complexity of these texts using the Quick Survey of Text Complexity chart, accounting for both Lexile and qualitative complexities. In what ways is each text complex?</li><li>Based on your text analysis, choose one anchor text for each week of your unit. (Example: For a four-week unit, choose four texts.) List your anchor texts.</li><li>Order your texts based on what would make the most sense for your students.</li></ul>
Step 3	<ul><li>Which standards are the most challenging for your students? How can you make sure your students are getting enough opportunities to focus on these challenge standards throughout the year?</li><li>How can you incorporate various standards into your unit even though the standard might not be "featured" in your unit assessment?</li></ul>	<ul><li>For your unit, which Common Core or state standard would be a good fit for a feature standard? Why? (Ex.: For a unit on mysteries, I might choose Standard 8 because of its emphasis on the reliability and validity of evidence and because it isn't always easy to match this standard to a unit of study in the elementary grades.)</li><li>For your unit, is there a standard that would be a useful supporting standard? (Ex.: For a unit on mysteries, I might choose Standard 5 as a supporting standard because students can always benefit from a review of genre characteristics.)</li></ul>

(Continued)

(Continued)

	Think About This Step in the Process . . .	How Might You Apply This Step as You Plan Your Own Unit?
Step 4	• In your school or at your grade level, what determines the length of your literacy units? How long is each unit? If you need to maintain a unit focus for more than four or five weeks, could you divide your units into two related parts? What would they be? (This would make teaching and learning more manageable.) • Would the basic organization of this Unit Curriculum Map work for you (initiation, instruction, assessment)? Why or why not? If it doesn't quite work, how would you modify it to make it more user friendly?	• Find a "kickoff" text to get students revved about the unit ahead. This should be short, not too complex, and worthy of discussion and divergent thinking. Identify your short text here. • Read your anchor texts. Decide tentatively what follow-up skill or strategy lessons you will teach after the Initial Close Reading Lesson. Fill in each week of the map with these lesson objectives and a brief phrase about the content of the lessons. See a Unit Curriculum Map for any of the units in this book for an example. Also, note that you can change your lesson objectives if your student data reveal different needs as you teach your unit. • Begin to think about the assessment question(s) you might ask about your texts at the end of the unit for the content assessment. Your questions should help students to integrate their learning from all of your texts. Also, begin looking for related short texts (including video clips and other resources) that could be used for your cold read standards-based assessments. Jot notes here about your initial thinking about these assessments.

Step 5	• What do you think about this idea of "learning pathways"? How could you use it beyond just an individual unit to support your students' literacy learning?
	
	• You don't really have to begin your unit with a kickoff lesson, but what would be the value of doing so?
	
	• Where could you look for short texts (literary or informational) that would engage your students and get them in the right frame of mind for the study ahead?
		• There are many suggestions here (and in the introduction to each unit) for initiating your unit. For a particular unit of your own, what would your unit preview include?
		  ○ How would you introduce the learning pathway?
		  ○ How would you introduce the unit focus?
		  ○ How would you introduce the inquiry question?
		  ○ How would you introduce the anchor texts?
		
		• What short text would you use to get students into the mindset of this unit? What questions would you ask for this text?

Step 6	• What instructional components will need the most tweaking for you to align your teaching practices with the kind of scaffolding advised for close reading? What changes will you want to make? • What novels or longer texts would you like to use for close reading with your students? Why would these be good choices?	• Using the Planning Template for Initial Close Reading Lesson (Appendix 1, at resources.corwin.com/boyleslessons), plan the way you will support students before, during, and after reading for the first anchor text in your unit. Then, plan the initial lesson for each of your other anchor texts. • To make sure you have addressed all of the Reading standards through your text-dependent questions, choose one of your lessons and identify the standard aligned to each question. What did you find? Were Standards 1–6 represented? (Standards 7–9 will likely be represented more fully in your follow-up lessons.) If you see that you are omitting certain standards, make a special effort to include them more consistently.

	Think About This Step in the Process . . .	How Might You Apply This Step as You Plan Your Own Unit?
Step 7	• Sometimes teachers provide the same level of practice to students over and over rather than gradually reducing instructional support. How do you gradually move students toward independence? Think of an example where you have led your students to independence step-by-step. • Identify some skills and strategies that seem to require much practice by your students to achieve success. Look for opportunities to build these skills and strategies through follow-up lessons.	• Choose a text for which you have written an initial close reading lesson and now plan a follow-up lesson. Write a short description of this lesson in the chart at the end of the lesson planning template or fill out the template for Follow-Up Skill or Strategy Lesson. Be sure to identify what you will reread. This lesson should not be just an "activity."
Step 8	• How do you help your students synthesize information and ideas from multiple texts? • Which questions from the chart on pages 41–42 might be new to your students and would help them integrate knowledge from multiple texts more thoroughly?	• Using the texts from a unit that you designed, list five or six questions that would help students integrate their knowledge from all texts. In what ways would these questions help them to develop deeper insights?
Step 9	• Do you agree with the thinking behind the use of two assessments rather than one? Why or why not? In what ways could both of these assessments be useful to you? • Look closely at the rubric criteria for both of the rubrics provided here. How could you provide your students with opportunities to demonstrate these characteristics in their thinking?	• Design both a content-based assessment and a standards-based assessment for a unit that you have created. Try to provide opportunities for students to demonstrate critical thinking across multiple texts. • Practice using the provided rubrics by evaluating one student using both the content and standards-based rubric and the critical thinking rubric: What did you learn about this student?
Step 10	• Take a look at some of the student work samples at the end of this book. Note my evaluation of different exemplars. Do you agree with my assessment? Do you see other points to consider? What conclusions would you draw, and where might you go next with instruction? • Is there anything you would add to the criteria I've suggested for either the feedback form for individual students or the reflection form for class trends? What would you add?	• Practice using one or more of these reflection forms for a specific literacy task to evaluate individual student performance or class trends. How can this systematic reflection guide your next instructional steps?

Learning Pathway

How to Study a Concept

What Makes Someone a Good Leader?

Unit Focus: Leadership

Photo courtesy of Wikimedia Commons

Let's begin the unit! This is one of eight units in this book that delivers just the "goods"—the questions, prompts, assessment tasks, and student reproducibles you'll need to implement robust close reading instruction within an inquiry unit. Just about all you need to do a few weeks in advance of starting is to look at the anchor texts on pages 64 and 65, and order those books. From there, the materials provided are all explained clearly in terms of when and how to use them. If you need clarification, look back at the ten steps that begin on page 15.

Introduction to the Unit

The Rationale

I chose this conceptual focus on leadership because it's so important for students in the intermediate grades to think about the personal traits and values that they want to guide the course of their lives now and in the future. What does a study of *leadership* entail? For intermediate grade students, I think this means building an understanding of leadership characteristics and then applying them to individuals who demonstrated these characteristics. We want students to understand that leaders are male and female, fictional and "real" and hail from diverse cultures and ethnic origins.

Some people may look at this *conceptual* focus and think of it as a "thematic" focus. I do not consider a one-word label (such as *leadership*) to be a theme or a main idea. I think a theme or main idea should be something *about* the concept. In this case, a related theme might be *persistence is an important leadership characteristic*. Or it could even be *young children can demonstrate characteristics of leadership*. These are central ideas that students might infer from reading a particular text or even several texts together.

With the concept of leadership as the focus of the unit, let's think about the ultimate goal of any unit teaching: helping students learn how to learn. I call it the learning pathway. With this unit, the pathway is How to Study a Concept. To that end, during your introductory lesson, you'll share with students the talking points in the following chart, Learning Pathway: How to Study a Concept.

The Inquiry Question and Discussion Points

The main question students will answer throughout this unit is **What makes someone a good leader?** There are so many angles from which we could approach this—and so many great books featuring great people and characters that could help to get us there—it's difficult to even know where to start. We also want students to understand the meaning of the term *concept* and that leadership is a concept: How do we study the concept of leadership? To launch, let's start with the discussion points indicated in Unit Preview Questions and Discussion Points for Studying a Concept: Leadership.

Next, because we want to know from the outset where we ultimately want to take students, I list questions under Questions for End-of-Unit Discussion About a Concept (Leadership) Integrating All Texts. These are questions you might pose at the end of this unit. That is, with any unit teaching, after completing all of the anchor books, we need to circle back to the inquiry question itself, to consider the books together. The questions help students synthesize their thinking across texts and wrap up the study in a thoughtful way.

Learning Pathway
How to Study a Concept

Share these prompts with students.

- *A concept is an idea, like injustice or conservation. A concept you study needs to be worth understanding. Why is it important to understand this concept?*

- *To study a concept, you first need to know what the idea is and to identify it clearly: What is the concept you are studying? Can you say it in your own words?*

- *A concept can mean different things to different people. A young person may understand only basic things about a concept, while an older person with more life experiences will have a deeper understanding. How might a younger child understand this concept? Why might a teacher or a parent care about this concept?*

- *In order to find meaning in any study, you need to consider how it might be important to you: How does this concept relate to you (past, present, future)?*

- *A concept is important because of what could happen if people don't understand it adequately. For example, if people don't understand pollution and make poor choices about caring for the environment, our world could develop many problems. What could happen if people don't understand this concept adequately?*

- *When you study a concept, you will learn more if you have some goals in mind: What do you hope to learn more about through the study of this concept?*

- *Where else could you research a concept other than in a book: Could you find newspaper or magazine articles about this concept? Could you examine a photograph or a piece of art work? Could you view a video clip or listen to an audio clip? Could you interview an expert who has studied this concept?*

Unit Preview Questions and Discussion Points

for Studying a Concept: Leadership

- *Introduce the term* concept *and its definition: "an idea of what something is or how it works" (www.merriam-webster.com/dictionary/concept)*

- *Discuss what it means to study a concept using the questions in* Learning Pathway: How to Study a Concept. *Select focus points and questions appropriate to your students' age and background knowledge about this type of study. Make a list of the "studying a concept" questions you will answer through this study of leadership.*

- *Now talk specifically about the concept of leadership: What is leadership, and how does it work? (Students should indicate that leadership involves influencing other people)*

- *Ask students what words they associate with leadership. (Students might indicate words such as* guide, direct, power, control.*)*

- *Ask students if all leaders are good leaders. Can they think of some good leaders and some bad leaders? What makes a leader good or bad?*

- *Introduce the inquiry question: What makes someone a good leader? (Students may have some initial responses to this question—which is fine. But don't get too far into this until they've acquired textual evidence.)*

- *Introduce the four leadership books selected for close reading. Show the cover and perhaps an illustration inside to pique students' interest. Do not explain the full story.*

Questions for End-of-Unit Discussion About a Concept (Leadership) Integrating All Texts

- Do you now feel that you can answer our inquiry question: *What makes someone a good leader?* Briefly summarize your response to this question.

- Which questions for Learning Pathway: How to Study a Concept can you answer after reading these books?

- Which book in this unit did you enjoy the most? Did you like this book because you liked learning about this leader? Or did you like the book because of the way it was written? Explain your thinking with textual evidence.

- How are the leaders we read about similar to one another? How are they different?

- What *obstacles* did these leaders face? How did each one overcome these obstacles? What leadership *values* were evident in overcoming these obstacles?

- Which author painted the most *believable* picture of a leader? How did this author make the person so believable?

- What advice would you give to other students studying the concept of leadership?

- Think about the article we read at the beginning of this unit: "To Be a Leader" (provided on pages 70 and 71). *After* completing this unit, what points in this article seem the most important? Why?

The Focus Standard

Any unit based on a *concept* will be well suited to the study of themes and central ideas since a concept *is* a central idea about some significant area of study. For that reason, the focus standard for this unit is CCRA R2: "Determine central ideas or themes of a text and analyze their development; summarize the key supporting details and ideas" (http://www.corestandards.org/ELA-Literacy/CCRA/R, Key Ideas section, para. 2). What themes emerge as readers consider the core values demonstrated through the lives of leaders studied through these texts? Hence, a lesson focusing on *theme* will be part of each week's study. But because these themes will reveal themselves through the lives of important individuals, real and fictitious, this unit is also a good opportunity to zoom in on *character*. This takes us to CCRA R3 as a supporting standard: "Analyze how and why individuals, events, or ideas develop and interact over the course of a text (http://www.corestandards.org/ELA-Literacy/CCRA/R, Key Ideas section, para. 3)." A lesson based on Standard 3 is suggested for most of these texts.

The Anchor Texts

The first text listed below is a short informational article intended to be read by the students themselves and discussed during a unit kickoff lesson. The remaining four texts are picture books, one of which will be read closely and studied during each week of the unit.

"To Be a Leader," a nonfiction article by Nancy Boyles (provided on page 70)

This text to be read by the students in a kickoff lesson (discussion questions are provided on page 71) is provided to get students thinking about what it is that leaders value. Initially, I thought of this as leadership characteristics. But a "characteristic" seems *fixed*, something immutable. My goal in having students read and discuss this article is for them to see that it's our values that guide our actions. And we can continually reconsider our values throughout our life so that they help us to make good choices. Some of those choices may, in fact, help us to become leaders.

Weslandia by Paul Fleischman

Weslandia is a perfect starting point for this unit. The main character in this fictional story is Wesley, a self-proclaimed outcast who marches to his own drum rather than to the beat of prevailing preadolescent priorities. One summer, in search of some relevance to his education, he creates his own fantasy civilization, which he names Weslandia. Resourcefulness, independent thinking, intelligence, and practicality lead to his success—and a new sense of respect from his peers. The wry humor in this book adds to its quirky charm and to its complexity. Other complexities include lots of new vocabulary words to learn and the inferential thinking required to discern the author's point of view about what is really important to maturing preadolescents. Lexile: 820. Grade level equivalent: 3.9.

Testing the Ice: A True Story About Jackie Robinson by Sharon Robinson

Testing the Ice is a personal narrative about Jackie Robinson written by his daughter. Of all the books I read to students, this remains one of their true favorites. More than just the story of a great baseball player, the strength of this text comes from the complexity of its double entendre: the father literally testing the ice for his children (despite his inability to swim) and the figurative interpretation related to Jackie Robinson's place in history as the first African American to play baseball on a major league team. Another complexity of this book is its structure, which moves back and forth between different time periods. Lexile: 800. Grade level equivalent: 5.3.

Night Flight: Amelia Earhart Crosses the Atlantic by Robert Burleigh

I chose this book in part for its depiction of a *female* leader, but as much for other reasons, too. Amelia Earhart became a leader in part because of her fearlessness, her courage to take almost unfathomable physical risks. I chose this book equally for its craft, the lyrical language so representative of books by Robert Burleigh. Take the time to appreciate all of the complexities this book has to offer: the craft, background about Amelia Earhart and this time in American history, and meaning regarding a person's motivations for taking such incredible risks. Do not be deterred by the low Lexile. This is a perfect example of why Lexile alone should never be our go-to factor in choosing complex texts. Lexile: 500. No grade level equivalent available.

Nelson Mandela by Kadir Nelson

Students will be drawn to this book, beginning on the cover. The full-color portrait of Mandela is everything we expect from Kadir Nelson, illustrator and author. It's alive with emotion, intensity, and character. The words inside paint an equally profound picture of the little boy in a faraway African village who started life with so little, made the most of educational opportunities along the way, recognized as a young adult the urgent need for justice in his South Africa, paid the price for his courage with decades of imprisonment, and at last realized his dream of equality for his people. Complexities include multiple themes requiring inferential thinking and lots of African words to test students' understanding through context. Lexile: 960. Grade level equivalent: 5.

Other Texts Useful for Studying Leadership

To extend this study of leadership or to use texts other than those identified above, you might want to consider the following titles. *The Empty Pot* is a Japanese folktale; the other books describe the lives of real people who made a difference in different ways. Of course, there are hundreds of other books that could also work for a study of leadership. Think about your population of students and what is most appropriate for your grade level.

- *The Empty Pot* by Demi
- *Brave Girl: Clara and the Shirtwaist Makers' Strike of 1909* by Michelle Markel
- *Elizabeth Leads the Way: Elizabeth Cady Stanton and the Right to Vote* by Tanya Stone
- *Harvesting Hope: The Story of Cesar Chavez* by Kathleen Krull
- *As Good as Anybody: Martin Luther King and Abraham Joshua Heschel's Amazing March Toward Freedom* by Richard Michelson

The Unit's Two Assessments

Featured Reading Standard 2: Theme/Main ideas in a text

Featured Writing Format: Opinion writing

See the Unit Curriculum Map for Close Reading for where these assessments might fit into your study of the Moon. Also, for more information about the rationale behind these two assessments and how they differ, as well as guidance for using the provided rubrics, refer to Step 9 on page 43 and Step 10 on page 50. For evaluating students' performance, see page 45 for the Rubric for Content-Based Assessment (Task 1) and Standards-Based Assessment (Task 2). Turn to page 293, The End of the Story: Reflecting on Student Work, for some sample student work and commentary.

Task 1: Content Assessment

It is said that the best leadership is not about making speeches or being liked. It is about what a person accomplishes and what they value. Decide which leader, in your opinion, was responsible for the most noteworthy accomplishment: Wesley, Jackie Robinson, Amelia Earhart, or Nelson Mandela.

Please do the following:

- Identify the leader you selected.

- Describe this person's major accomplishment and why it was so important.

- Name and explain *two* values that you think helped to make this person a leader, using examples from the article "To Be a Leader" and the book about the leader you selected.

- Finally, consider which other person that we studied would be the *most respected* by the leader you are writing about. Write at least two sentences about the reason for this respect using evidence from our reading.

Your writing should be done in the form of a newspaper article that could appear in your school newspaper. Be sure to include a headline and maybe some subheadings that get readers' attention.

Task 2: Learning Pathway and Standard Assessment

Access the articles below using these links. (Your teacher may tell you more specifically which articles to read.)

Possible articles (all retrieved for free from www.ReadWorks.org, a free site)

- Erik the Red: 840L: http://www.readworks.org/passages/north-america-erik-red-and-world%E2%80%99s-largest-island

- Harriet Tubman: 660L: http://www.readworks.org/passages/famous-african-americans-harriet-tubman-and-underground-railroad

- John Adams: 880L: http://www.readworks.org/passages/us-presidents-john-adams

- Jonas Salk: 780L: http://www.readworks.org/passages/just-what-doctor-ordered

- Marian Anderson: 610L: http://www.readworks.org/passages/famous-african-americans-marian-anderson

- Thomas Edison: 640L: http://www.readworks.org/passages/famous-inventors-thomas-edison

It is said that the best leadership is not about making speeches or being liked. It is about what a person accomplishes and what they value. Read three short articles about three different leaders (from the list above). Decide which leader, in your opinion, was responsible for the most noteworthy accomplishment while also living by important values.

Please do the following:

- Identify the leader you selected.

- Describe this person's major accomplishment and why it was so important.

- Name and explain *two* values that you think helped to make this person a leader, using examples from the article "To Be a Leader" and from the short texts about different leaders.

- Finally, consider which other person you read about in one of the short articles would be the *most respected* by the leader you are writing about. Write at least two sentences about the reason for this respect using evidence from your reading.

Your writing should be done in the form of a newspaper article that could appear in your school newspaper. Be sure to include a headline and maybe some subheadings that get readers' attention.

Unit Curriculum Map for Close Reading

What Makes Someone a Good Leader?

TEXT	MONDAY	TUESDAY	WEDNESDAY	THURSDAY	FRIDAY
				Unit Preview	Kickoff Lesson
				See Unit Preview Questions and Discussion Points	Read and discuss the article "To Be a Leader." Discussion questions are provided at the end of this document
Weslandia by Paul Fleischman	Objective: R1 Close Reading	Objective: SL1; R3 Close Reading Follow-Up	Objective: R2 Themes/Main Ideas	Objective: R6 Author's Purpose or Point of View	Objective: W3 Narrative Writing
	Read closely to answer text dependent questions	Complete the After Reading tasks including a collaborative task for identifying character traits	Identify multiple themes in this book, focusing particularly on "necessity is the mother of invention"	Identify places in the text where the author pokes fun at people's lack of independent thinking	What else might Wesley *need* for his civilization? Write a paragraph adding a new invention—complete with author's crafts
Testing the Ice by Sharon Robinson	Objective: R1 Close Reading	Objective: SL1; R3 Close Reading Follow-Up	Objective: R2 Themes	Objective: R7; R9 Nontraditional: Comparing Photos and Illustrations; Text-to-Text Connections	Objective: W2 Explanatory Writing
	Read closely to answer text dependent questions	Complete the After Reading tasks including a collaborative task for identifying character traits	Reread the text to identify possible themes and how they are important to the story	Compare a photograph of Jackie Robinson stealing home to the illustration on pp. 3–4	In what ways did Jackie Robinson show that he was a leader and role model?

TEXT	MONDAY	TUESDAY	WEDNESDAY	THURSDAY	FRIDAY
Night Flight: Amelia Earhart Crosses the Atlantic by Robert Burleigh	Objective: R1 Close Reading	Objective: R1 Close Reading	Objective: SL1; R2 Close Reading Follow-Up	Objective: R4 Word Choice	Objective: W2 Explanatory Writing
	Read the Afterword and first half of the book closely to answer text-dependent questions	Read second half of book closely to answer text-dependent questions	Complete the After Reading tasks including a collaborative task that relates to theme	Examine the author's crafts on page 10 and page 17. Create some shared examples of these crafts for independent application on Day 5	Using some of the crafts highlighted on Day 4, write a paragraph that Amelia might have written about her scariest moment in this flight
Nelson Mandela by Kadir Nelson	Objective: R1 Close Reading	Objective: SL1; R3 Close Reading Follow-Up	Objective: R2 Themes/Main Ideas	Objective: R7 Nontraditional: Video Clip	Objective: R9; W1 Opinion Writing Based on Text-to-Text Connections
	Read closely to answer text-dependent questions	Complete the After Reading tasks including a collaborative task for character traits	Explain how a quote represents Mandela's life	Identify images from a video that have significance in Mandela's life	Write an opinion piece comparing Mandela's leadership to the leadership of another character/person in this study
	Culminating Discussion	Content Assessment	Standards-Based Assessment		
	Respond orally to text-to-text connections for studying this topic. (*See* Questions for End-of-Unit Discussion Integrating All Texts)	Students complete the content-assessment task integrating all texts in this study	Students complete the standards-based assessment task using cold reads		

TO BE A LEADER

by Nancy Boyles

Every leader is different, so it's hard to paint a picture of a "typical" leader. Here are some values that many leaders live by that guide the decisions they make.

Lots of Decisions, Good Choices

Leaders understand the importance of making good choices. They make decisions based on goals, ethics, and examining their options. Having a clear objective or goal makes it so much easier to make a decision because you know what you are trying to accomplish. Each decision you make should move you a little closer to your goal. For example, if you want to be a star athlete on a major league team, you need to make good choices beginning in childhood. Should you practice your sport or hang out in front of the television all day? Which college will give you the best opportunity to perfect your sports skills in addition to providing you with a great education? Future leaders make smart choices that help make their dreams come true. Oh, and don't forget to follow through. Lots of people who would *like* to be leaders have great goals, but sometimes they don't stick to the plan. Eventually, other people stop believing in them.

Leading by Example

Leaders value hard work. Let's face it, if you are going to be a leader, you need to have someone (or lots of people) willing to follow you. How will you influence people? Do you get what you want by being popular, outgoing, and good looking? Sometimes in school, it may seem that way, but *real* leaders lead by example. They roll up their sleeves and work alongside the individuals they wish to lead. Do you want your classmates to vote for you for president of the "Clean Green Club?" Then you need to go out there with everyone else and pick up trash! People respect leaders who work hard, leaders who "put their money where their mouth is." Your energy will be contagious. If you are enthusiastic about your work, the people you want to influence will more likely be enthusiastic about what you have asked them to do. You will motivate them—another key ingredient to leadership!

Thinking With Your Head and Your Heart

Leaders represent their followers and think of their needs before their own. Leading is not about getting famous or rich. It is about meeting a need. To be a leader, you need to think with your head (your brain), but you also must think with your heart. Sometimes this is difficult. Suppose you are the "boss" at work. One of your employees is not very reliable. She often comes to work late, and she spends a lot of time on her phone. You consider firing her. But she has two little children at home, and her husband doesn't have a job. What should you do? It is not okay for personal issues to keep a person from meeting work responsibilities. But being a leader means considering all sides of a difficult situation and trying to come up with an acceptable situation for everyone involved. A good leader values what it *feels like* to be in the other person's shoes. This is called *empathy*.

Valuing the Vision

Good leaders value long range goals. This means having a *vision*. A vision is an idea of the way something could be if it worked out perfectly. A vision doesn't usually involve something you can imagine happening right away. It is more of a long-distance view. For example, a principal might have a vision of the kind of school she would create so that all children loved learning. An architect might have a vision of a playground that would be just right for kindergarten students if enough funds could be raised to build it.

Thinking Independently and Thinking Together

A couple of other qualities that many leaders value are creativity and resourcefulness. You can't do things "the same old way" if you want to accomplish something new and different. You need to be a problem solver. You need to think for yourself. You can't be afraid to stand out from the crowd or be the first to do something. Some people never accomplish the goals they've set out for themselves because they want to fit in with their friends and be just like them. They value safety more than adventure. Would

(Continued)

(Continued)

humans have ever landed on the moon without a sense of adventure? Would new lands have been discovered? Would inventions like the television or the Internet have been created? Leaders are bold without being reckless.

Leaders take on a lot of responsibility themselves, but they also make sure that everyone is involved and takes on some responsibility. This creates a sense of teamwork. With teamwork comes more excitement about projects, more good ideas, and even better results.

Most Important of All

Maybe what good leaders value most is the importance of living by all of these wonderful qualities even when no one is watching. It's sometimes easy to do the right thing when others are paying attention.

But when others are out of sight, some people think they can get away with actions that are not completely honest or responsible. The best leaders value *integrity*. That's a big word that means doing the right thing even when no one is looking.

Bibliography

The Characteristics of Leadership—7 Important Traits: http://www.leadership-toolbox.com/characteristic-of-leadership.html

Top 10 Qualities That Make a Great Leader: http://www.forbes.com/sites/tanyaprive/2012/12/19/top-10-qualities-that-make-a-great-leader/

23 Traits of Good Leaders: http://www.cnn.com/2011/LIVING/08/03/good.leader.traits.cb/

Think About

Think about the questions below as you reflect on the article and begin this unit on leadership.

- Why do you think this article was selected to introduce this unit?

- Which of the qualities described in this article do *you* especially value in a leader? Explain.

- Can you think of any leaders (living or dead) who lived by the values described in this article? Explain.

- Can someone be a leader if he or she just lives by one or two of these values—or do you need to live by *all* of these values to succeed as a leader? Explain.

- Can children demonstrate these same leadership values? How?

- How can this article guide us as we move through this unit on leadership?

Close Reading Lessons for Weslandia

Initial Close Reading Lesson

Text: *Weslandia*　　　　　　　　　　　　　　　　　　　**Author:** Paul Fleischman

Purpose: R1: Close reading for deep understanding of the text

Before Reading

Clues Based on Cover Illustration
• Notice evidence of fantasy in this illustration: child is standing on plant with flower taller than he is; child is wearing strange outfit
Clues Based on Title, Author
• No clues provided by title. Will need to pay attention during reading to determine significance
Probable Text Type (Literary or Informational); Possible Genre
• Appears to be a story; may be a fantasy
Vocabulary That May Need Pre-Teaching for ELLs or Low Language Students
• Outcast, shelter, fleeing, civilization, crop, schoolmates, traditional sports, language

During Reading

Questions Students Should Ask Themselves for Each Chunk of Text
• What is the author telling me?
• Any hard or important words?
• What does the author want me to understand?
• How does the author play with language to add to meaning?
Follow-Up Text-Dependent Questions for the Teacher to Ask About Each Chunk of Text
Pages 1–2
• What do you learn about Wesley on these pages? (doesn't fit in, doesn't give in to peer pressure, parents are worried that he isn't like everyone else)
• What is a civilization? (the culture characteristics of a time and place)
• Does the author seem to be poking fun at Wesley or at Wesley's parents? Explain (includes ridiculous examples: refused to shave his head, disliked pizza and soda)

Pages 3–4

- What is the author's purpose for including this detail: "two styles of houses—garage on the left and garage on the right" (to show how boring and unimaginative Wesley's world was)
- What is a tormentor? (someone who bullies you)
- What is shelter? (a place to live)
- Why do you think other kids tormented Wesley? (he wasn't like them)

Pages 5–6

- What does Wesley seem to think about school? (boring, what he learns doesn't really relate to him)
- What is Wesley's bright idea for a summer project? (found his own civilization)
- What is this book starting to be about? (following your own dreams, not following the crowd)

Pages 7–10

- How was Wesley's land "being planted"? (wind carried seeds)
- How does Wesley's garden show his independent spirit? (doesn't grow typical vegetables, no such thing as a weed, enjoyed the "unknown")

Pages 11–14

- What are the elements of fantasy here? (size of the plants)
- What is Wesley's attitude when his neighbor questions his plants? (confident, proud)
- What are you learning about Wesley with the invention of a cup made of fruit rind, a juice squeezing device, and new food recipes? (resourceful, a creative thinker)

Pages 15–16

- Now what was Wesley inventing? (clothing that was appropriate for his work, spinning wheel to make his fabric)
- Why did Wesley invent these particular things? (based on NEED—they solved a problem)
- What does *myriad* mean? (many)

Pages 17–18

- What does *scornful* mean? (critical)
- What was beginning to happen with Wesley's friends? (becoming interested, less critical; they wanted a turn at the mortar; they became *former* tormentors)
- Why is this *ironic*? (this was hard work; Wesley got to lounge around while his friends did his work)
- What were Wesley's latest inventions? Why did he create them? (suntan lotion and mosquito repellent—to solve other problems)

Pages 19–22

- What new features did Wesley add to his civilization? (system to tell time, new counting system, name: Weslandia, games that involved strategy)
- What do all of these inventions tell us about Wesley? (smart, independent thinker, resourceful, creative)
- Discuss words as needed: *traditional, spectators, strategy, complex, blunders*

Pages 23–26

- Do these new inventions follow the same kind of thinking? Explain (yes—all solved problems in a practical and creative way)

- What details do you observe in the picture on pp. 25–26 worth noting? (accept any reasonable answer)

Pages 27–30

- Look first at the illustration: How does Weslandia compare to the world around it? (not so boring and traditional)

- Do you notice any change here in Wesley's father? (seems to have more respect for Wesley)

- Why do you suppose Wesley's "morale" improved? (doing what he loved, had a *purpose*)

- Now what was Wesley creating? (language, ink, alphabet)

- What do you predict will happen with Wesley's friends when he returns to school? (should infer that he will be more respected)

Pages 31–32

- Look at the illustration: Not only did Wesley have friends, but he was also now regarded as _____? (the leader)

After Reading (Complete These Tasks on Day 2 of the Lesson Sequence)

Important Words to Talk About the Text

- Some possibilities include Wesley, Weslandia, tormentor, civilization, independent, resourceful, creative

Theme, Lesson, or Message (if Appropriate)

- There are multiple themes here such as, Don't be afraid to be an independent thinker, Your creative thinking and resourcefulness can lead to exciting new outcomes, "Necessity is the mother of invention," and others (Complete this task on Day 3 of the lesson sequence. See below)

Summary or Gist Statement

- This story might be better suited to a gist statement than a summary since it doesn't follow a traditional problem/solution format

Review of Text Type (Literary/Information) and Genre

- Fantasy (including many aspects of reality)

Collaborative Oral Task

- With a partner or small group, choose three qualities that you think made Wesley a leader. Be prepared to explain your thinking with evidence from the text

Follow-up lessons can be taught in a different order.

Day	Focus Standard	Content for Whole-Class Lessons and Guided Student Practice
2	Close reading follow-up discussion including an emphasis on character traits SL1; R3	Complete the After Reading tasks using a combination of partner/small group work and whole-class discussion: Identify important words to talk about the text, identify the genre, and generate a gist statement. Also, complete the *Collaborative Oral Task* (page 74) focusing on Wesley's leadership characteristics.
3	Theme/Main ideas R2	Reread this book or parts of the book to think about themes. There are several themes to consider. Ask students to name a few themes that they found. (They might say: *Think for yourself—don't follow the crowd, qualities that make a leader,* etc.) If students don't mention it, suggest that another important theme of this book goes along with the old saying: "Necessity is the mother of invention." Discuss the meaning of this. In pairs or small groups, students can find evidence for one of the themes.
4	Author's purpose or point of view R6	In this story, it is easy to figure out the author's point of view because he pokes fun at people who are not independent thinkers. Reread the book to find examples of this. Be sure to analyze the illustrations as well as the author's words.
5	Narrative writing W3	Now that students have probed the theme that new inventions are designed to solve a problem, ask them to think of something else that Wesley might need for his civilization. This should be something that is both *helpful* and *practical* (like the rest of his inventions.) Write one or more paragraphs about this invention that could be added to this story. Include author's crafts, such as dialogue, snapshots, thoughtshots, and gestures.

Close Reading Lessons for Testing the Ice: A True Story About Jackie Robinson

Initial Close Reading Lesson

Text: *Testing the Ice: A True Story About Jackie Robinson*   **Author:** Sharon Robinson

Purpose: R1: Close reading for deep understanding of the text

Before Reading

Clues Based on Cover Illustration

- Notice the father ice skating with children

Clues Based on Title, Author

- Title: Notice the title—pay attention to how this is important to the story
- Author: Notice that author is Sharon Robinson, probably related to Jackie Robinson—pay attention to what this connection really is

Probable Text Type (Literary or Informational); Possible Genre

- Looks like it's a story, but true (personal narrative)

Vocabulary That May Need Pre-Teaching for ELLs or Low Language Students

- World Series, Brooklyn Dodgers, New York Yankees, lake, trophy, Major League Baseball, guts, temper, insults, victory

During Reading

Questions Students Should Ask Themselves for Each Chunk of Text

- What is the author telling me?
- Any hard or important words?
- What does the author want me to understand?
- How does the author play with language to add to meaning?

Follow-Up Text-Dependent Questions for the Teacher to Ask About Each Chunk of Text

Pages 1–2

- What information are you getting on the first page? (date, Dodgers, beat Yankees)
- Who is Sharon Robinson? (daughter and narrator)

- Why do you think the author might have started the book in this way with all this information and no illustration? (sometimes you don't know right away why the beginning of a book is significant; come back to this later)

Pages 3–4

- Why do you think the author included only one line on this page? (must be very important)
- What strategy do you think the author wants us to use here? (wonder why it was such a big celebration?)
- How does the illustration add to the message here? (feel Jackie's tension)

Pages 5–6

- Do you think this scene is from the beginning of Jackie Robinson's career, or later in his career? Why? (big house—already famous, rich, liked privacy)
- The story says their father thought the best part was the woods. What does the illustrator feature here as well? Could this be a clue? (the water)

Pages 7–8

- What details might be important here? (kids really liked the water, but father did not)

Pages 9–10

- What details are we getting here? (information about Jackie's athletic accomplishments)
- Why is the author providing these details? (so we can appreciate Jackie's skill as an athlete)
- Look at last sentence on p. 10: What do you expect to find out about next? (entry into Major League Baseball)

Pages 11–12

- You can tell right away that this scene is earlier in Jackie's life. What are the clues in the illustration? (photo isn't color; Jackie looks older)
- What author's craft is this? (flashback)
- In your own words, explain what the author is telling us here. (Paraphrase examples of discrimination)
- Why does the author give us this information? (lets us know how much discrimination there was, tells challenges Jackie had to overcome)

Pages 13–14

- What is the tone of this conversation? (serious)
- What words does the author use to show this? (guts, touch, threatened, attacked)
- Why is the author using this tone here? (to show how important this issue was)
- What does the author mean, "doors opening to other blacks"? (opportunities)
- What does the author mean, "color barrier of baseball would be shattered"? (help to end discrimination in Major League Baseball)
- How does the illustration add to the power of these pages? (look of intensity)
- Does Jackie's response surprise you or not? Why? (accept all reasonable answers)

Pages 15–16

- Are we in the flashback or in the present? (flashback)

- What happened here—in your own words? (Jackie scored and got a victory for his team)

- Why is the author writing the last line in larger font, and why was it such a "sweet victory"? (it's really important; it's much harder to insult a person who leads his team to victory)

Pages 17–18

- Now are we in the flashback or in the present?

- What is this story beginning to be about? (how Jackie Robinson had guts, was brave, was a leader in sports in shattering the color barrier)

- Why does the author give us the additional details about Jackie's awards? (wants to emphasize that he was a great athlete)

- *Did* Jackie Robinson get into the Hall of Fame? (yes)

- Go back to front cover: What have we *not* heard anything about yet? (testing the ice, ice skating)

Pages 19–20

- Now what do we know about Jackie Robinson? (retired after 1956 season, did other work)

- Why do you think the author is giving us this information? (very accomplished in other areas, not just sports)

Pages 21–22

- What detail keeps coming back? (Jackie Robinson didn't like the water)

- Why might the author be doing this? (probably going to be important for some reason)

Pages 23–24

- What strategy do you think the author wants us to use here? (picture the scene)

- Why doesn't the author tell us right on this page what the question was? (raises suspense)

Pages 25–26

- How can you tell that Jackie isn't too eager to go skating? What word does the author use? (anxious)

- Why do you think he gives in? (wants his children to be happy)

Pages 27–28

- Is the tone on this page the same or different from the previous page? What is the evidence? (word *reluctantly*; slow motion image: *very slowly, he pulled on one giant black rubber boot then the other*)

- Why doesn't the author take us to the lake right away? (high point of the story, wants to build lots of suspense)

Pages 29–30

- What was Jackie going to do with the shovel and broomstick? (test the ice—notice how this connects to the cover)

Pages 31–32

- When you learned that Jackie Robinson couldn't swim, was this surprising or not? (Some students might respond *yes* because of his athletic ability; others might respond *no* because of the author's clues about not liking water)

- How does the author use font size to add to the message here? (large font—important moment in the story)

- Why doesn't the author let us know the outcome of this problem right on this page? (suspense)

Pages 33–36

- Why do you think the author ended p. 36 with the line in large font, "My dad is the bravest man alive"? (went out on the ice for the sake of his children although he couldn't swim)

- Was there any other way that J. R. showed bravery? (playing on a major league team)

- Think about the title of the book. *Testing the ice* is an expression that people use sometimes. What does it mean? Other than going out on the ice to see what would happen, is there any other way that J. R. "tested the ice" during his life? (discuss "testing the ice" as figurative expression for Jackie's role in opening Major League Baseball to non-white players)

Pages 37–38

- Read final page as confirmation of double meaning of "testing the ice." Then do *Collaborative Oral Task* (see below).

After Reading (Complete These Tasks on Day 2 of the Lesson Sequence)

Important Words to Talk About the Text

- Jackie Robinson, ice, Dodgers, Negro League, discrimination, temper, courage, testing the ice

Theme, Lesson, or Message (if Appropriate)

- Address both the literal and figurative meaning of testing the ice; even famous, important people have weaknesses and fears—just like the rest of us—and they have to test their courage

Summary or Gist Statement

- This is not really a good text to summarize due to flashbacks and multiple time frames. Instead, create a gist statement, such as Jackie Robinson tested the ice in two ways during his life: once when he was the first African American to play on a Major League Baseball team and, again, when he tested the ice for his children although he couldn't swim.

Review of Text Type (Literary/Information) and Genre

- Personal narrative (includes details about someone's life that only someone close to you could know)

Collaborative Oral Task

- With a partner, decide which you think required more courage for Jackie Robinson: testing the ice for his children or testing the ice as the first African American to play on a Major League Baseball team? Explain your thinking

Follow-Up Lessons: Digging Deeper Through Rereading

Follow-up lessons can be taught in a different order.

Day	Focus Standard	Content for Whole-Class Lessons and Guided Student Practice
2	Close reading follow-up discussion including an emphasis on character traits SL1; R3	As a whole class or in small groups, identify the important words to talk about this text, talk about the theme, create a gist statement, and briefly discuss the genre (personal narrative). Then, ask students to work in pairs to respond to the question for the *Collaborative Oral Task* (page 79).
3	Themes/Main ideas R2	Reread the text to identify possible themes. Some might include Jackie's love for this children and desire to make them happy; Jackie's bravery in testing the ice—for his children and Major League Baseball; Like all people, Jackie had strengths and weaknesses (couldn't swim). Find evidence for each theme.
4	Nontraditional: Interpreting photographs and illustrations R7	Project the photo from the website below that this illustrator (Kadir Nelson) used to create the illustration on pp. 3–4 of the book. Which do you think is the most powerful? Why? What are the qualities of each image that seem important? How are they different? Website: http://padresteve.com/2010/01/18/jackie-robinson-and-dr-martin-luther-king-they-changed-america/
5	Explanatory writing W2	What personal qualities do you think contributed to Jackie Robinson's leadership? Identify three qualities, and using evidence from the text, explain how they helped him to become a role model.

Close Reading Lessons for Night Flight: Amelia Earhart Crosses the Atlantic

Initial Close Reading Lesson

Text: *Night Flight: Amelia Earhart Crosses the Atlantic*　　　　　　**Author:** Robert Burleigh

Purpose: R1: Close reading for deep understanding of the text

In order to provide a context for this story, it might be helpful to read the Afterword at the end of this book before teaching the text itself. Without a bit of knowledge about Amelia Earhart, students will find it difficult to piece together the significance of the events that the author describes.

Before Reading

Clues Based on Cover Illustration

- Notice the plane (small, one propeller; pilot inside is a woman); notice the water below

Clues Based on Title, Author

- Notice the important words: night, Amelia Earhart, crosses the Atlantic
- Notice author's name: Robert Burleigh; look for keys to understanding his craft as you read

Probable Text Type (Literary or Informational); Possible Genre

- Appears to be an informational *story* (may want to identify this as *literary nonfiction*)

Vocabulary That May Need Pre-Teaching for ELLs or Low Language Students

- Flight, cockpit, runway, propeller, now or never, coastline

During Reading

Questions Students Should Ask Themselves for Each Chunk of Text

- What is the author telling me?
- Any hard or important words?
- What does the author want me to understand?
- How does the author play with language to add to meaning?

Follow-Up Text-Dependent Questions for the Teacher to Ask About Each Chunk of Text

Map inside front cover and quote on title page

- Note where flight originates (Newfoundland); flight destination (Ireland); distance (2,026 miles); date (1932)

- Note more details about plane (accept all text-based details)
- Note quote on title page: How long did Amelia expect this flight to last? (less than 15 hours)

Pages 1–2 (Begins: Harbour Grace, Newfoundland)

- What do you know based on this first page (Amelia was leaving at 7:12 p.m.; her plane was a red Vega; she was fairly confident)
- What do you notice already about the author's craft? (creates great imagery—students should give some examples)
- What strategy do you think the author wants us to use here? (picture the scene)

Pages 3–4

- Paraphrase each of these couplets, explaining them in your own words (discuss meaning of important words like *tundra, gleam, waning, froth, ascend*)
- What are you beginning to understand about Amelia: What was important to her?

Pages 5–6

- What additional evidence of author's craft do you find on these pages? (identify images)
- What additional evidence of Amelia's desire for adventure do you find on these pages? (*first time things, roller coasters; what she has seen from above*)

Pages 7–8

- How does the tone on these pages change? What words show you this? (the scary side of adventure emerges; terms include *dark and seething ocean*)
- What words does the author use to contrast to the ocean? (*gentle, soothed*)
- How does the author use *foreshadowing* on this page? (. . . *But she is wrong*).
- So what do you predict? (this will be a difficult trip)

Pages 9–10

- In your own words, what is happening here? (thunderstorm)
- What words stand out that contribute to the tone? (*erupts, heave, pummel, drown, wobbles, DANGER*)
- How is Amelia feeling now? What is the evidence in the text? (she's scared: *heart pounding*)

Since this is a complex text in various ways, and with the addition of the *afterword* before diving into the text itself, you may want to stop here, completing the initial close reading another day.

Pages 11–12

- Why was Amelia "flying blind"? (couldn't see beyond the storm and the darkness)
- What metaphor does Amelia use to describe this terrible night? (*friendly night becomes a graph of fear*)
- What is an altimeter? (measures how high you are—your altitude)
- Why is it dangerous that the altimeter meter is broken? (might go too high or not high enough)
- What is Amelia's plan for dealing with the storm? (tries to climb above it)

Pages 13–14

- What is going on now with the plane? Why is this so dangerous? (plane is getting icy; it adds too much weight)
- What do you picture in your mind? (Accept all reasonable responses based on text evidence)
- What words convey the plane's behavior: *pitching, struggles, sluggish, spins, dipping, nose dives*)
- What does Amelia realize? What words show you this? (this is a life or death moment—*now or never, all or nothing*)
- What does she need to do to survive? (accelerate to gain control)

Pages 15–16

- What is the new danger? (plane is dangerously close to the water)
- What words does the author use to let you know how she feels about the ocean at this point? (*uncaring eyes, breakers rise like teeth, angry mouth*)
- Why does the author use the term *ocean tomb*? (could be her death)

Pages 17–18

- What is happening with Amelia here? (she's getting tired, still scared, feels alone)
- What words show this? (*white knuckles, drowse, alone, alone, alone; counts out loud*)
- Look at Amelia in this picture. Now go back to her picture on the first page? How would you compare the mood of each? (first picture: happy, confident; this picture: stressed, worried)

Pages 19–20

- What is happening now, and what is the new problem? (finally, she's seeing daylight; gas leak)
- Is the daylight enough to make Amelia feel better about her situation? (no: *eyes burn, face clenched, stomach churns*)
- What seems to be Amelia's biggest frustration? (the water goes on and on)

Pages 21–22

- There's good news and bad news here: What is it? (approaching land—but there are mountains with rocks)
- What does the author mean: *An unseen clock is ticking*? (gas smell is getting worse—may be running out of gas)
- Does the last sentence on this page express a positive or negative tone? Explain (positive: *green fan beneath her*—creates nice image in your mind)

Pages 23–26

- Why didn't Amelia land at an airport? (there were very few airports in the early 1930s)
- How do you think Amelia feels at this point? (relieved, glad to be alive)
- What does she mean: "She knows she has crossed something more than an ocean"? (something few people and no women have ever done before)

Pages 27–28

- What small details does Amelia notice? Why? (insects, birds, grass; these are the small details of life that you overlook until you realize you may never have them again)

- Why do you think the farmer is *gaping*? (such an improbable sight—a plane AND a woman inside)
- Why do you think Amelia only says, "Hi, I've come from America"—and not something more detailed? (accept any reasonable answer based on evidence throughout text)

After Reading (Complete These Tasks on Day 3 of the Lesson Sequence)

Important Words to Talk About the Text

- Some possibilities include Amelia Earhart, Atlantic Ocean, cross, storm, frightened, adventurous

Theme, Lesson, or Message (if Appropriate)

- Adventure involves many risks though the outcome is sometimes worth the problems involved

Summary or Gist Statement

- A gist statement might work better for this text because it is more of an elaborated small moment than a traditional story with a problem and a solution

Review of Text Type (Literary/Information) and Genre

- Literary nonfiction: a story that provides accurate information

Collaborative Oral Task

- With a partner or small group, discuss why Amelia was willing to take this huge risk to fly across the Atlantic. Be sure to tie this to the central idea of the text

Follow-Up Lessons: Digging Deeper Through Rereading

Follow-up lessons can be taught in a different order.

Day	Focus Standard	Content for Whole-Class Lessons and Guided Student Practice
2	Close reading R1	Complete the close reading of this text.
3	Close reading follow-up discussion including an emphasis on theme SL1; R2	As a whole class or in small groups, identify the important words to talk about this text, talk about the theme, create a gist statement, and briefly discuss the genre (personal narrative). Then, ask students to work in pairs to respond to the question for the *Collaborative Oral Task* (see above).
4	Author's word choice R4	Identify the author's crafts on p. 10: sentence with a single word, very short sentences, metaphors, strong verbs, personification, surprising adjectives, all capital letters, imagery. Identify the author's crafts on p. 17: sentences that begin with the same word, repeated words, short sentences, dashes.
5	Informative writing W2	Write a paragraph in the style of Robert Burleigh, describing Amelia's scariest moment on this flight. Use some of the crafts discussed during the Day 4 lesson.

Close Reading Lessons for Nelson Mandela

Initial Close Reading Lesson

Text: *Nelson Mandela*   **Author:** Kadir Nelson

Purpose: R1: Close reading for deep understanding of the text

Before Reading

Clues Based on Cover Illustration

- A portrait; notice the dignity, the wrinkles, the feeling (peace?)

Clues Based on Title, Author

- Name: most likely a book about this leader (You may or may not have heard of Nelson Mandela. Pay close attention as we read to learn what makes him such a special leader)

Probable Text Type (Literary or Informational); Possible Genre

- Probably informational; possibly biography

Vocabulary That May Need Pre-Teaching for ELLs or Low Language Students

- Ancestors, schooling, apart, protested, power, jailed, peace

Other Supports Students Will Need

- Before reading this book, use a map or globe to show students the location of South Africa so they will have a better sense of where this story takes place

---

During Reading

Questions Students Should Ask Themselves for Each Chunk of Text
• What is the author telling me?
• Any hard or important words?
• What does the author want me to understand?
• How does the author play with language to add to meaning?
Follow-Up Text-Dependent Questions for the Teacher to Ask About Each Chunk of Text
Pages 1–2
• What do we learn on the first page? (child has no shoes; the way this child spent his time; one of thirteen siblings; only sibling allowed to go to school—because he was smart; teacher may have been from another culture—wouldn't use his native name, gave him English name: Nelson)

- How does the illustration contribute to your understanding of where this story takes place? (large stretch of beautiful undeveloped land, surrounded by nature)

Pages 3–4

- What does the author mean: "his father joined the ancestors in the sky"? (father passed away)
- What details on this page surprised you? (mother sent son away)
- How might you explain this? (family was very poor, different culture)
- What does the illustration add to your understanding of this action? (not easy for mother or son)

Pages 5–6

- In your own words, what is happening here? (Nelson is listening to elders' stories of "old Africa."
- What is the message here: "old" Africa versus "new" Africa? (land was beautiful; European settlers conquered the Africans, and now South Africa belonged to Europe)
- Discuss key words: *bountiful, fertile, elders*
- What do these phrases mean: "The settlers' weapons breathed fire"; "spirits dimmed"
- Why did Nelson feel sorry? (recognized all that blacks in South Africa had lost)

Pages 7–8

- In what ways was Nelson fortunate? (got to go to good schools, good education, became lawyer)
- How did his life contrast with others in South Africa? (poor and couldn't help themselves)
- How did Nelson help other South Africans? (defended those who couldn't defend themselves)

Pages 9–10

- What was the name of the *cruel, harsh policy*? (apartheid)
- In your own words, explain *apartheid*. (separated people according to European, Indian, African)
- Who seemed to get the best opportunities? (Europeans)
- What does this remind you of in the United States? (segregation and Jim Crow laws in the South)

Pages 11–12

- What did Nelson do to support black South Africans? (organized rallies, gave speeches)
- What was his message? (South Africa is for *all* South Africans)
- Look at the illustration: How does it add to your understanding of Mandela's mission? (see the passion, see hands as a symbol of empowerment)

Pages 13–14

- Was there freedom of speech in South Africa at this time? (no, against the law; arrested and jailed)
- How can you tell from this page that culture was important to the black South Africans? (they called their ancestors to join the fight; words on the page are in their language)

Pages 15–16

- How does the information on this page connect to what we just read? (continued the fight with a new wife, Winnie)

- What details in the illustration seem significant? What do you think they mean? (raised arms, clenched fists; power and solidarity)

Pages 17–18

- What does the author mean: Nelson went "underground"? (changed his identity, hid)
- What do you visualize here? (Mandela moving cautiously from one place to another)
- Does this remind you of anything in American history? (Underground Railroad)

Pages 19–20

- Why is this such an important page? (describes what Mandela did to renew his determination to win freedom for his people)
- What did Mandela witness outside of South Africa?
- What did the author mean: "returned to South Africa to cleanse his homeland of hate and discrimination"?

Pages 21–22

- What two contrasting feelings are present on this page? (hope and defeat)
- What created this sense of defeat? (Mandela was jailed)
- How does the illustration add to the emotion here? (jail bars, sadness in eyes, and downturned mouth)

Pages 23–24

- Describe Mandela's life in prison. (hard labor, poor food, cold; but he studied and tried to educate other prisoners)
- How does the author let you know how much time Mandela spent in prison? (weeks, months, years)

Pages 25–28

- As years passed, what happened in South Africa? (rallies, violence, new president, got rid of apartheid)

Pages 29–32

- What surprising detail does the author reveal here? (27 years in prison)
- To whom did Mandela credit his release? (ancestors in the sky)
- After his many years in prison, did Mandela have a positive or negative attitude? What words show this? (positive—forget our terrible past and fight for justice, walk last mile to freedom)

Pages 33–34

- How was Mandela rewarded for his life of hard work? (elected president)

After Reading (Complete These Tasks on Day 2 of the Lesson Sequence)

Important Words to Talk About the Text

- Nelson Mandela, prison, apartheid, South Africa, leader

Theme, Lesson, or Message (if Appropriate)

- Something like, A leader perseveres even in the face of many challenges to fight for what is right

Summary or Gist Statement

- A sequential summary would work well for this. Something like, Nelson Mandela was born into a very poor family but had the opportunity for a good education. He used his skills to fight apartheid in South Africa, though he was sent to prison for 27 years. In the end, he was released and at last became president of South Africa where he continued to fight for justice.

Review of Text Type (Literary/Information) and Genre

- This is a biography. It shows events of Mandela's life from the time he was a child to when he was an old man.

Collaborative Oral Task

- With a partner or small group, identify three character traits of Nelson Mandela that contributed to his success. Provide an example of each trait from the text.

Follow-Up Lessons: Digging Deeper Through Rereading

Follow-up lessons can be taught in a different order.

Day	Focus Standard	Content for Whole-Class Lessons and Guided Student Practice
2	Close reading follow-up discussion including an emphasis on theme SL1; R3	As a whole class or in small groups, identify the important words to talk about this text, talk about the theme, create a gist statement, and briefly discuss the genre (biography). Then, ask students to work in pairs or small groups to identify three of Nelson Mandela's character traits that led to his success. See *Collaborative Oral Task* above.
3	Theme/Main ideas R2	Watch the YouTube video showing important moments in Mandela's life: http://www.youtube.com/watch?v=QnnGiTCqJq8. There is a repeated line: "Fly like an eagle for you were born to fly." How does this line convey the theme of Nelson Mandela's life? Reread portions of the book to find examples.
4	Nontraditional: Nonprint text R7	Watch the same YouTube video again. Choose images that you think have great significance in Mandela's life. Why are each of these images so important.
5	Text-to-text connections; Opinion writing R9; W1	In your opinion, which individual that we have read about (Jackie Robinson or Wesley), is *most* like Nelson Mandela in terms of his leadership qualities? Explain, using evidence from each text.

Learning Pathway

How to Study a Person

Who Was Abraham Lincoln: Boy, Husband, Father, President?

Unit Focus: Abraham Lincoln

© Pictore/Thinkstock Photos.

Let's begin the unit! This is one of eight units in this book that delivers just the "goods"—the questions, prompts, assessment tasks, and student reproducibles you'll need to implement robust close reading instruction within an inquiry unit. Just about all you need to do a few weeks in advance of starting is to look at the anchor texts on pages 94 and 95 and order those books. From there, the materials provided are all explained clearly in terms of when and how to use them. If you need clarification, look back at the ten steps that begin on page 15.

Introduction to the Unit

The Rationale

From the earliest primary grades through advanced college level courses, students will learn about important people: great world leaders, artists, musicians, athletes, scientists, explorers, and other notable women and men from virtually every walk of life. But in elementary school, do we really teach them in depth the skills involved in studying a person? Think how much more efficient their learning would be the next time they were asked to research Louis Armstrong or write a report on Susan B. Anthony, if their "studying a person" search engine just kicked into gear. The intent of this unit is to develop the mindset in students that will help them read texts such as biographies, autobiographies, memoirs, and personal journals with a stronger capacity to understand the complexities of these individuals and the worlds in which they made their marks.

We also want to guide students to get away from thinking that what we want is for them to know a lot of facts or that the goal of school is to learn about a particular set of historical figures. Many teachers (and of course many students) were born into an American culture that instantly recognizes and reveres names such as George Washington, Abraham Lincoln, Rosa Parks, Amelia Earhart, and Benjamin Franklin, but many other people living in America come from different parts of the world. The traditional American heroes are not "household names." Therefore, for all students, we want to inspire them to study important people from a range of cultures, and we want to equip them with the tools to break past the gauzy, romanticized surface understandings of these individuals and into real depth of insight.

With Abraham Lincoln as the focus of the unit, let's think about the ultimate goal of any unit teaching: helping students learn how to learn. I call it the learning pathway. With this unit, the pathway is How to Study a Person. To that end, during your introductory lesson you'll share with students the talking points in the following chart, Learning Pathway: How to Study a Person.

Learning Pathway

How to Study a Person

Share these prompts with students.

- *There is usually a reason for studying a person. Why might you want to study this particular person?*

- *Sometimes, you might be asked to study a person you've never heard of before and someone that doesn't seem interesting to you. If this is the case, how can you make the study meaningful to you? As you read about the person, what are some ways to connect his or her life to your experience?*

- *When you study a person, you will want to learn what kind of contribution he or she made and how he or she made a difference to other people's lives: What kind of contribution did this person make? Was it positive or negative? How did other people's lives change because of this person?*

- *When you study a person, you want to learn important details of their life from birth to death: What important details should you remember about this person's early childhood? Adolescence? Adult years? End of life?*

- *Famous people didn't get their fame handed to them on a silver platter. They often endured personal and professional setbacks, naysayers, and rivals. When you study a person, you want to understand the challenges she or he faced and what helped the person overcome these challenges: What challenges did this person face, and how did she or he overcome them?*

- *When you study a person you want to know about any speeches the person gave, any famous quotes, or important words or ideas connected to this person: What famous words or quotes came from this person? What do they mean?*

- *When you study a person, where can you search for information beyond just books? If the person is still alive and famous for some reason, can you find information in a newspaper or magazine? Does the person have a website you could investigate? Are there any photographs or paintings of the person? Maybe there is someone who is an expert about this person whom you could interview. Many of these sources could be researched for people who are no longer living as well.*

The Inquiry Question and Discussion Points

In this unit, students will answer this question: **Who was Abraham Lincoln? Boy, husband, father, president?** Through their social studies text book or other encounters with Lincoln, students may have gleaned a one-dimensional view of this president who worked to unite the country and freed the slaves and was then assassinated. By contrast, the intent of this unit is to provide a more robust picture of Lincoln through a variety of lenses. To introduce students to the idea that Lincoln was a pretty interesting guy in many walks of life, begin with questions and discussion points indicated in the Unit Preview Questions and Discussion Points for Studying a Person: Abraham Lincoln.

Next, because we want to know from the outset where we ultimately want to take students, I list questions under Questions for End-of-Unit Discussion About a Person (Abraham Lincoln) Integrating All Texts. These are questions you might pose at the end of this unit. That is, with any unit teaching, after completing all of the anchor books, we need to circle back to the inquiry question itself, to consider the books together. The questions help students synthesize their thinking across texts and wrap up the study in a thoughtful way.

Questions for End-of-Unit Discussion About a Person (Abraham Lincoln) Integrating All Texts

- Do you now think that you can answer our inquiry question: *Who was Abraham Lincoln: Boy, husband, father, president?* Briefly summarize your response to this question.

- Which questions for How to Study a Person can you answer after reading these books?

- Which book in this unit did you enjoy the most? Why? Give evidence from the text to support your opinion.

- Which of these books would be best for a younger child? An older child? Explain using evidence from the text.

- From which book did you learn the most about Abraham Lincoln as a boy? Husband? Father? President?

- How has your understanding of Abraham Lincoln changed as a result of this study? Support your answer with examples from each text.

- What advice would you give to students studying Abraham Lincoln?

- Think about the quotes we read at the beginning of this unit: *Selected Quotes by Abraham Lincoln.* After completing this unit, what quote do you think best represents him as a boy? Husband? Father? President?

Unit Preview Questions and Discussion Points

for Studying a Person: Abraham Lincoln

● *Introduce what it means to study a person. (See chart for Learning Pathway: How to Study a Person, selecting focus points and questions appropriate to your students' age and background knowledge about this type of study). Make a list of the "Studying a person" questions you will answer through the study of Abraham Lincoln.*

● *Ask students to identify a few people they consider worthy of study— and why. In answering why, establish some criteria (e.g., made significant contribution, deserves to be more well known, influential right now, and so on). Also, ask if only famous people are worthy of study: Can we learn from the lives of people who aren't famous? What might we learn?*

● *Introduce the inquiry question:* Who was Abraham Lincoln: Boy, husband, father, president? *Discuss how this might be different from what students have learned about Abraham Lincoln in the past. (Students may have some initial responses to this question—which is fine. But don't get too far into this until they've acquired textual evidence.)*

● *Introduce the books about Abraham Lincoln that will anchor this study. Show the cover of each book and perhaps an illustration inside to pique students' interest. Do not explain the full story.*

The Focus Standard

The study of a person could provide an opportunity for reinforcing just about any standard, so in the units you plan, you may want to select a different comprehension focus. I chose CCRA R3: "Analyze how and why individuals, events, or ideas develop and interact over the course of a text" (http://www .corestandards.org/ELA-Literacy/CCRA/R, Key Ideas section, para. 3). Whenever you work with several books on the same topic, you want to first make students aware that each text will cover many of the same basic facts, but that each text is unique because the authors are different, and that as readers, they need to kind of "listen" for these nuances. Different authors approach a subject in different ways, offering different details, and sometimes focusing on a particular period in the subject's life more than another author might. You also want to make clear that you expect them to think about what they learned from *all* of the texts, thinking about not just the events themselves but also how the events of Lincoln's life fit together. This could lead to the creation of a nice timeline that would grow throughout the unit. I chose these texts with that goal in mind.

The Anchor Texts

The first text listed below is a selection of quotes from Abraham Lincoln. It is intended to be read by the students themselves and discussed during a unit kickoff lesson (discussion questions are provided on page 101). The remaining four texts are picture books, one of which will be read closely and studied during each week of the unit.

Selected Quotes by Abraham Lincoln (provided on page 100)

Finding an informational article about Abraham Lincoln would have served little purpose in this unit since the anchor texts are all nonfiction and cover the Lincoln territory quite thoroughly. Still I wanted to provide something within the realm of nonfiction in keeping with the intent to begin each study with some sort of nonfiction selection. Hence, I chose a few quotes that hint at some of the things Lincoln valued most: determination, reading, freedom for slaves, and more. These quotes, which can be read by the students themselves, can be used at the beginning of the unit to arouse students' curiosity about the study ahead—and at the end of the unit to connect to the knowledge about Lincoln they've gained.

Honest Abe by Edith Kunhardt

This is a basic biography of Abraham Lincoln and, thus, a good book to begin this unit. The large, colorful illustrations accompanied by comparatively sparse text may mistakenly lead one to believe this book is too easy for intermediate grade students; it's not. This book packs in a *lot* of information and does a nice job of hitting the highlights of Lincoln's life as a child, a young adult, and a president. Complexities include a possible lack of prior knowledge to ground students' thinking, lots of content specific vocabulary words, and lack of familiarity with biography as a genre. Lexile: 630; Grade level equivalent: 3.3.

Looking at Lincoln by Maira Kalman

Students love this book! This would not be a great text to begin the unit as it lacks a clear sequence. But it offers up a plethora of personal details that add interest to the study of Lincoln throughout all phases of his life story. The main complexity of this text is its structure as it moves between information retrieved about Lincoln by the young narrator—and her reflections regarding the information she finds. Do not be deterred by the low Lexile and grade level equivalent; there's a marked difference between reading a book for enjoyment and *studying* it for the nuances of its content and craft. Lexile: 460; Grade level equivalent: 1.6.

Abraham Lincoln Comes Home by Robert Burleigh

Although this book depicts a very somber subject, Lincoln's funeral train and his last ride from Washington, DC to his home in Springfield, Illinois, it features a topic seldom addressed in other sources about Lincoln: the end of his life beyond his infamous assassination. What makes this book special (and complex) is that readers feel they are *there*, standing along the tracks, experiencing the grief, honoring their president, and celebrating Lincoln's achievements. The author (in characteristic Burleigh fashion) conveys the mood through his word choice and imagery. Lexile: 560. No grade level equivalent available.

Abe's Honest Words: The Life of Abraham Lincoln by Doreen Rappaport

This book may at first appear repetitive as it describes the basic sequence of events in Lincoln's life. But the essence of this book is anything but basic. The intrigue (and complexity) of this text is in the way it embeds some of Lincoln's most famous quotes to support key moments in his life. With the three previous books in this unit under their belt, students will find these quotes now make sense, and they will be able to consider them meaningfully. Lexile: 820; Grade level equivalent: 4.9.

Other Texts Useful for Studying Abraham Lincoln

To extend your study of Abraham Lincoln or to adjust the complexity of the texts, you might want to consider these books that cover both the "basics" of Lincoln's life and the small details that add interest to the study of any individual.

- *I am Abraham Lincoln* by Brad Meltzer
- *A Picture Book of Abraham Lincoln* by David Adler
- *Lincoln and Grace: Why Abraham Lincoln Grew a Beard* by Steve Metzger
- *Abe Lincoln Goes to Washington: 1837–1865* by Cheryl Harness
- *Young Abe Lincoln* by Cheryl Harness

The Unit's Two Assessments

Featured Reading Standard 3: Story elements: Interaction of events

Featured Writing Format: Informative/Explanatory writing

See the Unit Curriculum Map for Close Reading for where these assessments might fit into your study of the Moon. Also, for more information about the rationale behind these two assessments and how they differ, as well as guidance for using the provided rubrics, refer to Step 9 on page 43 and Step 10 on page 50. Also, for evaluating students' performance on tasks, see page 45 for the Rubric for Content-Based Assessment (Task 1) and Standards-Based Assessment (Task 2). Turn to page 293, The End of the Story: Reflecting on Student Work, for some sample student work and commentary.

Task I: Content Assessment

Many people know that Lincoln was president of the United States and that he freed the slaves, but now you know so much more! Who was Lincoln—beyond these basic facts? On a separate piece of paper, write a speech that you could give to children about your age that includes details that are both *important* and *interesting*. Be sure to include information about

- His childhood

- How he got involved in politics and got to Washington

- His adult life as a husband and father

- His worries and accomplishments as a president

- His death

Use details from the texts we read in class to explain each of the bullet points above. Your teacher may tell you how many details to include in each section.

Task 2: Learning Pathway and Standard Assessment

Read and view the following sources about Marian Anderson, a famous singer:

- "As long as you keep a person down, some part of you has to be down there to hold him down, so it means you cannot soar as you otherwise might." (quote by Marian Anderson)

- http://www.youtube.com/watch?v=XF9Quk0QhSE (singing at the Lincoln memorial: One minute video clip)

- http://www.myhero.com/go/hero.asp?hero=m_anderson (brief biography about Marian Anderson)

On a separate piece of paper, write a speech you could deliver to your classmates: How did the quote (above) from Marian Anderson apply to

- Her life as a child?

- Her life as an adult?

- Did she soar? How? What did she accomplish?

- Who tried to keep her down? Use evidence from the video and biography to support your thinking

---

Available for download from **resources.corwin.com/boyleslessons**

Unit Curriculum Map for Close Reading

Who Was Abraham Lincoln: Boy, Husband, Father, President?

TEXT	MONDAY	TUESDAY	WEDNESDAY	THURSDAY	FRIDAY
				Unit Preview	Kickoff Lesson
				See Unit Preview Questions and Discussion Points	Read and discuss *Selected Quotes From Abraham* Lincoln. Discussion questions are provided at the end of this document
Honest Abe by Edith Kunhardt	Objective: R1 Close Reading	Objective: SL1; R5 Close Reading Follow-Up	Objective: R3 Story Elements: Sequence of Events	Objective: R9 Text-to-Text Connections	Objective: W2 Informative Writing
	Read closely to answer text-dependent questions	Complete the After Reading tasks including a collaborative task for identifying genre features	Begin a timeline showing how events of Lincoln's life fit together. (This timeline will be continued throughout the unit)	Read the poem *Abraham Lincoln* by Rosemary and Stephen Vincent Benét (at http://farmschool.wordpress.com/2008/02/15/poetry-friday-for-abraham-lincoln/.books?). Connect to *Honest Abe*	Using all sources, write about the events of Lincoln's life in order
Looking at Lincoln by Maira Kalman	Objective: R1 Close Reading	Objective: R3; SL1 Close Reading Follow-up	Objective: R3 Story Elements: Sequence of Events	Objective: R2 Theme/Main Ideas	Objective: R7 Nontraditional: Studying a Photograph or Painting
	Read closely to answer text-dependent questions	Complete the After Reading tasks including an emphasis on quotes from Lincoln	Add to the timeline that students started when reading *Honest Abe*	Study selected quotes from this text by Abraham Lincoln: Which one seemed the most significant? Why?	Examine Lincoln's eyes as they are depicted in a photograph or painting

TEXT	MONDAY	TUESDAY	WEDNESDAY	THURSDAY	FRIDAY
Abraham Lincoln Comes Home by Robert Burleigh	Objective: R1 Close Reading	Objective: SL1; R5 Close Reading Follow-up	Objective: R3 Story Elements: Sequence of Events	Objective: R6; W3 Author's Purpose or Point of View; Informative Writing	Objective: R7 Nontraditional: Interpreting an Illustration
	Read closely to answer text-dependent questions	Complete the After Reading tasks including a collaborative task for identifying genre features	Add to the timeline that students started when reading *Honest Abe*	Write a journal entry from the point of view of bystander awaiting Lincoln's funeral train	Identify an illustration in the book that has great meaning to you. Explain
Abe's Honest Words: The Life of Abraham Lincoln by Doreen Rappaport	Objective: R1 Close Reading	Objective: R1 Close Reading	Objective: R3 Story Elements: Sequence of Events	Objective: R6; SL4 Author's Purpose or Point of View; Oral Presentation	Objective: W1 Opinion Writing
	Read the first half of this book closely to answer text-dependent questions	Read the second half of this book closely to answer text-dependent questions	Add to the timeline that students started when reading *Honest Abe*	Choose a quote and use it in a speech	Write a book recommendation
	Culminating Discussion	Content Assessment	Standards-Based Assessment		
	Respond orally to text-to-text connections for studying this topic. (See Questions for End of Unit Discussion Integrating All Texts)	Students complete the content-assessment task integrating all texts in this study	Students complete the standards-based assessment task using cold reads		

SELECTED QUOTES BY ABRAHAM LINCOLN

Determination

Always bear in mind that your own resolution to succeed is more important than any other one thing.

—November 5, 1855, Letter to Isham Reavis

Reading

A capacity, and taste, for reading gives access to whatever has already been discovered by others. It is the key, or one of the keys, to the already solved problems. And not only so. It gives a relish, and facility, for successfully pursuing the [yet] unsolved ones.

—September 30, 1859, Address before the Wisconsin State Agricultural Society

Freedom for Slaves

And by virtue of the power, and for the purpose aforesaid, I do order and declare that all persons held as slaves within said designated States, and parts of States, are, and henceforward shall be free; and that the Executive government of the United States, including the military and naval authorities thereof, will recognize and maintain the freedom of said persons.

—January 1, 1863, Emancipation Proclamation

Equality

Four score and seven years ago our fathers brought forth on this continent, a new nation, conceived in Liberty, and dedicated to the proposition that all men are created equal.

—November 19, 1863, Gettysburg Address

Slavery

I have always hated slavery, I think as much as any Abolitionist.

—July 10, 1858, Speech at Chicago

Soldiers

I am greatly obliged to you, and to all who have come forward at the call of their country.

—August 22, 1864, Speech to the One Hundred Sixty-fourth Ohio Regiment

Source: http://www.abrahamlincolnonline.org/lincoln/speeches/quotes .htm

Think About

Use the following questions to discuss the quotes by Abraham Lincoln. These will be helpful to think about as you initiate your unit.

- You may think about Abraham Lincoln mainly because he was the president who freed the slaves. But these quotes show that he cared about many other things, too. What were some of the things Lincoln really cared about?

- Which of these quotes do you think might have been most important during the time in which Lincoln lived? Why?

- Which of these quotes do you think is the most important now? Why?

- Choose one of these quotes. What words in the quote do you need to understand more clearly in order to better understand the quote? Discuss these hard words. Now try to paraphrase the quote using words that are easier to understand.

- Why do you think we're reading and discussing these quotes *before* we study the books about Lincoln? How can these quotes help us to better understand Lincoln as we learn more about him?

Close Reading Lessons for Honest Abe

Initial Close Reading Lesson

Text: *Honest Abe*   **Author:** Edith Kunhardt

Purpose: R1: Close reading for deep understanding of the text

Before Reading

Clues Based on Cover Illustration

- Notice that the largest image on the cover is Abe Lincoln; he's putting a paper in his tall hat; notice pictures behind Lincoln: one looks like he might be in court; one looks like him and his wife and three boys; notice other details in the pictures: trees, ax, cat, logs

Clues Based on Title, Author

- Notice the word *honest*—think about what this might mean

Probable Text Type (Literary or Informational); Possible Genre

- Probably a literary (story) text with real facts about Abraham Lincoln

Vocabulary That May Need Pre-Teaching for ELLs or Low Language Students

- Honest, president, log cabin, lawyer, biography, shot

During Reading

Questions Students Should Ask Themselves for Each Chunk of Text

- What is the author telling me?

- Any hard or important words?

- What does the author want me to understand?

- How does the author play with language to add to meaning?

Follow-Up Text-Dependent Questions for the Teacher to Ask About Each Chunk of Text

---

Pages 1–2

- The author provides lots of information about Lincoln on these pages. What do we already know? (He was born in Kentucky to poor parents who couldn't read or write; he had an older sister; he walked two miles to school each day; he had only one year of school; he loved to learn and taught himself.)

- Why do you think the author gives us this information right at the beginning of the story? (sets the scene; we know Lincoln did not have an easy life; he loved learning)

Pages 3–6

- How does the information on these pages fit with what we already know? (more examples of how poor the Lincolns were; how they had to endure many hardships—give examples from pages)

Pages 7–8

- How does the information on these pages fit with the information we read previously? (Abe's life got better when his stepmother, Sally, came to live with them; she helped him learn)

Pages 9–10

- What traits do we see in Lincoln over and over? (his love of reading)
- What other traits are you beginning to see that may serve him well in the future? (he worked hard; people loved listening to him)

Pages 11–12

- What life-changing event happened to Abe when he was nineteen? Explain this in your own words. (Abe worked on a flatboat that traveled to New Orleans. There he saw slaves working for no pay. White people could sell them. Abe thought this was wrong.)

Pages 13–14

- What character traits are we seeing here again? (he worked hard; people liked his stories)
- How did Lincoln get the nickname *Honest Abe*? (walked a long distance to give pennies back to a person who overpaid him)

Pages 15–18

- How was Lincoln's life moving forward now that he was an adult? (became a lawyer, married Mary Todd, ran for Congress, debated Stephen A. Douglas about slavery)
- What detail from the cover is explained on this page? (kept papers in his tall hat)

Pages 19–22

- What were the changes in Lincoln's life now? (he became president and involved in the Civil War; son died; wrote the Emancipation Proclamation)
- Why was the Emancipation Proclamation considered a "milestone"? (ended slavery)

Pages 23–24

- What important information is the author giving us here? (a terrible battle occurred in Gettysburg, Pennsylvania; Lincoln later gave a speech there to dedicate a cemetery to those who had died: the Gettysburg Address)
- What famous line from the Gettysburg Address does the author include here? ("government of the people, by the people, for the people, shall not perish from the earth")
- In your own words, what does this line mean? (The government in the United States comes from people's needs, is run by our citizens, and is based on people's needs—or something close to this)

Pages 25–28

- In your own words, explain the events surrounding Lincoln's death. (went to the theater, got shot in the head by man who wanted slavery to continue, and died the next morning; body lay in the White House then body taken by train back to Illinois; funeral in ten different cities along the way, then burial in Springfield)

Important Words to Talk About the Text

- Abraham Lincoln, honest, slavery, Emancipation Proclamation, assassinated, lawyer, Civil War, Gettysburg Address

Theme, Lesson, or Message (if Appropriate)

- We remember Abraham Lincoln as an important president because he helped to end slavery

Summary or Gist Statement

- This text is well suited to a sequential summary. Complete this work on Day 3 of the lesson sequence (see below)

Review of Text Type (Literary/Information) and Genre

- This is a biography. It tells important information about Lincoln's life from his birth to his death and includes other features of a biography, too

Collaborative Oral Task

- With the whole class, review characteristics of a biography. (See Genre Checklists for Students chart in Appendix 3 at resources.corwin.com/boyleslessons.) Then, ask students to work with a partner or small group to identify three to five examples in the text that show that it is a biography

Follow-Up Lessons: Digging Deeper Through Rereading

Follow-up lessons can be taught in a different order.

Day	Focus Standard	Content for Whole-Class Lessons and Guided Student Practice
2	Close reading follow-up discussion including details from the text SL1; R5	As a whole group or in small groups discuss the important words needed to talk about this text and identify a couple of main ideas present in the text. Then, complete the *Collaborative Oral Task* (see above) for which students will find features of a biography in this book.
3	Story elements: Sequence of events R3	Divide the class into four groups: Lincoln's childhood, Lincoln's early adult life, Lincoln's presidency, and Lincoln's death. Ask each group to identify the important events and accomplishments in each stage. Be sure to show how events were *connected*: How did one event lead to another? As a class begin a timeline that summarizes Lincoln's life. (Students will add to this timeline throughout the remainder of the unit.)
4	Text-to-text connections; Fluency R9	Read the poem *Abraham Lincoln* by Rosemary and Stephen Vincent Benét (retrieved from this site or other sources: http://farmschool.wordpress.com/2008/02/15/poetry-friday-for-abraham-lincoln/.) What information is the same as the information in the biography? What is different? Also, this is a great poem for choral reading. Assign students to different stanzas. Practice reading fluently with expression.
5	Informative writing W2	Using information from both the book *Honest Abe* and the poem *Abraham Lincoln*, write about the important events and accomplishments in Lincoln's life from his birth to his death. Be sure to explain why his accomplishments were so important to the history of the United States.

Close Reading Lessons for Looking at Lincoln

Initial Close Reading Lesson

Text: *Looking at Lincoln*   **Author:** Maira Kalman

Purpose: R1: Close reading for deep understanding of the text

Before Reading

Clues Based on Cover Illustration

- Notice a child is looking at Lincoln. She appears very small; he looks really large

Clues Based on Title, Author

- Notice that *LINCOLN* is in all capital letters

Probable Text Type (Literary or Informational); Possible Genre

- Probably contains information, though it looks like more of a story

Vocabulary That May Need Pre-Teaching for ELLs or Low Language Students

- Abraham Lincoln, log cabin, lawyer, run for president, government, theater, slave, slavery, freedom

During Reading

Questions Students Should Ask Themselves for Each Chunk of Text

- What is the author telling me?
- Any hard or important words?
- What does the author want me to understand?
- How does the author play with language to add to meaning?

Follow-Up Text-Dependent Questions for the Teacher to Ask About Each Chunk of Text

Pages 1–4

- Who seems to be telling the story? (a child)
- What does the narrator mean: "We paid with a Lincoln"? (a five dollar bill—has the picture of Lincoln on it)
- What do you notice about the print on these pages? (looks like a child wrote it)

Pages 5–6

- What word is used to describe Lincoln (amazing), and what does the author tell us to show us how special Lincoln was? (16,000 books written about him?)

- What do you think this book will probably tell us about? (what made Lincoln so special)

- What does the narrator mean by "his unusual face"? (accept any reasonable answers)

Pages 7–8

- What are you learning about Lincoln here? (born in a log cabin; 1809; poor, dreamer; liked to read)

- Which of these facts do you think will make the biggest difference to Lincoln in the future? Why? (might predict *dreaming* and *reading* since it's good to have dreams and reading can help you achieve your dreams)

- What do you know about Lincoln's family life from page 8? (his stepmother adored him; she let him dream and read)

- Why do you think the author is telling us this? (wants us to know about Lincoln as a *regular* person, not just as a *famous* person)

- What do you notice about the print on page 7 and the print on page 8? (different—regular typing and handwriting)

- Why does the author use two kinds of writing? (typing = facts; handwriting = personal stories)

Pages 9–10

- Explain why the information on page 9 looks typed and the information on page 10 looks both typed and handwritten? (facts and personal reaction)

- How does the information on these pages help you to understand what is important to Lincoln? (loved learning, learned in spite of difficult circumstances)

Pages 11–12

- Based on the information on these pages, explain what made Lincoln a good lawyer? (he was a smart and honest man; he liked to argue—which is what lawyers do)

Pages 13–14

- How is this book different from a typical biography? (contains more personal information about Lincoln)

- What are we learning on this page that probably wouldn't be in a typical biography? (child's thoughts about nicknames)

- Would the information on page 14 be the kind of thing included in a biography? (yes—when he became president—this is a famous fact)

Pages 15–16

- Why do you think the author included the details about the cake and the hat? (make him seem more interesting)

- What characteristic of Lincoln keeps coming up? (*thinking*) Why do you think the author does this? (wants us to know that *thinking* was really important to Lincoln)

- What do you think the author is going to talk about next? (what Lincoln was *thinking* about)

Pages 17–18

- How does the author answer this question about thinking? (democracy, *Declaration of Independence*, *Constitution*, freedom, doing good)

- What do all of these "thinking points" show about Lincoln? (loved our country, wanted everyone in our country to be free and protected)

- After this serious thinking, why did the author include the information on page 18 about the whistle and pick-up sticks? (shows more of the human side of Lincoln, balances the public person with the private person)

Pages 19–20

- Which kind of information is the author including here—important facts about why Lincoln is famous, or personal stories that add interest? (personal)

- How can this approach to writing help you to be a better writer yourself? (what you think *about* something is also important—not just "the facts")

Pages 21–22

- Even before reading this page, do you think it will be about the "famous Lincoln" or the "family Lincoln"? Why? (famous Lincoln—it's the "typed" print)

- What does the word *plight* mean? (terrible situation)

- Put the information on these pages into your own words. (Lincoln loved all people and was against slavery because slaves were not *free*. He met with people like Sojourner Truth and Frederick Douglass to talk about the terrible life faced by slaves.)

Pages 23–24

- Explain the quote: "If slavery is not wrong, nothing is wrong." (accept reasonable responses)

- Why is this quote in such large font? (Author wants you to note its importance)

- Even if you don't know the meaning of *Emancipation Proclamation*, you can tell from this sentence on page 24 that it probably means _____. (freeing the slaves)

Pages 25–26

- Why do you think the author includes the factual information on page 25 about the war? (important to know the struggles that our country faced)

- What *were* the struggles faced by our country? (Southern states wanted their own country; the North [Union] believed slavery should be *abolished*)

- Why do you think the author includes the picture and details about the bullet hole in the soldier's uniform? (shows the human/personal side of war)

Pages 27–28

- What famous speech is mentioned here? (Gettysburg Address)

- Explain the meaning of the line that is quoted from the Gettysburg Address. (Our government is intended to protect all people and we do not want it to disappear.)

- What terrible fact does page 27 indicate about the Civil War? (almost a million people had been killed or wounded)

Pages 29–30

- Why does the illustrator use a gun to show the meaning of this page? (it was a gun like this that killed Lincoln)

- How does the author make Lincoln's death more personal and meaningful? (shows the rocking chair where Lincoln sat when he was shot)

Pages 31–32

- What stands out about the colors on this page? (dark, represents the mood of Lincoln's death)

- Why do you think the word *really* is in pink? (accept reasonable responses)

Pages 33–36

- Now what is the "pink" connection? (cherry blossoms, new life symbolized by Lincoln)

- Think about the meaning of the quote on the Lincoln Memorial: "With malice toward none, and charity for all." (After clarifying the word *malice*, students should be able to interpret this quote)

- What detail returns at the end of this book? (Lincoln's eyes). This is another possible author's craft to use: a circular ending that brings back an earlier detail

After Reading (Complete These Tasks on Day 2 of the Lesson Sequence)

Important Words to Talk About the Text

- Lincoln, slavery, thinking, reading, Emancipation Proclamation, freedom for all, Civil War, Gettysburg, assassinated

Theme, Lesson, or Message (if Appropriate)

- There is both a "famous" and "human" side to Lincoln—and both are important in order to understand his place in history

Summary or Gist Statement

- The summary of this text would be more based on the central ideas of Lincoln's life rather than events: something like, Lincoln was born a poor person, but his love of learning and love for all people helped him lead our nation through a difficult time. Unfortunately he was assassinated by someone who didn't share his beliefs about the value of freedom for all people

Review of Text Type (Literary/Information) and Genre

- This is a difficult book to classify. It is part biography and part personal narrative. Discuss why this book falls into both categories

Collaborative Oral Task

- This book contains several famous quotes by Lincoln. In pairs or small groups, ask students to identify the quote from the text that had the biggest impact on them—and explain why it was so powerful

Follow-Up Lessons: Digging Deeper Through Rereading

Follow-up lessons can be taught in a different order.

Day	Focus Standard	Content for Whole-Class Lessons and Guided Student Practice
2	Close reading follow-up discussion R3; SL1	As a whole class or in small groups, discuss the important words in the text, the story's theme, and genre and create a brief summary. Complete the *Collaborative Oral Task* (page 108), asking students to respond to famous Lincoln quotes showing their understanding of Lincoln as a person.
3	Story elements: Sequence of events R3	With the whole class, reread factual information in this book. Decide where it would fit in the biography of Lincoln (*Honest Abe*). Add to the timeline.
4	Theme/Main ideas R2	Reexamine significant quotes by Lincoln from the text. In small groups or pairs, ask students to consider which quote (from those identified by the teacher or students) made the biggest difference to their understanding of Lincoln. Be sure that they can also explain *why*.
5	Nontraditional: Studying a photograph or painting R7	In both the beginning and ending of this book, the author mentions Lincoln's eyes. Research pictures of Lincoln online—either photographs or paintings. Find one that you think shows the "magic" of Lincoln's eyes. Be prepared to share your picture, and why you think Lincoln's eyes are so outstanding in this graphic.

Close Reading Lessons for Abraham Lincoln Comes Home

Initial Close Reading Lesson

Text: *Abraham Lincoln Comes Home*   **Author:** Robert Burleigh

Purpose: R1: Close reading for deep understanding of the text

Before Reading

Clues Based on Cover Illustration

- Notice that Abraham Lincoln's face seems to be pictured in the night sky; notice the train passing by

Clues Based on Title, Author

- Notice key words: Abraham Lincoln, coming home

Probable Text Type (Literary or Informational); Possible Genre

- Seems to be a literary (story) text about a real person

Vocabulary That May Need Pre-Teaching for ELLs or Low Language Students

- Abraham Lincoln, funeral, buggy, train

During Reading

Questions Students Should Ask Themselves for Each Chunk of Text
• What is the author telling me?
• Any hard or important words?
• What does the author want me to understand?
• How does the author play with language to add to meaning?
Follow-Up Text-Dependent Questions for the Teacher to Ask About Each Chunk of Text

Page inside the cover, before the title page

- What stands out about this page? (flag that looks muted; important words: mourn, chief, fallen)

- Paraphrase the words on this page. (We are sad our president has died)

- What do you think this book will probably be about based on the information on this page? (Lincoln's death)

Pages 1–6

- How does the author set the scene for this story? (A boy and his dad are riding in a buggy at night; it was very dark; they were looking for a train)
- What question is the author *not* answering here? (why Luke and his father were looking for a train)
- Why do you think the author begins the story in this way? (raises suspense)

Pages 7–8

- What question has the author answered here? (why Luke and his dad were looking for the train: it carried Lincoln's body)
- Look at the picture on these pages. What details do you notice? How does it add to your thoughts and feelings about this situation? (accept all reasonable responses)

Pages 9–12

- Other than the fact that Lincoln was killed, why else might he have had "the saddest face" people had ever seen? (It was incredibly sad to be killed trying to bring freedom to all people)
- Why do you think that Luke and his dad and other people were standing near the railroad tracks? (waiting for the train to pay their last respects to Lincoln)

Pages 13–16

- What *symbolized* the love people had for Lincoln? (bonfires blazed, people waited, bells tolling, speeches, silence, black drapes, heaped roses, muffled drums)
- Which images paint a positive picture in your mind? Which paint a negative picture? (positive: bonfires, bells, roses; negative: silence, black drapes, muffled drums)
- Why do you think the author uses both kinds of images here? (Positive images stand for the respect and love; negative images stand for Lincoln's death and the reason for his death)

Pages 17–20

- How does the author help you visualize the train coming into view? (first as a tiny speck then larger until it appeared immense)
- What words described the torches? (flared; swoosh, like giant fireflies)
- What was the point of the torches? (to light Lincoln's way)
- Go back to the title: Can you figure out the meaning of the title yet? (going "home" to be buried)
- What does the author mean, "The ground *shivered*"? (vibrated from the power of the train)
- What do you think a "cow catcher" is? (something to push cows off the track so they wouldn't get run over)

Pages 21–24

- Why was the orange glow "eerie"? (very bright, but signified a really sad event)
- Why do you think this moment was so emotional for Luke's father? (accept all reasonable responses)
- In your own words, what does the author mean by, "Engulfed in the harsh roar of iron on iron, . . ."? (something like, The loud roaring of the train's wheels against the tracks seemed to be everywhere)
- What is a coffin? (casket where Lincoln lay)

Pages 25–28

- Explain what was happening with the train now? (it had passed by and was moving on)

- What words does the author use to show the train? ("The prairie swallowed the *clack-clack-clack*, all the way to nothing.")

- What was the voice? Do you think it was a *real* voice? (accept all reasonable responses)

- What do you notice about the ending? (the ending is about the same as the beginning)

- Why do you think the author chose this ending? (Even after a terrible event like Lincoln's death, life just goes on for the rest of us—or something like that)

Afterword and Interesting Facts about the Lincoln Funeral Train

- You will not need to read these final pages with the closeness of the rest of the book for craft as well as content. However, it would be good to share these pages with students; they clarify lots of the actual details of the funeral train that the story itself omits.

- Where ultimately was "home"? (Springfield, Illinois)

After Reading (Complete These Tasks on Day 2 of the Lesson Sequence)

Important Words to Talk About the Text

- Abraham Lincoln, train, coffin, mourn, respect

Theme, Lesson, or Message (if Appropriate)

- Something like, People were overcome by a mixture of grief and respect as they waited for the passing of Lincoln's funeral train

Summary or Gist Statement

- Something like, A young boy and his dad joined thousands of other mourners waiting by the side of the tracks for the train carrying Lincoln's body to pass by

Review of Text Type (Literary/Information) and Genre

- Historical fiction: Luke and his dad may not have been real people, but the funeral train passing by was a real event, and their feelings would have been similar to the feelings of other people who witnessed this sad event

Collaborative Oral Task

- Following a review of the features of historical fiction, ask students to work with a partner or small group to identify three or more details from this text that are probably factual and three or more details that may be fictionalized. Why do they classify each detail as they do?

Follow-Up Lessons: Digging Deeper Through Rereading

Follow-up lessons can be taught in a different order.

Day	Focus Standard	Content for Whole-Class Lessons and Guided Student Practice
2	Close reading follow-up discussion including details from the text SL1; R5	With the whole class or in small groups, discuss the important words in the text and the theme/main ideas and create a brief summary. Then, discuss the features of historical fiction. Ask students to work in pairs or small groups to complete the *Collaborative Oral Task* (page 112) to distinguish between factual and fictionalized details in this story.
3	Story elements: Sequence of events R3	Reread pages of this text that show significant details to be added to the timeline of Lincoln. As a class, add these details explaining the connection between events.
4	Author's purpose or point of view; Narrative writing: Describing a scene showing tone R6; W3	Reread the portion of the text where bystanders are awaiting Lincoln's funeral train. With a partner or small group, pretend that *you* were standing at the train tracks awaiting Lincoln's funeral train. Write a journal entry describing the scene. Remember to describe the train, your feelings, and the dark night. To make your scene even more dramatic, read it against a backdrop of the music for *Lincoln's Funeral March* retrieved from this site: https://www.youtube.com/watch?v=G3OtdOXBTho
5	Nontraditional: Interpreting an illustration R7	With a partner or small group, choose an illustration in this book that you found especially meaningful. Why do you consider this picture so powerful? How has the illustrator created this sense of strong emotion? How do the colors add to the feeling in the picture?

Close Reading Lessons for Abe's Honest Words: The Life of Abraham Lincoln

Initial Close Reading Lesson

Text: *Abe's Honest Words: The Life of Abraham Lincoln*　　　　**Author:** Doreen Rappaport

Purpose: R1: Close reading for deep understanding of the text

This book will probably take two days to read closely due to its length and the quotes on each page that will need to be discussed and interpreted.

Before Reading

Clues Based on Cover Illustration

- Front cover: Notice picture of Abraham Lincoln with the American flag in the background; no title

Clues Based on Title, Author

- Back cover: Notice important words: honest; *The Life of Abraham Lincoln*

Probable Text Type (Literary or Informational); Possible Genre

- Probably another biography

Vocabulary That May Need Pre-Teaching for ELLs or Low Language Students

- Abe (nickname for Abraham), honest, honesty, quotes

During Reading

Questions Students Should Ask Themselves for Each Chunk of Text

- What is the author telling me?
- Any hard or important words?
- What does the author want me to understand?
- How does the author play with language to add to meaning?

Follow-Up Text-Dependent Questions for the Teacher to Ask About Each Chunk of Text

Page inside the front cover

- Where have you seen this quote before? (The book *Looking at Lincoln*)
- Why do you think the author chose to begin with this quote? (very important to Lincoln's life)

Pages 1–2

- What can you already tell about the way this book is different from the other books we've read about Lincoln? (it's written like a poem with lots of descriptive language; it includes a quote in a different font)

- Talk about these words: wilderness, sorrow, tend, haste

- Are you getting any information here that adds to what you already knew about Lincoln? (liked to hunt and fish)

- What two contrasting feelings does the author include here? (sorrow and joy)

- Reread the quote: Where might Abe Lincoln have written this? (sounds like something he may have scratched into a tree—almost like graffiti)

Pages 3–4

- Why does the author choose this particular quote for this page? (matches the main idea: Abe loved to read)

- What are you learning here about where Abe got his love of storytelling? (his dad loved to tell stories, too)

- What is a "mite" of schooling? (a wee little bit)

- How does this quote show Abe's true love of reading? ("my best friend is the man who'll git me a book I ain't read"—Abe absolutely *loved* to read)

Pages 5–6

- What "different voices" did Abe hear in his heart? (storytellers, lawyers, preachers)

- Explain the quote: "A house divided against itself cannot stand." (accept reasonable responses)

- How did this quote *foreshadow* future events in Lincoln's life? (This would be the problem during the Civil War—the country was divided against itself)

Pages 7–8

- Describe the two contrasting images Lincoln saw in New Orleans. (rich people who enjoyed a beautiful life, slaves who had a miserable life)

- What do you picture in your mind when Lincoln says, "strung together like so many fish upon a trotline"? (Slaves were chained together like fish are sometimes strung together)

- What is the meaning of "perpetual" slavery? (forever)

- What was Abe's observation about slavery that made him hate it so much? (how it took people away from their family and friends)

- How does the illustration on this page add to your understanding of what the author is saying? (accept all reasonable responses)

Pages 9–10

- How did Abe Lincoln get his education? (reading whenever he had a spare minute)

- Reread the quote on this page: Would you say that mostly applied to the time in which Lincoln lived, or can it be applied to other times, too? Explain your thinking. (accept all reasonable responses; make sure that students respond with evidence from *this* text, too)

Pages 11–12

- Why did Lincoln want to get involved in politics? (to help people and the country move forward)

- Reread the quote on this page. Say it in your own words. (I am young and poor with no rich or famous people to support me.)
- Why do you think Lincoln ran for office if he knew he probably couldn't win? (wanted to get known)

Pages 13–14

- According to Abe Lincoln, what was the most important character trait a person could have? (honesty)
- Take another look at the title. Why do you think the author chose this title? (it had a lot to do with what was important to Lincoln throughout his life)

Pages 15–16

- What surprising *statistic* does the author share on this page? (four million black people were enslaved in Southern states)
- What evidence did Lincoln use to show we should get rid of slavery? (it went against the Declaration of Independence)
- What line in the Declaration of Independence did Lincoln think was especially important? ("all men are created equal")
- Why do you think the author includes this information? (shows us that slavery was actually against the law—right from the beginning)

Pages 17–18

- What problems did Lincoln face as soon as he was elected president? (Civil War started; seven Southern states left the Union)
- Why do you think the Southern states left the Union? (wanted a "country" where slavery was allowed)
- What did Lincoln say to try to convince the Southern states to return to the Union? ("We are not enemies, but friends.")

Pages 19–20

- What event started the Civil War? (Southern troops attacked Fort Sumter)
- Reread the quote on this page. Say it in your own words. (All of the states are part of *one* country. No state has the right to say they don't belong to the United States.)

Pages 21–22

- What were people's concerns about Lincoln? (several details—that he couldn't do this job)
- How did Lincoln respond? (said he'd keep trying until the end)
- Do you think this was an acceptable response? Explain. (accept all reasonable responses)

Pages 23–24

- In addition to freeing slaves, what else did Lincoln ask for with his Emancipation Proclamation? (asked black men to join the Union army)
- Look at the illustration on this page. How does it show the response to the Emancipation Proclamation? (many African Americans joined the Union army)

Pages 25–26

- What surprising information does the author share on this page? (many Northerners opposed the Emancipation Proclamation)

- Why might some Northerners have been opposed to freeing the slaves? (This is complicated—accept reasonable responses and consider researching this point at a later time.)

- How did Lincoln respond to his lack of support? (He believed he was right with all his *soul*.)

Pages 27–28

- From other books we have read about Lincoln, why was he speaking at the Gettysburg battlefield? (site of a brutal battle where many soldiers died, came to dedicate a cemetery)

- Reread this quote. Try to say it in your own words. (Eighty-seven years ago our ancestors created a new country based on freedom where all people are equal.)

Pages 29–30

- What was the problem with the Emancipation Proclamation? (It freed only slaves in the rebellion states.)

- Reread the quote on this page. Explain it in your own words. (must get rid of slavery to save the nation)

- How did Lincoln convince lawmakers to get rid of slavery in *all* states? (the quote: "slavery must die that the nation might live!")

Pages 31–32

- What were some of the problems in the country as the war raged on? (many men had died; nation was divided; Northerners wanted to punish the Southerners for starting the war; Southerners were angry that the North had destroyed their cities, homes, and crops)

- Explain the line: "With malice toward none; with charity for all . . ." (no bad feelings toward anyone, only a giving heart)

Pages 33–34

- Reread the quote. Explain it in your own words. (Those of us who survived the war need to make sure that we carry on with freedom so the soldiers who died will not have died for no reason.)

- Did Lincoln's words succeed in guiding the nation forward even after his death? Explain. (accept all reasonable responses—should include the thought that we are still one free nation)

After Reading (Complete These Tasks on Day 2 of the Lesson Sequence)

Important Words to Talk About the Text

- If this book is read as the final text in this unit, there will not be many new words.

- Add: quotes, nation, Fort Sumter, perpetual, assassin, Union

Theme, Lesson, or Message (if Appropriate)

- Something like, Lincoln showed great strength of character throughout his whole life, believing in liberty and justice for all and one nation united

Summary or Gist Statement

- The main events and accomplishments of Lincoln's life have been summarized through previous texts. As a collaborative task, add details to the basic timeline established when reading *Honest Abe* by Edith Kunhardt

Review of Text Type (Literary/Information) and Genre

- This is a biography, but it also includes quotes from *primary sources*. (Explain this term to students.)

Collaborative Oral Task

- Ask students to work with a partner or small group to add *three new pieces of information* to the timeline about Lincoln's life

Follow-Up Lessons: Digging Deeper Through Rereading

Follow-up lessons can be taught in a different order.

Day	Focus Standard	Content for Whole-Class Lessons and Guided Student Practice
2	Close reading R1	Complete the close reading of this text, resuming from wherever you finished on the previous day.
3	Story elements: Sequence of events: Add to the timeline R3	Since the first three texts in this unit addressed many of the same words, a similar theme, and Lincoln's basic biography, use this time to add to the timeline with new details about Lincoln that were not present in the other texts using some of the additional vocabulary introduced in this book. Ask each partnership or small group to identify three additional pieces of information to be added to Lincoln's timeline. Be sure students understand *where* each item should be placed.
4	Choose a quote and use it in a speech Author's purpose or point of view R6; SL4	Ask students to choose one of the quotes in this book. Now pretend they are Lincoln and use that quote in a speech created by them: What is the occasion for this speech? The quote should make sense in its use for this event, and it should be evident that the student understands what the quote means.
5	Write an opinion piece W1	Now that students have completed all four books about Lincoln, ask them which one they would recommend to (choose one): a student about their age, a younger child, an older child. Ask them to support their opinion with evidence from the text. (They may also use evidence from other texts to explain why other books might *not* be a good choice for their identified audience.)

Learning Pathway

How to Study a Topic

How Do You Prefer to See the Moon—As an Astronomer, an Astronaut, a Native American, or a Storyteller?

Unit Focus: The Moon

© Eraxion/Dreamstime.com

Let's begin the unit! This is one of eight units in this book that delivers just the "goods"—the questions, prompts, assessment tasks, and student reproducibles you'll need to implement robust close reading instruction within an inquiry unit. Just about all you need to do a few weeks in advance of starting is to look at the anchor texts on pages 124 and 125 and order those books. From there, the materials provided are all explained clearly in terms of when and how to use them. If you need clarification, look back at the ten steps that begin on page 15.

Introduction to the Unit

The Rationale

There are thousands of topics that are engaging and worthwhile for intermediate grade students to study. They crisscross science, social studies, the arts—you name it! Why did I select the Moon as a good model of how to study a topic? Because it can be viewed through a variety of literary and informational lenses that are accessible to students. For example, students can study the Moon as an astronomer or an astronaut. Students could also study Native American Moon traditions or consider the Moon from a storyteller's perspective.

With the topic of the Moon as the focus of the unit, let's think about the ultimate goal of any unit teaching: helping students learn how to learn. I call it the learning pathway. With this unit, the pathway is How to Study a Topic. To that end, during your introductory lesson, you'll share with your students the talking points in the following chart, Learning Pathway: How to Study a Topic.

The Inquiry Question and Discussion Points

Throughout this unit, students will explore the question **How do *you* prefer to see the Moon—as an astronomer, an astronaut, a Native American, or a storyteller?** Why such a tightly focused question? Because no matter what one's age, the biggest challenge in learning about a topic is to decide which aspect of it to explore in depth. For example, if I launched into studying the Moon in general with a class, I'd quickly find myself experiencing a zero-gravity floating sensation in front of twenty-plus kids. It's just too vast. In framing the question so it's "bite size," students can more ably answer this question for themselves—and in a way that offers them some choice: *How do you prefer to see the Moon—as an astronomer, an astronaut, a Native American, or a storyteller?* We can all view the Moon in a variety of ways, but which lens speaks to *you* most strongly? Along the way, there are other questions we will want students to consider. We can ask some of these as we initiate the unit. To prepare for introducing the unit, see Unit Preview Questions and Discussion Points: for Studying a Topic: The Moon.

Next, because we want to know from the outset where we ultimately want to take students, I list questions under Questions for End-of-Unit Discussion About a Topic (The Moon) Integrating All Texts. These are questions you might pose at the end of this unit. That is, with any unit teaching, after completing all of the anchor books, we need to circle back to the topic itself, to consider the books together. The questions help students synthesize their thinking across texts and wrap up the study in a thoughtful way.

Learning Pathway
How to Study a Topic

Share these prompts with students.

- *When you study a topic, you have a particular purpose in mind, which means you need to narrow your topic: How might you narrow this topic?*

- *When you study a topic, you need to research it and find sources that will give you great information: What sources could give you great information about this topic?*

- *When you study a topic, you think about the most important big ideas and the facts or details that show these big ideas: How will you keep track of the important facts and details you learn about this topic?*

- *When you study a topic, you use key words that are important to understanding the topic: What key words do you need to understand to talk about this topic in a smart way?*

- *When you study a topic and want to write about it, you need to decide which genre would be the best for sharing your information so that it is clear and interesting: What genre would you choose to write about this topic? Why?*

- *When you study a topic and want to research it, where else can you look beyond books: Could you find information in a video or audio clip? Would photographs help you? Could you interview an expert? Are there reliable websites on this topic?*

Unit Preview Questions and Discussion Points

for Studying a Topic: The Moon

- Introduce the term *topic* and what it means to study a topic. Reference the questions for How to Study a Topic. Customize these points and questions according to the developmental level of your students. Chart the questions you will try to address through the unit.

- Introduce this topic and ask why it might be important to study this topic?

- Introduce the inquiry question: How do you prefer to see the Moon: As an astronomer, a Native American, an astronaut, or a storyteller? (Students may have some initial responses to this question—which is fine. But don't get too far into this until they've acquired textual evidence.)

- Introduce the Moon books selected for close reading. Show the cover and perhaps an illustration inside to pique students' interest. Do not explain the full story.

Questions for End-of-Unit Discussion About a Topic (The Moon) Integrating All Texts

- After reading the four anchor texts in this unit and the article by Bob Crelin, do you now feel you can answer the inquiry question: *How do* YOU *prefer to see the Moon . . .?* State your preference with two good reasons.

- Which questions for How to Study a Topic can you answer after reading these books?

- How do you see the Moon differently now than before studying these books?

- Which of these texts was easiest to understand and the most interesting? What did the author do to make it so interesting and easy to understand?

- After reading all of these texts, do you have any unanswered questions about the Moon? What questions?

- How else could the author of each text have presented the information to make it more interesting or easier to understand?

- Before beginning this study, you gave some reasons why people should study the Moon. Based on the books we've read, would you add anything to that list? Explain.

The Focus Standard

Many standards are included within the close reading follow-up lessons of this unit. However, the unit is designed around CCRA R6: "Assess how point of view or purpose shapes the content and style of a text" (http://www.corestandards.org/ELA-Literacy/CCRA/R, Craft and Structure section, para. 3) That means that a lesson related to author's purpose or point of view is included for every book. For this unit, you will always find this focus embedded in the work for Day 2 of the lesson sequence.

The Anchor Texts

The first text listed below is a short autobiographical piece by the author Bob Crelin. It's intended to be read by the students themselves and discussed during a unit kickoff lesson (discussion questions are provided on page 130). The remaining four texts are picture books, one of which will be read closely and studied during each week of the unit.

"Reflections on the Moon and Astronomy," an article by Bob Crelin (provided on page 130)

This brief article is by the author of *Faces of the Moon,* and students can read it independently. It describes one person's fascination with the Moon from the point of view of astronomy. Follow-up questions are included to get students thinking about their own Moon fascination.

Faces of the Moon by Bob Crelin

This book was selected for its clear, kid-friendly explanation of phases of the Moon. It's a rhyming text with interesting text features, such as tabs, to easily reference each Moon phase. The end of the book provides rhyming couplets, *Moon Mems,* to help students remember the meaning of each phase. Complexities of this book include the quantity of information included and the technical language. The Lexile is 950.

Thirteen Moons on Turtle's Back by Joseph Bruchac

This is a gorgeous book in part because of the beautiful language through which each Moon legend is told but also for the amazing illustration of each Indian Moon by Thomas Locker. This will be a challenging text for students because many of them will lack the cultural background inherent in Native American belief systems. The Lexile is 960.

Moonshot: The Flight of Apollo 11 by Brian Floca

There are many books available to students on the topic of Moon exploration, in particular the flight of Apollo 11. In the end, I chose this one because I thought the level of sophistication for intermediate grade students was just right: plenty of facts and useful vocabulary to build understanding of this Moon mission but as well lots of small details to add interest. The strong sense of voice makes you feel like you're actually on this journey with Aldrin, Armstrong, and Collins. The Lexile is 990.

The Man in the Moon (Guardians of Childhood) by William Joyce

There are numerous legends and even nursery rhymes that feature stories of the Moon. But this unit is for students beyond the early primary grades, and we want a text with sufficient complexity. I think I found the perfect match in this tale by William Joyce. His illustrations alone qualify as art worthy of extended study, so intricate are his images. But the story itself is fascinating, based on the idea that there are "guardians of childhood" among them: the Sandman, the Tooth Fairy, and the Man in the Moon. Students will need to attend closely to catch all the plot twists and turns. The Lexile is 830.

Other Texts Useful for Studying the Moon

If you'd like to use additional texts to extend this unit, or texts other than the ones for which lessons have been provided, consider the books below which also cover the full range of "Moon perspectives":

- *Long Night Moon* by Cynthia Rylant (the Moon from a Native American perspective)

- *Moonstick: The Seasons of the Sioux* by Eve Bunting (the Moon from a Native American perspective)

- *The Moon Book* by Gail Gibbons (the Moon from an astronomer's point of view)

- *Why the Sun and the Moon Live in the Sky* by Elphinstone Dayrell (An African folktale about the Moon)

- *One Giant Leap* by Robert Burleigh (the Moon from an astronaut's point of view)

The Unit's Two Assessments

Featured Reading Standard R6: Author's purpose or point of view

Featured Writing Format: Informative/Explanatory writing

See the Unit Curriculum Map for Close Reading for where these assessments might fit into your study of the Moon. Also, for more information about the rationale behind these two assessments and how they differ, as well as guidance for using the provided rubrics, refer to Step 9 on page 43 and Step 10 on page 50. Also, for evaluating students' performance, see page 45 for the Rubric for Content-Based Assessment (Task 1) and Standards-Based Assessment (Task 2).

Task 1: Content Assessment

You have studied a topic (the Moon) where different authors each had a different purpose in writing about this topic.

- One author's purpose was to help you understand the Moon from an *astronomer's* point of view

- One author's purpose was to help you understand the Moon from a *Native American's* point of view

- One author's purpose was to help you understand the Moon from an *astronaut's* point of view

- One author's purpose was to help you understand the Moon from a *storyteller's* point of view

On a separate piece of paper, answer these questions with a short informative paragraph about each bullet point:

- How do *you* see the Moon most clearly—as an astronomer, a Native American, an astronaut, or a storyteller? Why?

- What three or four key words are important in order to talk about the Moon from this point of view? Why is each word important?

- Explain two interesting facts about the Moon from this point of view using examples from the book we read or videos we watched.

- If you were writing about the Moon from this point of view, what genre would you choose? Why? Name at least two features of this genre you would be sure to include.

Task 2: Learning Pathway and Standard Assessment

Read the two selections below on the topic of tigers.

- *The Ungrateful Tiger: A Korean Folktale:* http://www.planetozkids.com/oban/ungrate.htm

- *Tiger Tale: What Dangers Do Big Cats Face?:* https://www.readworks.org/passages/tiger-tale

On a separate piece of paper, answer these questions with a short informative paragraph about each bullet point:

- What was the author's purpose in the *Ungrateful Tiger?* Write a brief summary of this text.

- What was the author's purpose in *Tiger Tale?* Write a brief summary of this text.

- How do you prefer learning about tigers—through stories or information? Explain.

- Explain the genre of the tiger text that you like best. Explain *three features* of this genre with examples from the text.

Unit Curriculum Map for Close Reading

*How Do You Prefer to See the Moon—As an Astronomer,
an Astronaut, a Native American, or a Storyteller?*

TEXT	MONDAY	TUESDAY	WEDNESDAY	THURSDAY	FRIDAY
				Unit Preview	Kickoff Lesson
				See Unit Preview Questions and Discussion Points	Read and discuss "Reflections on the Moon and Astronomy" by Bob Crelin. Discussion questions are provided at the end of the article
Faces of the Moon by Bob Crelin	Objective: R1 Close Reading	Objective: SL1; R6 Close Reading Follow-Up	Objective: R3 Story Element: Sequence of Phases	Objective: R7; R2 Nontraditional: Using Illustrations; Theme/Main Ideas	Objective: R9; R8 Text-to-Text Connections; Critiquing Text
	Read closely to answer text-dependent questions	Discussion addressing author's purpose, research, development of main idea, genre, key words	How does one Moon phase lead to the next?	Illustrate and paraphrase a Moon memo rhyme from the back of the book	Watch video clip to compare information; critique text for ease of understanding
Thirteen Moons on Turtle's Back by Joseph Bruchac	Objective: R1 Close Reading	Objective: SL1; R6 Close Reading Follow-Up	Objective: R4; R2 Word Choice: Summary With Key Words; Theme	Objective: R7 Nontraditional: Using illustrations	Objective: W1 Opinion Writing
	Read closely to answer text-dependent questions	Discussion addressing author's purpose, research, development of main idea, genre, key words	Summarize a legend including central idea and key words	Create a Moon symbol and provide a caption	Which legend in this book is the most magical? Provide evidence

TEXT	MONDAY	TUESDAY	WEDNESDAY	THURSDAY	FRIDAY
Moonshot: The Flight of Apollo 11 by Brian Floca	Objective: R1 Close Reading	Objective: SL1; R6 Close Reading Follow-Up	Objective: R3 Story Elements: Sequence of events	Objective: R7 Nontraditional: Using a Video Clip	Objective: W2 Informative Writing
	Read closely to answer text-dependent questions	Discussion addressing author's purpose, research, development of main idea, genre, key words	Include key events in a sequential summary	Identify additional information about the Moon landing from a video clip	Write a summary of the Apollo 11 Flight
The Man in the Moon (The Guardians of Childhood) by William Joyce	Objective: R1 Close Reading	Objective: SL1; R6 Close Reading Follow-Up	Objective: R4 Word Choice	Objective: R9 Text-to-Text connections	Objective: W3 Narrative Writing
	Read closely to answer text dependent questions	Discussion addressing author's purpose, research, development of main idea, genre, key words	Identify words chosen by the author that represent a "play on words" about the Moon	Compare this story to the poem *The Moon* by Robert Louis Stevenson	Write your own fairy tale about how something came to be
	Culminating Discussion	Content Assessment	Standards-Based Assessment		
	Respond orally to text-to-text connections for studying this topic. (See Questions for End-of-Unit Discussion Integrating All Texts)	Students complete the content-assessment task (below) integrating all texts in this study	Students complete the standards-based assessment task (below) using cold reads		

REFLECTIONS ON THE MOON AND ASTRONOMY

by Bob Crelin

My parents recalled that "Moon" was the first word I spoke as a baby, and for as long as I can remember the Moon has been my touchstone to the "great beyond." While growing up, my curiosity led me to explore all the sights, sounds, tastes, smells, and textures of the world around me. But there in the sky, out of my reach, hung this place of untold secrets.

During my childhood in the 1960s, the realm of outer space captivated our society's imagination. Manned rockets were being built and launched farther and farther beyond Earth's atmosphere. A new, futuristic age was dawning, and I read books and comics that vividly imagined what a visit to the Moon, Mars, or distant star systems would be like. I was ten years old when the entire world witnessed the first Moon landing in the summer of 1969. The experience was breathtaking and exhilarating—we were watching history unfold live on television! From then on, when I gazed upon the Moon, I knew we had actually been there, but it did not lessen my curiosity about our celestial neighbor. In particular, a school trip to a museum planetarium, where the experience of a fifteen-minute show inside the darkened theater felt like an entire night under the stars, changed my life.

Over the decades, the Moon and the stars have become deeply imprinted in my heart. Through the windows of my life, I have always noticed the Moon, her changing face peeking between branches, behind clouds, or simply suspended in the twilight, above the silhouettes of buildings and trees. I was easily mesmerized at the sight of the Moon—it seemed to transcend any other urgency of the moment. The Moon was a celestial beacon, marking the threshold to even greater mysteries beyond.

The purchase of my first telescope opened a whole new and intriguing chapter in my life, and I sought to understand as much as I could about our vast universe. As I learned more over the years, I began to share my knowledge of astronomy with others, and always made sure to include children. By remembering what was fun and easy to grasp about the Moon, stars, and planets, I was able to share the profound excitement of discovering worlds and places far, far beyond our little home planet. It seemed a natural next step for me to write books that invite the reader to notice the stars, or the Moon. My goal was simply to engage the reader's curiosity by connecting what they see in the sky with things they already know—making simple sense of something so grand.

Source: © Bob Crelin/BobCrelin.com

Think About

Use the questions below as discussion points for this article and as a way of initiating the *Moon* unit.

- How does Bob Crelin seem to feel about the Moon, and what words in the article show this feeling?

- In this article, Bob Crelin explains his purpose in writing a book about the Moon. What is his purpose? How will this information help you as you read his book, *Faces of the Moon*?

- How does Bob Crelin try to convince you that studying the Moon is "something so grand?" Are you convinced? Why or why not?

- What details in this article seem especially important? Why?

- Why do you think this article was selected to introduce this unit?

Close Reading Lessons for Faces of the Moon

Initial Close Reading Lesson

Text: *Faces of the Moon*   **Author:** Bob Crelin

Purpose: R1: Close reading for deep understanding of the text

Before Reading

<table>
<tr><td>

Clues Based on Title, Author

- Important words to notice: faces, Moon

Clues Based on Cover Illustration

- Notice cut-out full circle; not sure what design represents

Clues Based on Page Layout (Columns, Stanzas, Bolded Words, etc.)

- Notice the tabs and cut-outs inside the book and how they support meaning

Vocabulary That May Need Pre-Teaching for ELLs or Low Language Students

- Moon, faces of the Moon, month, orbit, sunbeams, quarter, full Moon, dusk, dawn

</td></tr>
</table>

During Reading

Questions Students Should Ask Themselves for Each Chunk of Text
• What is the author telling me?   • Any hard or important words?   • What does the author want me to understand?   • How does the author play with language to add to meaning?
Follow-Up Text-Dependent Questions for the Teacher to Ask About Each Chunk of Text
Pages 1–2   • What words on this page would a scientist need to know? (dusk, dawn, midday, orbit)   • What other words do we need to know? (transforms, shrinks, steady, reveal)
Pages 3–4   • What is another term for *changing face*? (lunar phase)   • What does the author mean by "changing face"? (lunar phase)

- Explain in your own words what the author means in the first stanza "Each changing face. . ." (The Moon has different "looks" depending on its phase.)

- Why are we able to see the Moon? (reflection)

- What words does the author use to help us understand this? ([the Sun] "paints her shadowed face with light . . .")

Pages 5–6

- "For as she orbits Earth in space . . .": Who is *she*? (the Moon)

- What happens to the Moon from night to night and day to day? (spins around the Earth)

- What words would a scientist need on this page? (wax, wane) What does each mean? (get bigger, get smaller)

Pages 7–8

- What is the first phase of the Moon called? (new Moon)

- Explain in your own words why you can't see the Moon when it's in its first phase? (Moon is between Sun and Earth with sunlit side turned away)

- How does the tab on this page help you to understand what a new Moon is? (no Moon on the tab)

Pages 9–10

- What does the author mean: "The Moon's less shy"? (we can see it more easily)

- What type of figurative language is this? (personification)

- Find another example of personification on this page. ("Her smile lights the twilight sky.")

- What word would a scientist need on this page? (crescent)

- What is a *crescent* Moon? (a curving sliver of a Moon between a new moon and a quarter)

- What clues on this page help you understand what a *crescent Moon* is? (cut-out and tab)

Pages 11–12

- What is this phase of the Moon called? (quarter Moon)

- How many days does it take for the Moon to reach its *quarter* phase?

- Why do you think this is called the *quarter* phase?

Pages 13–14

- After the first quarter Moon, what does the Moon look like? (almost round)

- When can you see this Moon? (from midday to late at night)

Pages 15–18

- What is the Moon's most famous phase? (full Moon)

- At what point during the month do you get a full Moon? (fourteen days/halfway through the month)

- How do the Earth, Moon, and Sun "line up" during a full Moon? (Sun—Earth—Moon)

- When does the full Moon rise and set? (rises at sunset, sets at dawn)

Pages 17–18

- When does the waning Moon rise? (mid-evening)
- And when does it set? (after sunrise)
- *Embark* is another word for _____? (rise)

Pages 19–20

- Now it's the last quarter. When does this Moon rise and set? (rises around midnight, sets around noon)

Pages 21–22

- When can you see the "waning crescent Moon"? (hours before sunrise to mid-afternoon)

Pages 23–24

- Now the Moon is "dark" again. What is the order of the Earth, Sun, and Moon? (Sun—Moon—Earth)

Pages 25–26

- Why doesn't the Moon always look the same to us? (The Earth and the Moon are both spinning)

After Reading (Complete These Tasks on Day 2 of the Lesson Sequence)

Important Words to Talk About the Text

- Name words from this book that a scientist would need in order to talk about the Moon. (There are many choices. Select words based on students' level of understanding about the Moon.)

Retell/Summarize (if Appropriate)

- Use these labels to explain how the Moon looks different at different points in the month: new Moon, waxing crescent Moon, full Moon, waning crescent Moon

Theme, Lesson, or Message (if Appropriate)

- Provide a *brief summary* that explains what happens to the Moon throughout the month

Collaborative Oral Task (May Add Written Task if Appropriate)

- With a partner or small group, draw a diagram of one phase of the Moon that includes the Earth, Sun, and Moon and be ready to explain your drawing using "moon words" that a scientist would use

Follow-Up Lessons: Digging Deeper Through Rereading

Follow-up lessons can be taught in a different order.

Day	Focus Standard	Content for Whole-Class Lessons and Guided Student Practice
2	Close reading follow-up discussion addressing Author's purpose or point of view SL1; R6	Complete the After Reading tasks. Discuss as a whole group or in small groups: • What was the author's purpose in writing this book? (How did this author want you to see the Moon?) • What did this author need to research to write this book? • What is the genre, and what did the author need to know about it to write this book? • What are the big ideas we should know from this book? How did the author show these big ideas? • What are the important words we should know from this book?
3	Story element: Sequence R3	Reread the text focusing especially on the phases of the Moon and how one phase leads to another. Ask students to complete the *Collaborative Oral Task* (page 133) at the end of this lesson.
4	Nontraditional: Illustrations that enhance meaning R7	Choose one of the Moon Memo Rhymes at the end of this book. Illustrate it to demonstrate its meaning. Then, paraphrase the rhyme explaining it in your own words.
5	Text-to-text connections; Critiquing text R9; R8	Watch this YouTube video about the Moon: https://www.youtube.com/watch?v=gHlMReTpJXw. What additional information does it give you? (explains about eclipses). Was this video clip easier or more difficult to understand than the book? Explain.

Close Reading Lessons for Thirteen Moons on Turtle's Back

Initial Close Reading Lesson

Text: *Thirteen Moons on Turtle's Back: A Native American Year of Moons*

Author: Joseph Bruchac (and editor Jonathan London)

Purpose: R1: Close reading for deep understanding of the text

Before Reading

Clues Based on Cover Illustration

- Notice the full Moon in the background; notice the larger-than-life turtle in the foreground

Clues Based on Title, Author

- Notice the important words: thirteen Moons, turtle's back, Native American

Probable Text Type (Literary or Informational); Possible Genre

- Probably literary; can't be sure yet about the genre

Vocabulary That May Need Pre-Teaching for ELLs or Low Language Students

- Native American, Moon, legend

During Reading

Questions Students Should Ask Themselves for Each Chunk of Text
• What is the author telling me?
• Any hard or important words?
• What does the author want me to understand?
• How does the author play with language to add to meaning?
Follow-Up Text-Dependent Questions for the Teacher to Ask About Each Chunk of Text
Pages 1–2
• What information is the author giving us right away? (The grandfather is telling his grandson that there are thirteen Moons in each year; the thirteen scales on a turtle's back represent the thirteen Moons; this is an Abenaki, Native American, legend)

Pages 3–4: Moon of Popping Trees

- Why was this Moon called *Moon of Popping Trees*? (the trees made a cracking sound in the bitter cold)

- What does the author mean by the "Frost Giant"? Was this a real person? (not a real person; this meant that the weather was really, really cold)

- In your own words, what did coyote have to do with this legend? (when coyote was out, the weather wasn't quite as cold, and children could go out)

Pages 5–6: Baby Bear Moon

- In your own words, tell this legend. (A mother bear once protected a human child throughout the winter. Now we do not disturb a mother bear for we know she protects her children)

- What do you think the author means: "small bears are like our children"? (they need protection and care)

Pages 7–8: Maple Sugar Moon

- Long ago, how did people get maple sugar, and why did this change? (Long ago, maple syrup dripped from trees all year long, but people got lazy and just slept under the maple trees.)

- Now how do people get maple syrup? (They have to boil down the sap, and this happens only once a year.)

Pages 9–10: Frog Moon

- How many winter Moons are there, and why is this Moon called *Frog Moon*? (There are five winter Moons; this one got its name because at the end of winter frogs sing.)

- What does the author mean by a "victory song"? (It is a victory because winter is over.)

Pages 11–12: Budding Moon

- Explain this legend in your own words. (One time Winter wouldn't leave. The Sun came to visit Winter and breathed on him. This made Winter grow smaller, and it went back to the north. Flowers began to grow.)

- What happens during the budding Moon? (animals wake up)

Pages 13–14: Strawberry Moon

- In your own words, explain this legend. (A little boy was given strawberries for being helpful. He returned as a man and shared with his people what he had been taught. The Senecas remember this each year with songs of praise for the Moon's gift.)

- What part of this legend couldn't possibly be true? (The young boy went away for four days and returned a man.)

- What is special about Strawberry Moon? (its sweetness)

Pages 15–16: Moon When Acorns Appear

- In your own words, explain this legend. (After the world was created, Earth Elder created a tree. The acorns were the first food.)

- What words tell you the time of the year for this Moon? ("the sun shining bright"—summer)

Pages 17–18: Moon of Wild Rice

- Who was Thunder Eagle? (a thunder and lightning storm)

- What are the gifts that are being celebrated here? (water, corn, fire, and wild rice)

- What time of year does this seem to be, based on the picture? (late summer or early fall)

Pages 19–20: Moose-Calling Moon

- Now what season is it? What words provide evidence? (fall—"the season when leaves begin to turn color")

- Why are the moose's horns flat? (He threatened to harm people with them.)

- The author says the moose is "strong as the northeast wind." Why does he use this comparison? (The northeast wind can be very strong—and the moose is strong.)

Pages 21–22: Moon of Falling Leaves

- In your own words, explain the legend of the falling leaves. (All trees were told to stay awake seven days and nights, but only the pine and spruce obeyed, so their leaves can always be green. But other trees must shed their leaves.)

- Explain the sentence: "This journey the leaves are taking is part of that great circle which holds us all close to the earth." (The falling leaves are part of the circle of life.)

Pages 23–24: Moon When Deer Drop Their Horns

- Now what is the season? (winter)

- In your own words, what is the legend that explains why the deer drop their horns? (They fought and hurt each other at the start of winter trying to prove their strength, so now they must drop their horns at the beginning of this season.)

- How does the author create a beautiful image of these dropping horns? ("drop onto earth, white with peaceful snow.")

Pages 25–26: Moon When Wolves Run Together

- Why do the wolves climb hills and sing together? (They are celebrating the stars honoring the footsteps of their forefather.)

- What is the message that the Wolf Trail teaches us? ("Our lives and songs are stronger when we are together.")

Pages 27–28: Big Moon

- In what way is this legend about the circle of life, too? (The Changer came back to this beautiful lake when his time on life was done.)

- Why might this Moon have been named the Big Moon? (accept all reasonable responses)

After Reading (Complete These Tasks on Day 2 of the Lesson Sequence)

Important Words to Talk About the Text

- Thirteen, Moon, Native American, legend, season, turtle

Theme, Lesson, or Message (if Appropriate)

- Identify themes for individual legends rather than for the text as a whole

Summary or Gist Statement

- Summarize or provide a gist statement for these legends individually

Review of Text Type (Literary/Information) and Genre

- This is a descriptive narrative

Collaborative Oral Task

- Working in pairs or small groups, ask students to choose different Moons in this book and briefly summarize the legend behind it

Follow-Up Lessons: Digging Deeper Through Rereading

Follow-up lessons can be taught in a different order.

Day	Focus Standard	Content for Whole-Class Lessons and Guided Student Practice
2	Close reading follow-up discussion addressing Author's purpose or point of view SL1; R6	What was the author's purpose in writing this book? (How did this author want you to see the Moon?) What did this author need to research to write this book? What is the genre, and what did the author need to know about it to write this book? Look at one legend: What are the important words in this legend? What is the central idea? How did the author show this central idea and make it interesting with supporting details?
3	Word choice; Theme/Main ideas Summary including central idea and key words R4; R2	Ask students to work in small groups or pairs to choose a different Moon legend from this book (not the one modeled on the previous day), identify the key words, and use the key words in a summary that includes the central idea of the legend and supporting details.
4	Nontraditional: Create a Moon symbol R7	This site contains Moon signs for each month, though they are not exactly like the ones described in *Thirteen Moons on Turtle's Back:* http://www.whats-your-sign.com/native-american-moon-signs.html. Show these symbols to students and ask them to create their own Moon symbol for one of the book's thirteen Moons. Provide a caption that explains the meaning behind the graphic.
5	Opinion writing W1	In your opinion, which Moon legend in this book is the most magical? Explain using details from the story itself.

Close Reading Lessons for Moonshot: The Flight of Apollo 11

Initial Close Reading Lesson

Text: *Moonshot: The Flight of Apollo 11*   **Author:** Brian Floca

Purpose: R1: Close reading for deep understanding of the text

TOPIC

Before Reading

Clues Based on Cover Illustration

- Notice the spaceship and the Moon and the patterns on the surface of the Moon; notice the dark sky and the stars, which look like tiny specks

Clues Based on Title, Author

- Notice the word *moon* in moonshot. Think about what a "moonshot" might be. Notice *Apollo 11*

Probable Text Type (Literary or Informational); Possible Genre

- This text probably gives us information

Vocabulary That May Need Pre-Teaching for ELLs or Low Language Students

- Moon, landing, astronaut, spaceship

Additional Supports

- Notice the double-page spread at the beginning of the book (before the title page). Spend a couple of minutes with students observing some of the diagrams on this page and talking about them—briefly

---

During Reading

Questions Students Should Ask Themselves for Each Chunk of Text

- What is the author telling me?
- Any hard or important words?
- What does the author want me to understand?
- How does the author play with language to add to meaning?

Follow-Up Text-Dependent Questions for the Teacher to Ask About Each Chunk of Text

Pages 1–2

- By using words like *cold, quiet, no air,* and *no life,* what kind of image of the Moon is the author trying to create? (silent, lonely, eerie)
- What one word contrasts with this image? (glowing)
- Why do you think the author adds this word? (it makes us think that maybe the Moon isn't so "boring" after all)

Pages 3–4

- How does the author get us interested in this Moon mission? (shows step-by-step how the astronauts got ready, like we're going on this adventure, too)

Pages 5–6

- What are they: *Columbia, Eagle, Saturn V* (*Columbia* and *Eagle* are two small spaceships on top of the rocket, *Saturn V*)
- What words does the author use to show the power of Saturn V? (*monster, thirty stories, six million pounds, tower of fuel and fire, too big to believe, mighty*)
- What senses does the author want us to use here when he describes the astronauts getting into the spaceship? (picturing them squeezing into their seats, *hearing* the clicks and the hums)

Pages 7–8

- Why does the author give us this information about the Launch Control and Mission Control Centers? (wants us to know how complex this mission was and all of the people supporting the astronauts)
- There was so much suspense when the astronauts went to the Moon. How does the author begin to create that suspense here? (*Go, Go, Go*)

Pages 9–10

- How does the author continue to raise suspense? (the countdown)
- What is the author showing in the illustrations on these pages? (how excited people were to be part of this experience, the power of the rocket, the anticipation of the astronauts)

Pages 11–12

- Why is the word **LIFTOFF** written in such large, upper case letters? (the importance of this moment)
- Do you get the sense that the rocket is going up quickly or slowly? Why? (slowly: *foot by foot, pound by pound*)

Pages 13–14

- Now what does the author want us to focus on? (the **ROAR** of the rocket)
- What sound words can you practically hear on this page? (*cracking* flame, *shakes* the air, *shakes* the Earth)

Pages 15–16

- What progress has been made at this point? (the rocket has shed some of its parts; the rocket flies faster; it is one hundred miles high; the rocket's last stage fires again, releasing Columbia and Eagle)
- Why does the author describe Eagle as "more bug than bird, a folded spider"? (its legs reach out like a spider's legs; it looks like a "bug")
- How does the author help us understand how heavy the men feel? (heavy as clay—talk about this)

Pages 17–18

- Now what progress has been made? (Columbia locks to Eagle; the last stage of Saturn is left behind)

- The author repeats some words here that we saw earlier in the book. Why do you think he does this? (wants us to remember how lonely and lifeless the Moon is)

Pages 19–20

- Why does everything float around in the spaceship? (lack of gravity)

- Look at the picture on this page. What would be strange about this? (accept all reasonable answers that reflect the evidence in the illustration)

Pages 21–22

- What are some of the inconveniences about being an astronaut? (crumbs float around, soup starts out as dust and has to have water added, don't have regular toilets, no fresh air, gets smelly)

Pages 23–24

- What do you notice in the words here? (the same words about the lifelessness of the Moon are repeated—but now they're getting closer to it)

- What do you notice in the illustration? (The Moon is not smooth; there are all kinds of craters on its surface)

Pages 25–26

- Explain in your own words what happens as Columbia and Eagle get to the Moon. (Collins stays in Columbia; Armstrong and Aldrin are in Eagle and go lower; they are running out of fuel)

- Why are so many people watching this? (these three men are making history)

Pages 27–28

- What is the problem that has occurred now? (The Eagle flew past its safe landing spot; the ship is running out of fuel; there is no level landing place)

Pages 29–30

- What details let you know this was a really close call? (only sixty seconds of fuel left)

- What words help you imagine how it felt to land the Eagle? (spray of dust, slow and slower, low and lower)

- How did the length of the phrases add to the suspense? (very short phrases with only one word in the last line: *landing!*)

- What words, now famous, did Armstrong say? ("The Eagle has landed.")

- How does the illustration on this page add to your understanding? (accept all reasonable responses)

Pages 31–32

- Now what is the "life" on the Moon? (Aldrin and Armstrong)

- Where will these astronauts find the "secrets" of the Moon? What secrets are they hoping to find? (secrets are in the rocks and dust; they want to know where the Moon came from, its age, and what it is made of)

- Now what word is used to describe the Moon? Why? (magnificent—it is totally different from any place on Earth)

- What does the author mean: "The sky is *pitch*"? (pitch black)

- Why is it so dark? (The Moon has no light; it just looks light to us when the sun is shining on it, and we see the reflection)

Pages 33–36

- Now how does the point of view change about the Earth and the Moon? (now the Earth is far away and looks lonely glowing in the sky—despite the fact that we know there is life on Earth)

Pages 37–40

- What details do we know about the trip home? (they brought back pictures, stones, stories, and secrets of the sky)

- What do these details show? (the trip had been a huge success)

- Why do you think the author includes the details about what they were returning to on Earth? (it's always good to come back home after a big trip)

- Why do you think the author includes the words "To warmth, to light" on the last page? (contrasts with the Moon: cold and dark)

After Reading (Complete These Tasks on Day 2 of the Lesson Sequence)

Important Words to Talk About the Text

- Moon, Earth, Eagle, Columbia, Saturn, rocket, astronauts, Aldrin, Armstrong, Collins, landing

Theme, Lesson, or Message (if Appropriate)

- With careful planning, hard work, and skill, you can accomplish amazing things—even things that have never been accomplished before

Summary or Gist Statement

- This would be a good text for creating a sequential summary showing a central idea (journey to the Moon) and key details. Students should include the main steps in this journey but leave out the small details intended to add human interest

Review of Text Type (Literary/Information) and Genre

- This is a great example of literary nonfiction. Be sure to discuss the characteristics of this genre

Collaborative Oral Task

- Ask students to work in pairs or small groups to identify three to five small details that added interest to this story. How did each detail add interest? Groups can share their findings at the end of the session

Follow-Up Lessons: Digging Deeper Through Rereading

Follow-up lessons can be taught in a different order.

Day	Focus Standard	Content for Whole-Class Lessons and Guided Student Practice
2	Close reading follow-up discussion addressing Author's purpose or point of view SL1; R6	Complete the After Reading tasks. Discuss as a whole group or in small groups: • What was the author's purpose in writing this book? (How did this author want you to see the Moon?) • What did this author need to research to write this book? • What is the genre and what did the author need to know about it to write this book? • What are the big ideas we should know from this book? How did the author show these big ideas and make them interesting? Extend with *Collaborative Oral Task* (page 142). • What are the important words we should know from this book?
3	Theme/Main ideas Identifying the sequence of events R2	Reread portions of the text that show the sequence of events, distinguishing the main events from small details. Ask students to work in pairs or small groups to list 6–8 pieces of information they would include in a summary of this text.
4	Nontraditional: Video clip of the Moon landing R7	Access a video clip of the Moon landing, such as from www.youtube.com/watch?v=xLu0Ak9Blog (1.24 minutes). This includes the quote, "The Eagle has landed," as well as Armstrong's famous words, "That's one small step for man; one giant leap for mankind." Be sure to discuss the meaning and significance of this quote. Ask: What new details does this video provide for you that were not included in the book? How does this video add to your understanding of the Moon landing?
5	Informational writing Write an informational summary W2	Ask students to write a summary of the Apollo 11 flight showing how one step in this process was connected to the next. Be sure to include information from both the text and the video.

Close Reading Lessons for *The Man in the Moon*

Initial Close Reading Lesson

Text: *The Man in the Moon*　　　　　　　　　　　　　**Author:** William Joyce

Purpose: R1: Close reading for deep understanding of the text

Before Reading

Clues Based on Cover Illustration

- Notice a giant blue butterfly/moth; notice a man who looks a little like the Man in the Moon; he's holding some kind of spear

Clues Based on Title, Author

- Notice this is about *The Man in the Moon*; notice the subtitle: *The* Guardians *of Childhood*

Probable Text Type (Literary or Informational); Possible Genre

- Probably a story, possibly some kind of fantasy; look for story parts

Vocabulary That May Need Pre-Teaching for ELLs or Low Language Students

- Man in the Moon, night light, nightmares, shooting star, telescope, guard (guardian)

During Reading

Questions Students Should Ask Themselves for Each Chunk of Text

- What is the author telling me?

- Any hard or important words?

- What does the author want me to understand?

- How does the author play with language to add to meaning?

Follow-Up Text-Dependent Questions for the Teacher to Ask About Each Chunk of Text

---

Pages 1–2

- Based on the examples on this page, what do you think the author means by *"guardians of childhood"*? (someone who takes care of children)

- What is the question this story is going to answer for us? (How did the Moon get to be the guardian of childhood?)

- When the author says, "Many once upon a times ago," what is he telling us about the kind of story this is going to be? (fairy tale)

- What do we expect to find in a fairy tale? (magic, good vs. evil, takes place in a land far away, a problem that doesn't get solved right away, a happy ending, a lesson)

- If this is a story, does it have a problem yet? (no)

- Reread the last sentence: What is the author *transitioning* to do here? (tells us about a time of hope and happiness)

Pages 3–8

- What is the author doing to get the story started? (tells us the characters, tells what made life so great)

- On p. 8 the author says, "As long as Nightlight watched over him, MiM was safe from nightmares." Where do you think the author is going next with this? (a problem: nightmares)

Pages 9–10

- What part of the story are we getting now?

- In your own words, explain what the problem was here. (accept reasonable paraphrasing)

- What is the *tone* on this page? (scary)

- What words does the author use to create this tone? (*waves of fear; plundering, extinguishing, scuttling*)

Pages 11–12

- Notice that the setting is changing here. Where is it now? (Earth)

- Why do you think the author is moving the setting to Earth? (The Man in the Moon belongs to our Earth Moon)

- Do you expect the problem to be solved in this attack? (no, there have to be more attempts)

Pages 13–14

- What is an oath? (a pledge or promise)

- Why do you think MiM's parents made Nightlight take this oath? (they might not survive)

- What magic is the author giving us here? (tear turned to a diamond dagger)

- Why do you think the author gave Nightlight this magic? (this will help to solve the problem)

Pages 15–22

- *Did* Nightlight use the magic of his diamond dagger? (yes)

- What was the outcome of the battle? (parents were gone—they had become new constellations of stars in the sky; Nightlight fell to Earth as a bright shooting star; MiM became the little Man in the Moon)

Pages 23–28

- Was MiM's new life a happy one? How do you know? (yes, saw his parents' constellation; dreamed of the Golden Age; played on the "moon playground"; ate Moon treats)

- Is the story over? Does the author have anything else to tell us? (story isn't over because we don't yet know how MiM became the Guardian of Childhood)

Pages 29–34

- What important clue did the author give us on page 29 when MiM looked through the telescope? (There were *children* on Earth)

- Why is this important? (getting us closer to MiM *guarding* children)

- Who did MiM really find who could help children? (Santa, Easter Bunny, Tooth Fairy, Mother Goose)
- Has MiM become a guardian yet? (no!)

Pages 35–40

- What was the one remaining problem for children? (nightmares)
- What does MiM want to do for the children? (bottom of p. 36: find them a friend like Nightlight)
- What do you think MiM's idea was as he kicked the rocks into sand? (accept reasonable answers)
- On p. 39 the last sentence says, "the Man in the Moon smiled and summoned the Lunar Moths"—but the author doesn't tell us the answer yet. Why not? (wants to keep the suspense going)

Pages 41–46

- In your own words, explain what MiM had done. (kicked the sand into a happy face that would smile brightly at the children—like a night light)
- Now is the problem solved? (yes—MiM was now a guardian of children)
- What is MiM's final action? (gets all his friends to take the oath)
- Why do you think the author includes this? (to remind readers that this is what we want most for all children)

After Reading (Complete These Tasks on Day 2 of the Lesson Sequence)

Important Words to Talk About the Text

- Man in the Moon, Nightlight, guardian, hopes and dreams, nightmare

Theme, Lesson, or Message (if Appropriate)

- All children should feel protected, safe, and loved and should have hopes and dreams

Summary or Gist Statement

- This is suitable for a problem/solution summary

Review of Text Type (Literary/Information) and Genre

- This is a fairy tale. Find elements of a fairy tale with examples from the story

Collaborative Oral Task

- With a partner or small group find the elements of a fairy tale in this story using examples from the text

Follow-Up Lessons: Digging Deeper Through Rereading

Follow-up lessons can be taught in a different order.

Day	Focus Standard	Content for Whole-Class Lessons and Guided Student Practice
2	Close reading follow-up discussion addressing Author's purpose or point of view SL1; R6	Complete the After Reading tasks. Discuss as a whole group or in small groups: • What was the author's purpose in writing this book? (How did this author want you to see the Moon?) • What did this author need to research to write this book? • What is the genre, and what did the author need to know about it to write this book? Extend with *Collaborative Oral Task* (page 146) • What are the big ideas we should know from this book? How did the author show these big ideas and make them interesting? • What are the important words we should know from this book?
3	Word choice R4	In this story, the author has used words very cleverly to go with the "Moon" topic. Some examples from page 4 are *Moonbot, Primer of Planets, Moonmice, Nightlight, Moon Clipper.* Find examples of other cleverly chosen words and names on other pages.
4	Text-to-text connection R9	Read the poem *The Moon* by Robert Louis Stevenson. You can find this at http://www.lnstar.com/mall/literature/rls/Moon.htm or in many poetry books. Is the Moon described here as a *guardian*? What is the evidence? Is there anything *different* about the way the Moon is described in this poem compared to the Moon in the story?
5	Narrative writing W3	Write your own fairy tale about how we got the tooth fairy, how we got Jack Frost, how we got the sandman, or anything else you would like to turn into a fairy tale about how something came to be. Remember to include magic, a setting far away, a problem, good and evil characters, and a happy ending. Try to make your story suspenseful by not solving the problem right away.

Learning Pathway

How to Study a Genre

How Many Ways Can You Tell a Fairy Tale?

Unit Focus: Fairy Tale

© Double_Bubble/Thinkstock Photos

Let's begin the unit! This is one of eight units in this book that delivers just the "goods"—the questions, prompts, assessment tasks, and student reproducibles you'll need to implement robust close reading instruction within an inquiry unit. Just about all you need to do a few weeks in advance of starting is to look at the anchor texts on pages 154 to 156 and order those books. From there, the materials provided are all explained clearly in terms of when and how to use them. If you need clarification, look back at the ten steps that begin on page 15.

Introduction to the Unit

The Rationale

Students read plenty of different genres throughout their academic careers, so it's easy to assume they are getting a balanced diet and have sufficient "muscle memory" of genre characteristics.

In fact, we've gotten an extra nudge about this from the Common Core—which seeks an equal proportion of informational and literary text in the elementary school. But remember that text type alone (literary or informational) doesn't guarantee a distribution of genres within either category. For example, are students reading widely from biography, personal narratives, primary sources, narrative nonfiction, charts, maps, and other varieties of information? Or are they mostly reading one kind of informational text? The same question prevails for literary genres.

Moreover, *sampling* genres is not the same as *studying* genres. Knowing the characteristics of any genre is a helpful contributor to students' comprehension. It gives them a framework for understanding. Is it a fairy tale? Then there should be evidence of some of those iconic fairy tale words (*once upon a time, happily ever after*). There should be good guys and bad guys (or girls), perhaps a "royal" setting, a bit of magic, and the power of three. In the end, honor should prevail over evil, from which we can all learn a lesson. If students realize that they should be looking for these elements when reading *The Princess and the Pea* or any fairy tale, they'll be more intentional about finding them—and recognizing when their thinking has gone offtrack.

A single unit such as this one can't ensure the kind of balance we want long term, but it can provide a model of what we mean by explicit genre instruction.

With fairy tales as the focus of the unit, let's think about the ultimate goal of any unit teaching: helping students learn how to learn. I call it the learning pathway. With this unit, the pathway is How to Study a Genre. To that end, during your introductory lesson you'll share with students the talking points in the following chart, Learning Pathway: How to Study a Genre. Also, see Appendix 3, at **resources.corwin.com/boyleslessons,** for Genre Checklists for Students that students can use independently to analyze any text for its genre features.

Learning Pathway
How to Study a Genre

Share these prompts with students.

If you know the genre, think about what you expect to find:

- *Genres build characters in different ways: What kinds of characters do you expect to meet in this genre?*

- *A genre develops problems in different ways; some genres do not contain any problem: Does this genre include a problem? If so, what kind of problem will characters probably encounter in this genre and what will go into solving the problem?*

- *A genre is usually based on either fantasy or reality and sometimes a combination of both: Will you expect fantasy, reality, or a combination of both in this genre?*

- *Particular "genre words" are often associated with a genre: What kind of words are often connected to this genre (like detective, moral, once upon a time)*

- *Most genres have text features related to the genre: What text features might you see in this genre (such as headings, bolded words, chapter titles)?*

If you aren't sure about the genre, start with what you do know and narrow the possibilities:

- *In order to determine the genre, you need to first decide if a text is literary or informational: Does this text look like it will be a story, or is it more like a nonfiction article with information? Why?*

- *To determine a literary genre it's also helpful to consider whether it is mostly fantasy or reality: If it's a story, does it look like it could be true—or is it definitely a fantasy? Why?*

- *Sometimes even if you're not sure about the genre, you can make a good guess based on what you have observed: Based on your best guess, what genre might this be? (Think of a couple of possibilities.)*

The Inquiry Question and Discussion Points

The main question students will answer throughout this unit is **How many ways can you tell a fairy tale?** When I first considered a unit on fairy tales, I was thinking about various versions of one tale, for example, *Cinderella*. But *Cinderella*, even in its multiple iterations, is still, well, *Cinderella*, and didn't seem complex enough to warrant an entire month of study for intermediate grade students. But what about examining all of the kinds of things an author could do with a fairy tale to change it up? An author could change the setting—or modernize it—or switch the point of view—or choose a different format for telling the story. The list goes on, but those will be the fairy tale varieties addressed here. You'll want to get this unit going with some questions to transport students' thinking back to the magic of fairy tales, as well as helping them focus on what it means to study *any* genre. To get started, see Unit Preview Questions and Discussion Points: for Studying a Genre: Fairy Tales.

Next, because we want to know from the outset where we ultimately want to take students, I list questions under Questions for End-of-Unit Discussion About a Genre (Fairy Tales) Integrating All Texts. These are questions you might pose at the end of this unit. That is, with any unit teaching, after completing all of the anchor books, we need to circle back to the inquiry question itself, to consider the books together. The questions help students synthesize their thinking across texts and wrap up the study in a thoughtful way.

Questions for End-of-Unit Discussion About a Genre (Fairy Tales) Integrating All Texts

- Which fairy tale variation did you personally enjoy the most and why?

- If you had the opportunity to speak to a children's book publisher, what fairy tale variation would you advise that person to consider for future books? Why?

- In which of the texts that we read were the genre characteristics (features of a fairy tale) the most obvious to you? Explain your thinking with specific examples from the text you chose.

- Which of the fairy tales we read seemed the most creative to you? Why? Give examples.

- What advice would you give to students studying a genre in general?

- What advice would you give to students studying the fairy tale genre?

- Think about the blog post we read at the beginning of this unit: "*Why We Need Fairytales.*" After completing this unit, do you agree more or less with that author? Explain your thinking.

Unit Preview Questions and Discussion Points

for Studying a Genre: Fairy Tales

- *Introduce the term genre and name a few genres. Discuss what it means to study a genre. (See the chart Learning Pathway: How to Study a Genre.)*

- *Now, talk specifically about the characteristics of a fairy tale and what to look for when that is the genre of the text you are reading. Ask students to name a few fairy tales.*

- *Introduce the inquiry question: How many ways can you tell a fairy tale? Ask students for some examples of nontraditional fairy tales. (To get them started, you might need to give an example such as The True Story of the Three Pigs, which tells the story from the wolf's point of view.)*

- *Introduce the four fairy tale books selected for close reading. Show the cover and perhaps an illustration inside to pique students' interest. Do not explain the full story.*

The Focus Standard

The study of any genre is a good match for College and Career Readiness Anchor (CCRA) Standard 5: "Analyze the structure of texts, including how specific sentences, paragraphs, and larger portions of the text (e.g., a section, chapter, scene, or stanza) relate to each other and the whole." (http://www.corestandards.org/ELA-Literacy/CCRA/R, Craft and Structure, para. 2). I think this is especially well suited to a genre study that looks at variation within the genre because then students get to probe complexities beyond just the expected genre features. Don't forget, too, the more subtle features of structure (the second part of this standard): how parts of a text are connected to each other. This can easily be applied to the study of fairy tales—but should apply equally to the analysis of all texts. The specific work around Standard 5 in this unit will appear in different places each week depending on where it fits most authentically within the systematic close reading of the text.

The Anchor Texts

The first text listed below is a blog post intended to be read by the students themselves and discussed during a unit kickoff lesson (discussion questions are provided on page 160). The remaining four texts are picture books, one of which will be read closely and studied during each week of the unit.

"Why We Need Fairytales," an article adapted from a blog post by Emerald Lugtu (provided on page 160)

This article, to be read by the students themselves, initially came from a blog post that caught my attention. The blogger was a high school student at the time, and her articulation of the value of fairy tales even for mature readers seemed the perfect introduction to this unit for intermediate grade kids who just might think they're too cool for "baby stories." It was a little long, and the author (who blogged under the name *Aliceinreaderland*) allowed me to adapt (shorten) it so it could work for this book. Lexile: 730.

The Princess and the Pizza by Mary Jane Ausch and Herm Ausch

I teach close reading lessons with numerous modernized fairy tales when I visit classrooms. I tried *not* to include this one in this curriculum because, honestly, I use it a *lot* and wanted to explore new options. But in the end, it's still one of my all-time favorites; I thought other teachers and students should have the opportunity to enjoy it for close reading too. This is a book where complexity and fun come together. Complexities include a humorous voice that relies on plays on words (you'll discover how the authors arrived at the clever title, a spin on the original *Princess and the Pea*). Then, there's intertextuality where characters from other fairy tales make cameo appearances in this story. And notice, too, the new take on the fate of the princess—not the typical outcome for a damsel in distress. Don't be deterred by the Lexile of 540 and the grade equivalent of 3.8, which don't account for these nuances.

The Cowboy and the Black-Eyed Pea by Tony Johnston

Read this book next to examine yet another version of the *Princess and the Pea* and compare it to the *Princess and the Pizza*. This one is set in the Wild West and illustrates how setting can make a difference to a story. Examine the story details that make good use of Wild West dialect, gear, clothing, and the like. The Lexile measure is 510, but the grade level equivalent is 5.1.

Extra! Extra!: Fairy-Tale News From Hidden Forest by Alma Flor Ada

This book's format as a series of newspaper articles—local news, sports, international news, op-ed pieces, kiddie page, advertisements, and more, speaks to both its creativity and its complexity. In this book, characters from numerous fairy tales come together as well-known tales are depicted as "news." The lead local item is young Jack's disappearance up a sinister looking beanstalk—and many townsfolk weigh in about what to do next. Reports are updated on three different dates along with the results of the race between the tortoise and the hare (sports), and an international crisis—tracking the whereabouts of Geppetto, father of Pinocchio. Complexities include knowledge demands: the text-to-text connections and prior knowledge of fairy tales, and structure, a story told as a series of newspaper articles of various formats. No Lexile or readability measure is available.

Once Upon a Cool Motorcycle Dude by Kevin O'Malley

Above all, this book shows how point of view makes a difference in writing. A boy and a girl have been charged with writing a fairy tale together. The story starts with the girl telling the story, and it's all-pastel ponies and damsels in distress, pretty much what you'd expect from a stereotypic "girl world." The young boy, however, is having no part of this, and he lobbies for a hero named Ralph who is a motorcycle dude. The writers volley back and forth for the supremacy of their own voice. In the end, happily ever after emerges as a compromise. The complexity here is in the structure of the text: multiple speakers with different points of view. Lexile: 550.

Other Texts Useful for Studying Fairy Tales

To extend this study of fairy tales or to use texts other than those identified above, you might want to consider the following titles. One cautionary note is that the Lexile levels are apt to be lower than those prescribed for the intermediate grades. Recognize that these levels do not reflect the concept of *studying* these tales as a *genre* or of analyzing the features that set them apart from more traditional tales.

- *Goldilocks and Just One Bear* by Leigh Hodgkinson

- *Little Red Writing Hood* by Joan Holub

- *Seriously, Cinderella is SO Annoying* by Trisha Shaskan (and many other titles in this series, *The Other Side of the Story,* published by Capstone)

- *The True Story of the Three Little Pigs* by Jon Scieszka

- *Once Upon a Time: Writing Your Own Fairy Tale* by Nancy Loewen

- *Frozen* (Little Golden Book) by R. H. Disney

The Unit's Two Assessments

Featured Reading Standard 5: Genre and structure

Featured Writing Format: Narrative writing

See the Unit Curriculum Map for Close Reading for where these assessments might fit into your study of fairy tales. Also, for more information about the rationale behind these two assessments and how they differ, as well as guidance for using the provided rubrics, refer to Step 9 on page 43 and Step 10 on page 50. Also, for evaluating students' performances, see page 45 for the Rubric for Content-Based Assessment (Task 1) and Standard-Based Assessment (Task 2). Turn to page 293, The End of the Story: Reflecting on Student Work, for some sample student work and commentary.

Task 1: Content Assessment

In this unit you have studied a genre: fairy tales. Specifically, you have studied fairy tales told in different ways. Please respond to the questions below. Your answers should relate to the four anchor stories we have read:

- *The Princess and the Pizza*

- *The Cowboy and the Black-Eyed Pea*

- *Extra! Extra!: Fairy-Tale News From Hidden Forest*

- *Once Upon a Cool Motorcycle Dude*

1. Which tale that we read do you consider to be the closest to a traditional fairy tale based on what you have learned about characteristics of a fairy tale? Explain using evidence from the text you selected.

2. Compare two of the fairy tales we studied. What is the same about each one? What is different? You can talk about the plot (what happens), but you also need to talk about the structure (how the story was put together).

3. Choose one of these fairy tales and rewrite it, telling it in another way. For example, if the story is not written as a newspaper article, you could rewrite it as a newspaper article or as if two people were writing the story together or as if the story is taking place in a different setting. You could also consider including fairy tale characters from other stories.

Task 2: Learning Pathway and Standard Assessment

Access the texts below using these links. You will read *Thumbelina*. You will view *The Story of Leaping Beauty* and the original story of *Sleeping Beauty*.

- *Thumbelina:* http://shortstoriesshort.com/story/thumbelina/

- *The Story of Leaping Beauty*: https://www.youtube.com/watch?v=edS6i-2z4H0 (YouTube)

- The original story of *Sleeping Beauty*: http://www.agendaweb.org/videos/short-tales/sleeping-beauty.html (YouTube)

1. Watch the video of the original story of *Sleeping Beauty*. In what ways is this a *traditional* fairy tale? Write an explanatory paragraph giving at least three reasons with examples from the video.

2. Compare *The Story of Leaping Beauty* to the original story of *Sleeping Beauty*. Find three similarities and three differences. Use examples from both stories as evidence.

3. Read the story of *Thumbelina*. Rewrite it as a newspaper article, or as if it were happening somewhere else, or as if two people were writing it together. You could also consider including fairy tale characters from other stories.

Unit Curriculum Map for Close Reading

How Many Ways Can You Tell a Fairy Tale?

TEXT	MONDAY	TUESDAY	WEDNESDAY	THURSDAY	FRIDAY
				Unit Preview	Kickoff Lesson
				See Unit Preview Questions and Discussion Points	Read and discuss the blog post "Why We Need Fairytales" by Emerald Lugtu. Discussion questions are provided at the end of the article
The Princess and the Pizza by Mary Jane and Herm Ausch	Objective: R1 Close Reading	Objective: SL1; R5 Close Reading Follow-Up	Objective: R6 Author's Purpose or Point of View: Identifying Point of View	Objective: R9 Text-to-Text Connections: Compare Two Versions of the Same Story	Objective: W3 Narrative Writing
	Read closely to answer text-dependent questions	Discussion addressing the text's key words, summary message; collaborative task relating to genre characteristics	Reread the story to identify and elaborate on the author's point of view about princesses	Compare *The Princess and the Pizza* to the original tale of *The Princess and the Pea* by Hans Christian Andersen	Rewrite the ending of this story to change it in some way
The Cowboy and the Black-Eyed Pea by Tony Johnston	Objective: R1 Close Reading	Objective: SL1; R5 Close Reading Follow-Up	Objective: R4 Word Choice: Vocabulary	Objective: R3 Story Elements: Setting	Objective: W3 Narrative Writing
	Read closely to answer text-dependent questions	Discussion addressing the text's key words, summary message; collaborative task relating to genre characteristics	Reread the story to identify vocabulary that fits with the "Wild West" setting	Reread the story to focus on setting and how the story would change with a different setting	Rewrite the story so that it takes place in a different setting

TEXT	MONDAY	TUESDAY	WEDNESDAY	THURSDAY	FRIDAY
Extra! Extra!: Fairy-Tale News From Hidden Forest by Alma Flor Ada	Objective: R1 Close Reading for First Half of Text	Objective: R1 Close Reading for Second Half of Text	Objective: SL1; R2 Close Reading Follow-Up	Objective: R5 Genre and Structure: Characteristics	Objective: W2 Explanatory Writing: Write a News Article About a Fairy Tale
	Read closely to answer text-dependent questions	Read closely to answer text-dependent questions	Reread three *Hidden Valley News* articles in order to summarize the story of *Jack and the Beanstalk*	Review the kinds of newspaper articles in this text; look for evidence of the five Ws, *who, what, when, where*, and *why* plus *how* questions	Write a news article about a previously read text in this unit (*The Princess and the Black-Eyed Pea* or *The Princess and the Pizza*)
Once Upon a Cool Motorcycle Dude by Kevin O'Malley	Objective: R1 Close Reading	Objective: SL1; R5; R6 Close Reading Follow-Up	Objective: R6 Author's Purpose or Point of View	Objective: R4 Word Choice	Objective: W3; R6 Narrative Writing; Author's Purpose or Point of View
	Read closely to answer text-dependent questions	Discussion addressing the text's key words, summary, and message; collaborative task relating to genre characteristics and point of view	Reread parts of the text to dig deeper into point of view: What did the girl care about? What did the boy care about?	Reread selected parts of the text to identify how author's word choice strengthens the story's point of view	Write a fairy tale with a partner and think about how point of view made a difference to your story and the process of writing your story
	Culminating Discussion	Content Assessment	Standards-Based Assessment		
	Respond orally to text-to-text connections for studying this topic. (See Questions for End-of-Unit Discussion Integrating All Texts)	Students complete the content assessment task integrating all texts in this study	Students complete the standards-based assessment task using cold reads		

GENRE

How to Study a Genre 159

WHY WE NEED FAIRYTALES

by Emerald Lugtu

Once upon a time . . .

No matter our age, most of us can remember those words that began fairytale adventures. Most of us can also remember the fuzzy feeling that settled over us like fairy dust by the time the story ended. Perhaps that's one good reason why fairytales are important: they make us happy.

The funny thing is that many fairytale heroes and heroines are not very heroic at all. Jack from *Jack and the Beanstalk* was a thief. The Princess from *The Princess and the Pea* was not a very gracious guest. She did a *lot* of complaining about that uncomfortable bed.

Yet we still want to root for fairytale characters. Why? Because they're human. We look at them and in some ways, we see ourselves. Sometimes *their* mistakes are sort of like the mistakes *we've* made. We can learn lessons from them—like don't take apples from strangers (*Snow White*). Don't forget to invite everyone to your party (*Sleeping Beauty*). Read the fine print when signing contracts (*Rumplestiltskin*).

Fairytales also give us a chance to see the good things about ourselves. They help us realize that good often triumphs over evil and that if we work hard, we can succeed. Sometimes fairytales make us feel brave. Maybe if we'd been given the chance we would have tamed the dragon. We would have gone to the ball. We would have been strong enough to pull the sword from the stone. We, too, could have been heroes!

Some people say that fairytales are ridiculous because they don't show life the way it really is. Wishes on stars don't come true. If you fall down a rabbit hole you'll probably sprain your ankle, not have tea parties with mad hatters. Some parts of fairytales *aren't* true. But they do send us messages that are real—like "don't be afraid," or "you can do this!" and "they all lived happily ever after."

Maybe the best part about fairytales is that they remind us to dream. They help us dare to believe that there's our very own happy ending somewhere out there just waiting to happen. Yes, with imagination and creativity there really can be [a] happy ending.

Source: Adapted from an essay by aspiring writer Emerald Lugtu titled "Why We Need Fairytales."

Think About

This article was adapted from a post by Emerald Lugtu on her blog Alice in Readerland. When she wrote this, she was a high school student. Think about the questions below as you reflect on this article and begin this unit on fairy tales.

- Why do you think Emerald Lugtu wanted to write this post for her blog? What was her purpose?

- What details in this post seem especially important? Why?

- What do you think the author means when she says, "We look at them [fairy tale characters] and in some ways, we see ourselves?"

- The author gives us lots of reasons why we need fairy tales. In your opinion, what is the most important reason of all? Explain using examples of fairy tales that you know.

- Why do you think this post was selected to introduce this unit? How can it guide us as we read the fairy tales in this unit?

Close Reading Lessons
for *The Princess and the Pizza*

Initial Close Reading Lesson

Text: *The Princess and the Pizza*

Author: Mary Jane Ausch and Herm Ausch

Purpose: R1: Close reading for deep understanding of the text

Before Reading

Clues Based on Cover Illustration

- Notice that a "cartoonish" looking princess is carrying a pizza

Clues Based on Title, Author

- Notice key words: *Princess* and *Pizza*; notice the similarity to the title *The Princess and the Pea*

Probable Text Type (Literary or Informational); Possible Genre

- Probably a fairy tale

Vocabulary That May Need Pre-Teaching for ELLs or Low Language Students

- Princess, pizza

During Reading

Questions Students Should Ask Themselves for Each Chunk of Text

- What is the author telling me?

- Any hard or important words?

- What does the author want me to understand?

- How does the author play with language to add to meaning?

Follow-Up Text-Dependent Questions for the Teacher to Ask About Each Chunk of Text

Pages 1–2

- What is different here from the original story of *The Princess and the Pea*? (The princess is not rich and doesn't live in a castle.)

- What does the authors' point of view seem to be about princesses? What is the evidence? (They seem to be poking fun at princesses and "princessing": walking the peacock, surveying the kingdom from the castle tower, doing the princess wave.)

Pages 3–4

- How do the details on this page relate to what we learned on the previous page? (The author shows that these "princess behaviors" don't work out as well in Paulina's new life: made holes in the roof, people thought she was swatting at flies.)

- How are these authors making this story humorous? (poking fun at princesses)

Pages 5–6

- What does Paulina seem to think about being a princess? What is the evidence? (She wanted to be a princess—ball gown, tiara, wanted to marry the prince)
- What odd details does the author include on this page? (took along some garlic and herbs)

Pages 7–8

- Does Paulina talk and act like a princess? Explain. (No: "Oh, for Pete's sake"; "the old princess-and-the-pea trick.")
- What does Paulina mean: "That's so once-upon-a-time"? (She is referring to fairy tales.)

Pages 9–10

- Why were the princesses who looked bright-eyed sent home? (they were able to sleep with the pea under their mattress—so they weren't real princesses)
- In a fairy tale there are often three tests. What was the first test that Paulina had to pass? (write an essay about her mother-in-law)
- Why was the topic of this essay so humorous? (Queen Zelda was definitely *not* "exquisitely beautiful.")
- How does Paulina respond when Queen Zelda explains the second test? Do you expect this in a fairy tale? (Paulina argues back—definitely not a princess quality)
- What is a "sharp look"? (angry look)

Pages 11–12

- This page includes references to several other fairy tales. What are they? Explain the references. (The two big-footed princesses were like the stepsisters in *Cinderella*; the seven strange little men were like the dwarfs in *Snow White*; the princess with the long braid was like Rapunzel.)
- How does the illustration add to the humor on this page? (accept all reasonable responses)
- If you were to use one word to describe Paulina, what might it be based on her actions and words so far? (outspoken, bold, rude, etc.)

Pages 13–14

- How do the authors continue to use other fairy tales in a clever way? (The characters from other fairy tales are back again—and get in the way of Paulina's success.)
- Notice the ingredients that are left for Paulina. Do you think she can create a feast out of these? Explain. (accept all reasonable responses: will students recognize that these are the ingredients for pizza?)

Pages 15–16

- What strategy do you think the authors want us to use as they describe Paulina's "feast"? (visualize)
- What other fairy tale character is mentioned on this page? (fairy godmother)
- Why do you think the authors are having Paulina take a nap right now? (raises suspense about who will win)

Pages 17–18

- What is the meaning of *beheaded*? (off with your head)
- What is the fairy tale referenced here? (*Rumplestiltskin*)

- What do you think the authors are trying to show with the arguments back and forth between Queen Zelda and Paulina? (They are both strong women; don't want to be pushed around.)

Pages 19–22

- What details from earlier in the book are returning here? (garlic and herbs—the authors included these details for a reason)

- What was Paulina creating? (pizza)

- How are the authors using other fairy tales here? (Paulina considered climbing down Rapunzel's braid to escape)

Pages 23–26

- How did pizza get its name? ("Pete's. . . . ah")

- How did the authors create a surprise ending here? (Paulina says she doesn't want to marry the prince.)

- What do you think Paulina's new plan is? (accept all reasonable responses)

Pages 27–30

- How do the authors tie details together from the beginning of the story? (Paulina opens a pizza restaurant; the restaurant includes the carved furniture her father makes; Drupert and Queen Zelda come to the restaurant; people now notice the princess wave.)

- How do the authors let you know there might be one more surprise? ("She was still worried about one little thing.")

Pages 31–32

- Explain what Paulina is worried about. (Her dad might marry Queen Zelda—which would make Zelda Paulina's stepmother)

After Reading (Complete These Tasks on Day 2 of the Lesson Sequence)

Important Words to Talk About the Text

- Paulina, Queen Zelda, pizza, fairy tales, Drupert

Theme, Lesson, or Message (if Appropriate)

- Being a princess isn't for everyone—even though it might look great at first

Summary or Gist Statement

- This is a great story to summarize because of its classic problem/solution structure. Students can identify what happens at the beginning, middle, and end

Review of Text Type (Literary/Information) and Genre

- This is a fairy tale with modern twists. It also incorporates characters from other fairy tales into its plot

Collaborative Oral Task

- To reinforce understanding of genre characteristics, ask students to work in pairs or small groups to identify five fairy tale characteristics in this story. (You might want to review fairy tale characteristics before asking students to complete this task.)

Follow-Up Lessons: Digging Deeper Through Rereading

Follow-up lessons can be taught in a different order.

Day	Focus Standard	Content for Whole-Class Lessons and Guided Student Practice
2	Close reading follow-up discussion related to After Reading tasks (above) SL1; Collaborative task for R5 (Genre and structure)	With the whole class, identify key words in the text and use them to create a summary that includes all story elements: characters, problem, events, solution. Also identify the message. Review features of a fairy tale. As a collaborative task, ask students to work in pairs or small groups to identify five fairy tale characteristics they found in *The Princess and the Pizza*. See the *Collaborative Oral Task* (page 163).
3	Identifying Author's purpose or point of view R6	In this story, the authors seem to be making fun of princesses. Reread the story (or selected pages) where the authors are making princesses and fairy tales seem a little silly. Find at least five examples that show this point of view.
4	Narrative writing: Compare two versions of the same story R9	Reread *The Princess and the Pizza* to note ways that this version of the story is different from the original story by Hans Christian Andersen. You will probably also need to read the original *Princess and the Pea*, so students have a clear sense of the original tale. Make a list (as a whole class or in small groups) of five differences between *The Princess and the Pizza* and *The Princess and the Pea*.
5	Narrative writing: Rewrite the ending of the story W3	How else might this story have ended? What if Paulina didn't win the cooking contest? What if she decided to marry Prince Drupert? What if one the characters from another fairy tale won instead? Rewrite the ending of the story so the outcome is different. Try to tie everything together just like the authors did.

Close Reading Lessons for *The Cowboy and the Black-Eyed Pea*

Initial Close Reading Lesson

Text: *The Cowboy and the Black-Eyed Pea*　　　　　　　　**Author:** Tony Johnston

Purpose: R1: Close reading for deep understanding of the text

Before Reading

> **Clues Based on Cover Illustration**
>
> - Notice the cowboy riding on a horse piled high with blankets; notice the cactus growing and the wide open, flat land
>
> **Clues Based on Title, Author**
>
> - Notice the words *cowboy* and *black-eyed pea*. Notice the similarity to another fairy tale: *The Princess and the Pea*
>
> **Probable Text Type (Literary or Informational); Possible Genre**
>
> - Probably literary; probably a fairy tale
>
> **Vocabulary That May Need Pre-Teaching for ELLs or Low Language Students**
>
> - Black-eyed pea, cowboy, saddle, saddle blanket

During Reading

> **Questions Students Should Ask Themselves for Each Chunk of Text**
>
> - What is the author telling me?
> - Any hard or important words?
> - What does the author want me to understand?
> - How does the author play with language to add to meaning?

> **Follow-Up Text-Dependent Questions for the Teacher to Ask About Each Chunk of Text**
>
> **Pages 1–2**
>
> - What do you already know from this first page? (Woman's name was *Farethee Well*; the story seems to be happening "out" West—woman is wearing cowboy boots, mention of *coyotes, sagebrush*; the woman is pretty)
> - What does it mean, *"The sagebrush grays the land"*? (Sage is a grayish-green color. It makes the land look gray.)

Pages 3–6

- What are some more clues that this is happening in the West? (herd of longhorns, corral, great state of Texas)

- What does the author mean: "Men will flock like flies to pralines"? (You will probably need to tell students that pralines are sweet candies.)

- What does the author mean "came from hither and yon"? (from everywhere)

- What is similar to the traditional story of *The Princess and the Pea*? What is different? (accept all reasonable answers)

Pages 7–8

- In your own words, explain Farethee Well's problem and her plan. (She needed to find a *real* cowboy.)

- What is the meaning of *sensitivity*? (You notice every little detail—and it bothers you.)

- How is Farethee Well's plan different from that of the princess in the original story or of Paulina's in *The Princess and the Pizza*? (other two stories were about princes and princesses; they both involved using a pea to see if their prince/cowboy was the real deal)

Pages 9–11

- What similes does the author use to describe the first cowboy? How does each one help you get a good picture in your mind? (*tall as a tree, mustache as big as tarnation, fresh as a Texas morning, prideful as a rooster.* Mind pictures: he was a tall man with a big mustache; he felt refreshed when he came back; he was a bragger)

- What words did the author choose to let you know that this cowboy was mad? (*he hissed mean as a snake*; "*HOGS*" is in capital letters; he *roared* and *stomped his feet*)

Pages 12–14

- Look at the picture: What stands out about this cowboy? (very fancy, looks rich)

- What does the author mean: *bristling with pistols and brag?* (he had pistols; he was a bragger, too)

- How can you tell he was rich? (tooled leather boots, fringes galore, swagger clothes)

- What did Farethee Well mean: he didn't know the front end of a horse from the rear? (didn't really know how to be a cowboy)

- What tone is the author creating on this page? What words let you know this? (Angry: glared with a look hard as petrified grits)

- What kind of pattern do you notice here? What do you expect to happen next? (Fairy tales often have *three* events. This is the second cowboy that hasn't been "real." Maybe the third one will be the real cowboy.)

Pages 15–18

- What seems different about this third cowboy? (he doesn't try to impress her; he doesn't ask to marry her; he is bothered by the pea)

- In your own words, explain why this cowboy went back to the ranch. (Something was uncomfortable; he went back to ask for more saddle blankets, so the saddle would feel better.)

Pages 19–22

- Does this seem to be a real cowboy? Explain. (Yes, he is bothered by the one small pea under the saddle blanket.)

- How is this story becoming more and more like the original story of *The Princess and the Pea*? (his saddle is piled high with blankets)

- What words show you how uncomfortable the cowboy was? (*twisted, twitched, culprit, no end of pain, gritted his teeth*)

Pages 23–26

- How is the cowgirl different from typical fairy tale princesses? (She is strong and helps solve the cowboy's problem; usually it's the *prince* who saves the *princess*.)

- How did this cowboy describe his uncomfortable ride? ("*Setting on this saddle is like setting on sheer stone.*")

Pages 27–29

- Is the ending of this story more like the traditional *Princess and the Pea* or *The Princess and the Pizza*? (more like *Princess and the Pea* because the girl marries the prince/cowboy)

- Why do you think the cowboy and cowgirl brought along a mule piled high with blankets? (in case something else got under the saddle)

After Reading (Complete These Tasks on Day 2 of the Lesson Sequence)

Important Words to Talk About the Text

- Farethee Well, cowboy, saddle, saddle blanket, fake, real, black-eyed pea, uncomfortable, marry

Theme, Lesson, or Message (if Appropriate)

- People should love you (or like you) for who you are, not your money or your appearance

Summary or Gist Statement

- Because it is a traditional fairy tale, this is a good story to summarize using a problem/solution format

Review of Text Type (Literary/Information) and Genre

- This is a modernized fairy tale with modifications that relate mostly to the *setting*

Collaborative Oral Task

- Ask students to work in small groups or pairs to complete a T-chart showing three genre *similarities* between the original story of *The Princess and the Pea* and *The Cowboy and the Black-Eyed Pea* and three *differences*

Follow-Up Lessons: Digging Deeper Through Rereading

Follow-up lessons can be taught in a different order.

Day	Focus Standard	Content for Whole-Class Lessons and Guided Student Practice
2	Close reading follow-up discussion related to After Reading tasks (above) SL1 Collaborative task for R5 (Genre and structure)	With the whole class, identify important words in the text and use them to create a summary that includes all story elements: characters, problem, events, solution. Also identify the message. Review features of a fairy tale. As a collaborative task, ask students to work in pairs or small groups to identify three similarities and three differences between the original story of *The Princess and the Pea* and this tale of *The Cowboy and the Black-Eyed Pea:* How do *both* stories include fairy tale elements?
3	Word choice: Vocabulary W4	There are many "Wild West" words and phrases in this book, which make it sound like the story really is happening "out" West with cowboys and cowgirls. Reread the story to locate these words and phrases. Ask students to explain the similes and phrases in their own words. They could illustrate some of the new words or create a dictionary of "Wild West Words."
4	Story elements: Changing the setting R3	To prepare students for the next day's narrative writing task, reread the story to think about how it would be different if it were set at the beach. Who would the characters be? (What would they look like; How would they talk?) Where would the pea be placed? What events would precede the solution to the problem? Would the ending follow that of the traditional tale—or is this a "strong girl"—like Paulina? Reread parts of this text as you make decisions about the modifications for a new setting.
5	Narrative writing: Rewrite the story so that it takes place in a different setting W3	Ask students to rewrite this story as if it is happening in a different place. They could consider Alaska, Hawaii, New York City, even the town or city where they live. How will the characters be different? How will the problem be different and the way the problem is solved? (Students may need to research their new location before using it as the setting of their story so that they get the right details.)

Close Reading Lessons for Extra! Extra!: Fairy-Tale News From Hidden Forest

Initial Close Reading Lesson

Text: *Extra! Extra!: Fairy-Tale News From Hidden Forest*　　　　　**Author:** Alma Flor Ada

Purpose: R1: Close reading for deep understanding of the text

The close reading lesson for this text will probably take two days due to the length of the book.

GENRE

Before Reading

Clues Based on Cover Illustration
• Notice the rabbit (Peter Rabbit?) with the bag of newspapers over his shoulder; notice the newspaper wrapped up that says *Hidden Forest News*
Clues Based on Title, Author
• Notice the word repeated and the exclamation points: *Extra! Extra!* Notice the subtitle: *Fairy-Tale News*
Probable Text Type (Literary or Informational); Possible Genre
• It seems to be a story, maybe a fairy tale
Vocabulary That May Need Pre-Teaching for ELLs or Low Language Students
• Newspaper, fairy tale, Peter Rabbit, Jack (from Jack and the Beanstalk)

During Reading

Questions Students Should Ask Themselves for Each Chunk of Text
• What is the author telling me?
• Any hard or important words?
• What does the author want me to understand?
• How does the author play with language to add to meaning?
Follow-Up Text-Dependent Questions for the Teacher to Ask About Each Chunk of Text
Pages 1–2: Hidden Forest News
• What do you notice right away about the way this story is set up? (It looks like a newspaper with different articles)
• In your own words, explain the problem described in this article? (a giant beanstalk is growing and neighbors are worried about it)

- What fairy tales and fairy tale characters are included in this article? (Mr. McGregor from *Peter Rabbit*, Mrs. Bear and Baby Bear from *Goldilocks and the Three Bears*, Jack from *Jack and the Beanstalk*)

Page 3: Opinion-Editorial

- What is the point of view expressed on page 3? (The beanstalk should be removed because it is dangerous.)
- What evidence is cited by different characters? (Mr. Wolfy Lupus: *Anything we don't understand is dangerous*; Mr. McGregor: *It is unfair competition*)
- Discuss these words: *menace, detrimental, competition, eliminating, threat*
- Discuss the significance of the characters' names: *Mr. Wolfy Lupus, Mr. Fer O'Cious, L. Feline*

Page 4: Opinion-Editorial

- What is Hetty Henny's point of view? (Just because something is new, it doesn't mean it's bad.)
- What details support Hetty's point of view? (you can explore new species; maybe it will cure an illness; it is an example of diversity)
- Discuss the meaning of "there's richness in diversity"
- How do the cartoons on these two pages add to the text's meaning? (accept all reasonable responses)

Page 5: International

- Why is this considered "International News"? (It is happening in Italy and Mexico.)
- What is the gist of the article about Mr. Geppetto? (he is missing; neighbors think he may have gone to look for Pinocchio)
- *Half-Chicken* is the story of a weathervane. (You may need to explain this to students and why this would be a "half chicken.")
- Discuss the word *unique*

Page 6: Sports

- What fairy tale does this feature? (*Tortoise and the Hare*)
- How does the graph help you better understand the article? (shows the number of people who support each animal)
- Discuss the words *resilient, resourceful*
- Notice the other newspaper feature on this page: *Rhyming Contest*

Pages 7–8: Back Page

- What newspaper feature is on the back page? (advertisements)
- Discuss the connection between each service and the service provider: (ex.: fur by Speedy Raccoon; brick ovens by Pig Three)

Pages 9–10: Hidden Forest News

- How does the information on this page connect to what you read earlier in this book? (the beanstalk *did* prove to be dangerous)
- In your opinion, should the beanstalk be chopped down now? Use evidence to support your thinking (could support either "yes" or "no" based on evidence on these pages)

Pages 11–12: Opinion-Editorial

- What can you infer about the *real* reason Mr. Fer O'Cious wants the beanstalk taken down? (The children who climb it are his "dinner.")

- What sentences show Mr. Fer O'Cious's intentions? (What would happen "if all young delicious morsels climb. . . . What will be left . . . to pursue?")

- What is Hetty Penny's point of view? (vine is beautiful, need to live in harmony, Jack might have climbed the vine)

Pages 13–14: International-Sports

- What details stand out to you on this page? (accept all reasonable responses)

- How do these details connect to information from earlier in this book? (recognize that these articles show next steps in the whereabouts of Geppetto, the journey of Half-Chicken, the race between the tortoise and the hare, and the future of the beanstalk)

Pages 15–16: Back Page

- Which of these advertisements seems the cleverest to you? Why? (probably the ad where the wolf is offering chicken recipes)

Pages 17–18: Extra

- Why do you think this page is titled "Extra"? (*Extra* is often a special edition of a newspaper that includes important news updates or breaking news.)

- What are the "important news updates" here? (Geppetto and Pinocchio reunited, Half-Chicken was almost cooked)

Page 19: Hidden Forest News

- In your own words, explain what happened with the beanstalk. (Jack returned home; his mom cut it down before the giant could descend; she thought she saw the giant's face in the clouds—but it could have been a thunder cloud.)

Page 20: Opinion-Editorial

- In these editorials, what is the main issue? (whether or not to plant the beans that came from the beanstalk)

- What does L. Feline think about planting the beans? What does Hetty Henny think about this? What do YOU think? Why?

Pages 21–22: International

- What part of a fairy tale are we getting on these pages? (the "happily ever after" part)

- What details from earlier in this book have reappeared in the article about Half-Chicken? (Fire, Water, and Wind came back to help him.)

- In what ways is Pinocchio living happily ever after?

- What is a "harrowing ordeal"? (a scary and dangerous experience)

- What is Jack's happily ever after? (brought back a goose that lays golden eggs)

- How is this version of the story different from the original version? (Jack wants to donate the hen to the community, hoping to build a community center.)

Pages 23–24: Back Page

- Which advertisement do you like the best? Why? (accept all reasonable responses)

Important Words to Talk About the Text

- Newspaper, article, Hidden Forest, international, editorial-opinion, beanstalk, Jack, Half-Chicken, Pinocchio, Geppetto

Theme, Lesson, or Message (if Appropriate)

- The fairy tales in this text represent various themes. For *Jack and the Beanstalk,* some possible themes might be, Leaving home on an adventure without telling someone where you are going is probably not a good idea, When you take unnecessary chances you sometimes end up in trouble

Summary or Gist Statement

- This would not be a good text to summarize as a whole due to its complex structure. Alternately, summarize just the *Hidden Forest News* that describes the step-by-step story of Jack's beanstalk adventure

Review of Text Type (Literary/Information) and Genre

- This is not a clearly identifiable text type. Several fairy tales are retold here in a series of newspaper articles

Collaborative Oral Task

- Students work in pairs or small groups to create a brief summary of this version of the *Jack and the Beanstalk* story based on the three *Hidden Forest News* articles related to this

Follow-Up Lessons: Digging Deeper Through Rereading

Follow-up lessons can be taught in a different order.

Day	Focus Standard	Content for Whole-Class Lessons and Guided Student Practice
2	Close Reading R1	Complete the close reading of this text.
3	Close reading follow-up discussion related to After Reading tasks (above); SL1 Collaborative task for summary R2 (Theme/Main ideas)	Review the three *Hidden Forest News* articles. Discuss the theme of *Jack and the Beanstalk* and key words in the text as a whole class. Ask students to work in pairs or small groups to create a brief summary accounting for all story parts: characters, setting, problem, solution, extended ending.
4	Genre and structure: Characteristics R5	Review the different kinds of newspaper articles included in this text: local (Hidden Forest) news; opinion-editorials; international news, sports, advertisements. Explain that newspaper articles typically answer six basic questions: Who, what, when, where, why, how. Examine different articles in the text, looking for these components. (Using the Hidden Forest [local] news will probably be easiest.)
5	Explanatory writing: Informational (news) writing W2	Write a news article about one of the other previously read texts in this unit: *The Princess and the Pizza* or *The Cowboy and the Black-Eyed Pea.* Students could also create an ad that would appear on the same page as their article.

Close Reading Lessons for Once Upon a Cool Motorcycle Dude

Initial Close Reading Lesson

Text: *Once Upon a Cool Motorcycle Dude*

Author: Kevin O'Malley

Purpose: R1: Close reading for deep understanding of the text

Before Reading

Clues Based on Cover Illustration

- Notice that there are two pictures: one shows a sad princess with a pony; one shows a tough guy riding a motorcycle

Clues Based on Title, Author

- Notice that "Once upon a . . ." sounds like fairy tale language; notice that "cool motorcycle dude" does *not* sound like fairy tale talk

Probable Text Type (Literary or Informational); Possible Genre

- Probably a story; probably a fairy tale

Vocabulary That May Need Pre-Teaching for ELLs or Low Language Students

- Fairy tale, cool, motorcycle, princess

During Reading

Questions Students Should Ask Themselves for Each Chunk of Text

- What is the author telling me?

- Any hard or important words?

- What does the author want me to understand?

- How does the author play with language to add to meaning?

Follow-Up Text-Dependent Questions for the Teacher to Ask About Each Chunk of Text

Pages 1–4

- Who is telling this story? (a boy and a girl)

- In what ways is the beginning of this girl's story a "typical" fairy tale? (the setting is a castle, there's a princess with a typical princess name—*Princess* Tenderheart, she played with her eight ponies)

- Why does the boy say, "Please . . . don't call him Buttercup. Call him Ralph or something"? (he doesn't like "girlie" stories)

Pages 5–8

- What are other typical fairy tale features of the girl's story? (A bad giant takes away several of the cute little ponies)

- What is the boy's reaction? Why? ("get a grip, princess!"; he doesn't think the story is very exciting)

- What do you expect to happen once the boy starts to tell the story? (It will probably have some boy characters; there will be more action)

Pages 9–10

- What sounds like a fairy tale here? What is different? (There is still a castle. But a guy on a motorcycle is the one who comes to help—not a prince.)

- What is the girl thinking about? What is the evidence? (She's thinking about what the prince looks like: "He's not even cute or anything.")

Pages 11–14

- What seems like the biggest difference to you between the girl's and the boy's point of view? (The girl wants a sweet story and a gentle princess; the boy wants lots of action and gross stuff)

- What evidence shows what the boy wants here? (giant had four rotten teeth in his mouth; breath smelled like rotten, moldy, stinky wet feet; wanted to make pony stew; big sword; volcanoes were exploding)

- How does the girl feel about this? What is the evidence? (She's horrified, says his story is gross, wants to know where the volcanoes came from)

Pages 15–18

- How does the boy's story end? (the princess keeps making thread; the dude gets rich because the princess keeps giving him the gold thread)

- Why do you think the girl is upset about the way the story ends? (the dude has all the power; the princess just sits around)

Pages 19–24

- How is the girl now changing her story? (the *princess* is becoming strong—she tells the dude to make his own thread)

- Who is the hero in the girl's story? (the princess: she gets the giant to run back to his cave; the dude makes the gold thread)

- How does the boy turn the story around now? (the dude turns the thread into a blanket that makes him invisible and then goes to rescue the ponies)

Pages 25–26

- How does the girl get her way? (the princess goes with the dude)

- Who finally frees the ponies? (no one—the giant gets scared and jumps off the cliff)

Pages 27–29

- Now what is the boy upset about? (doesn't want the dude to be a prince, doesn't want the princess and the dude to fall in love and get married)

- Is there a clear ending to the story? What's the evidence? (No, they're still disagreeing: is the baby a boy or a girl?)

Important Words to Talk About the Text

- Princess, motorcycle dude, giant, point of view, boy, girl, disagree)

Theme, Lesson, or Message (if Appropriate)

- Our own point of view makes a huge difference to the stories we write

Summary or Gist Statement

- This is a story within a story and doesn't really work for summarizing. However, students could generate a gist statement about how the boy and the girl had different points of view and couldn't agree about what would happen in their story

Review of Text Type (Literary/Information) and Genre

- As you discuss the genre of this book, point out that the central idea of the text is how point of view impacts *anything* we write; it's not really limited to fairy tales

Collaborative Oral Task

- Ask students to work in pairs or small groups to answer these questions:

    1. Do you think the story would have been better if only the *girl* was telling the story? Explain

    2. Do you think the story would have been better if only the *boy* was telling the story? Explain

    3. Do you think the story was better because both the boy and the girl were telling it together? Explain. What fairy tale elements were contained in each version of the story?

(Note: There are no "right" and "wrong" answers to the questions about point of view.)

Follow-Up Lessons: Digging Deeper Through Rereading

Follow-up lessons can be taught in a different order.

Day	Focus Standard	Content for Whole-Class Lessons and Guided Student Practice
2	Close reading follow-up discussion related to After Reading tasks (above); SL1 Collaborative task for R5 (Genre and structure)	With the whole class, identify important words in the text, discuss the theme/central idea, and create a gist statement showing why the author wrote this book. For a collaborative task, ask students to think about which version of this story they liked best: the story told by the girl, the story told by the boy, or the one they invented together. Did both the boy and the girl include fairy tale elements in their version of the story? Explain. See *Collaborative Oral Task* (page 175).
3	Author's purpose or point of view R6	How did point of view matter in this story? Reread parts of the story to find places where the girl's point of view was evident: What was important to the girl? Find places in the story where the boy's point of view was evident: What was important to the boy? How did the story change because the boy and the girl were writing it together? What kinds of decisions do you need to make when writing a story?
4	Word choice W4	Reread selected pages of this book to note the kinds of words used by the girl when telling the story and the kinds of words used by the boy. What differences do students notice? How does word choice strengthen point of view?
5	Narrative writing: Writing with a partner W3, R6	Ask students to work with a partner to create a fairy tale: When you finish, think about how you did working as a team: Did you and your partner have the same point of view or different points of view? How did you make decisions when you disagreed? Was it helpful or not helpful to have a partner—and why? Was your story better or worse because you wrote it with someone else—and why?

Learning Pathway

How to Study an Author

*How Does Robert Burleigh Write
Such Interesting Informational Books?*

Unit Focus: Robert Burleigh

Photo courtesy of Robert Burleigh

Let's begin the unit! This is one of eight units in this book that delivers just the
"goods"—the questions, prompts, assessment tasks, and student reproducibles
you'll need to implement robust close reading instruction within an inquiry unit.
Just about all you need to do a few weeks in advance of starting is to look at the
anchor texts on pages 182 to 184 and order those books. From there, the materials
provided are all explained clearly in terms of when and how to use them. If you
need clarification, look back at the ten steps that begin on page 15.

Introduction to the Unit

The Rationale

Many teachers with whom I work often tell me that studying an author is valuable and engaging for children, and some teachers do incorporate units on authors as part of their literacy curriculum. In the primary grades, I often see studies of authors such as Kevin Henkes and Dr. Seuss. As students move into the intermediate grades, the focus often turns to Cynthia Rylant, Jane Yolen, Eve Bunting, and Patricia Polacco. I love all of these authors and applaud teachers for helping students to explore the literary magic of their craft. But as I thought about the author unit to include in this book, I decided to choose someone who is a master of craft but less well known, so teachers and students would have someone new to study and enjoy. Thus, I chose the author Robert Burleigh.

Here's what drew me to him initially: Many of his titles relate to informational topics, and his "literary nonfiction" style is chock-full of the kind of craft that draws students in. Finding well-crafted informational texts is not the easiest mission for classroom teachers. The books I have chosen by Burleigh for this unit (and the two others incorporated into other units) show children that indeed informational text can be interesting and exceptionally well written.

With Robert Burleigh as the focus of the unit, let's think about the ultimate goal of any unit teaching: helping students learn how to learn. I call it the learning pathway. With this unit, the pathway is How to Study an Author. So what does it really mean to *study* an author—any author? Essentially, we want students to analyze elements like an author's topics, themes, and writing style. The depth to which you investigate an author will depend a bit on the age of your students and their prior experience with the author's craft. Your focus points will also depend on the author you choose: Which features of this author's work really stand out? To get you started, during your introductory lesson discuss with students the talking points in the following chart, Learning Pathway: How to Study an Author.

Learning Pathway

How to Study an Author

Share these prompts with students.

- *When choosing an author to study, it's helpful to be able to say in your own words why he or she is worth studying. What are a few things that you notice and like about the books?*

- *An author makes choices about topics and themes: What sorts of topics or themes does this author choose? If it's a topic, how does the author limit the topic?*

- *An author makes choices about genre: Does this author usually write in the same genre? Different genres? What genre seems to dominate?*

- *An author uses words carefully to create images: How does this author create strong visual images? (For example, does the author include lots of metaphors, personification, or strong verbs?)*

- *An author creates sentences carefully: How does this author typically construct sentences? Are they mostly short? Are they long and complicated? Is there anything that stands out about the way the author creates sentences?*

- *An author tries to get readers' attention right from the beginning of a book: What kinds of leads does this author use to hook readers?*

- *An author works to create interesting characters that seem real: How does this author create characters in a way that makes you care about them?*

- *An author keeps readers engaged: How does this author create suspense, use humor, or create an emotional connection?*

- *An author makes the ending memorable: How does this author bring his/her books to an end? What stands out?*

The Inquiry Question and Discussion Points

The question students will answer in this unit is **How does Robert Burleigh write such interesting informational books?** When students study a text, they typically focus most directly on its meaning, with attention to craft and structure a negligible part of their literary analysis. While all of the texts selected for this unit are also rich in meaning, you will see that a large proportion of the text-dependent questions for each close reading lesson do, in fact, emphasize CCRA Standards for Reading 4, 5, and 6. You can begin to shift students' attention to these standards with the questions and discussion points indicated in Unit Preview Questions and Discussion Points: for Studying an Author: Robert Burleigh.

Next, because we want to know from the outset where we ultimately want to take students, I list questions under Questions for End-of-Unit Discussion About an Author (Robert Burleigh) Integrating All Texts. These are questions you might pose at the end of this unit. That is, with any unit teaching, after completing all of the anchor books, we need to circle back to the inquiry question itself, to consider the books together. The questions help students synthesize their thinking across texts and wrap up the study in a thoughtful way. Doing so is particularly fruitful in this unit, as students can look at all of Burleigh's books together to draw some conclusions about his craft.

Questions for End-of-Unit Discussion About an Author (Robert Burleigh) Integrating All Texts

- After reading the four anchor texts in this unit and the article by Robert Burleigh, do you now feel you can answer the inquiry question: *How does Robert Burleigh write such interesting informational books?* Answer this question briefly with one or two main reasons.

- Which questions for How to Study an Author can you answer after reading these books?

- Which book of Robert Burleigh's did you enjoy the most? Was it because of the topic or because of the way it was written? Explain.

- What elements of Robert Burleigh's craft stand out to you the most? Why? Give some examples from his books.

- Which book that we read in this unit seems the most different from the others? Why? What is the evidence?

- If you wanted to write in the style of Robert Burleigh, what particular points would you keep in mind?

- What advice would you give to students doing an author study?

- How will doing this author study help you study other authors more effectively in the future? What will you look for?

- Think about the article we read at the beginning of this unit: *Robert Burleigh Talks about His Writing*. Now that you've read several of his books, especially the book *Home Run*, is there anything in this article that has more meaning to you? Explain.

Unit Preview Questions and Discussion Points

for Studying an Author: Robert Burleigh

- *Introduce the term author study and discuss what it means to study an author. (See the chart Learning Pathway: How to Study an Author, selecting focus points and questions appropriate to your students' age and background knowledge about the author's craft.) Make a list of the features of an author's craft that you will focus on in the unit.*

- *Ask students to identify a few authors they know and a couple of basic observations about each author's craft. (Choose well-known authors such as Shel Silverstein: He wrote a lot of poetry; many of his poems were silly; they rhyme)*

- *Introduce the inquiry question: How does Robert Burleigh write such interesting informational books? (If you have already taught the leadership unit with Burleigh's book* Night Flight *and the Abraham Lincoln unit with his book* Abraham Lincoln Comes Home, *students may have some initial insights to share.*

- *Introduce the Robert Burleigh books that will anchor this study.*

- *Show the cover of each book and perhaps an illustration inside to pique students' interest. Do not explain the full story.*

The Focus Standard

When planning any author study, I would look first to reading anchor Standards 4, 5, or 6 for the focus of your unit. It's not that other standards wouldn't work. It's that with units that do not focus on an author you won't always have such a golden opportunity to zero in on the *way* a story is told or information is conveyed: its imagery, structure, or point of view. All of these standards will be reflected in the text dependent questions for this unit. But Burleigh's true gift is the imagery that emerges from his choice of words and the way he puts words together. That makes this a perfect unit for focusing on CCRA Standard 4: "Interpret words and phrases as they are used in a text, including determining technical, connotative, and figurative meanings, and analyze how specific word choices shape meaning or tone" (http://www.corestandards.org/ELA-Literacy/ CCRA/R, Craft and Structure section, para. 1).

The Anchor Texts

The first text listed below is a short reflection by the author Robert Burleigh. It's intended to be read by the students themselves and discussed during a unit kickoff lesson (discussion questions are provided on page 190). The remaining four texts are picture books, one of which will be read closely and studied during each week of the unit.

"Robert Burleigh Talks About His Writing," a reflection on craft by Robert Burleigh (provided on page 190)

When I was contemplating this unit, I was initially stumped as to what kind of nonfiction piece would best support the content. I could have looked to another selection on any of the individuals featured in these anchor texts to compare them stylistically. That could work for an author study. But on a whim, I went to Robert Burleigh's website and saw that it listed his personal e-mail. I contacted him, explaining my book project and requested a short piece to include about a few things that are important to him as an author of children's books. He responded right away, and the article he wrote is now part of this unit for the benefit of all children. In his piece, to be read by the students themselves, Burleigh speaks most directly about his book *Home Run*, the initial anchor text in our unit. I love that he really does describe how he approaches a topic and some of the issues he grapples with as an author—both useful insights for students to appreciate.

Home Run: The Story of Babe Ruth by Robert Burleigh

Kids love this book. They feel like they're really up at bat with The Babe, experiencing the same tension and exhilaration he faces as the ball barrels toward him: Will he hit it? Ah! A fun feature of this book is the additional information presented as "factoids" in the form of baseball cards on nearly every page. I save these cards for a lesson when I return to the text; they really do provide a nice opportunity to dig deeper into some of Babe's statistics and the details of his life. Complexities of this text include the craft, particularly the sophisticated use of words for imagery; the multiple layers of meaning within the main text and in the details on the baseball cards; and the structure, which is essentially free verse poetry. Lexile: 280. Grade level equivalent: 1.8. (This in no way reflects the qualitative complexities of this text.)

Flight: The Journey of Charles Lindbergh by Robert Burleigh

Burleigh again takes a significant moment in someone's life—in this case, Lindbergh's first solo flight across the Atlantic—and creates a "you are there" perspective through powerful words and images. Burleigh transports his audience of 21st century techie kids back to 1932 so they can view this history-making event with a level of intensity similar to that of the American public so many decades ago. They will celebrate the glory of Lindbergh's achievement along with the perils that he survived along the way. Complexities again include the use of free verse and the imagery as well as lack of knowledge about this period in American history. Lexile: 570. Grade level equivalent: 3.

Look Up! Henrietta Leavitt, Pioneering Woman Astronomer by Robert Burleigh

I'm always looking for female role models for young girls, stories that depict women as strong, competent individuals capable of achieving anything that their male counterparts could achieve. Henrietta Leavitt qualifies as such a person. Her field was science, a great connection to Science, Technology, Engineering, and Mathematics (STEM) initiatives in today's schools. And Henrietta made her mark on astronomy in the earliest years of the 20th century when it was significantly harder than today for a woman to gain respect in any scientific domain. I also chose this book because its style departs a bit from that of the other Burleigh texts in this unit. This book reads more like a running narrative with complete sentences that tell the story in quite a straightforward manner. By comparison, the other anchor texts in this unit are structured more as descriptive, free verse poems. Noting this discrepancy will be an important complexity to consider for this text, along with recognition of the role of women in the early 20th century. No Lexile or grade level equivalent was available.

Tiger of the Snows: Tenzing Norgay: The Boy Whose Dream Was Everest by Robert Burleigh

One of the features I liked about this book from the outset is that like the story of Henrietta Leavitt, most students probably do not know about Tenzing Norgay. In fact, many children may even be unfamiliar with the name *Sir Edmund Hillary* or, for that matter, the location of Nepal or Mount Everest. So lack of background knowledge is likely to be a complexity when reading this book. The vocabulary in this text from which Burleigh crafts images is also particularly sophisticated. The pictures are in black and white only, which really works with the whiteness of the mountain and the starkness of the lonely climb. Lexile level: not available. Grade level equivalent: 5.1.

Other Texts Useful for an Author Study About Robert Burleigh

Robert Burleigh has written many, many picture books. Every one of them that I perused was worthy of study, so examine them for yourself to see what would work best for your students. To expand your study, some of these books also revolve around fiction (Pandora and Hercules) and some nonfiction topics focus on something other than people (for example: volcanoes, the sea, chocolate). For intermediate grade students, I especially like the books noted below:

- *One Giant Leap* by Robert Burleigh

- *Black Whiteness: Admiral Byrd Alone in the Antarctic* by Robert Burleigh

- *Edward Hopper Paints His World* by Robert Burleigh

- *Into the Woods: John James Audubon Lives His Dream* by Robert Burleigh

- *Night Flight: Amelia Earhart Crosses the Atlantic* by Robert Burleigh

The Unit's Two Assessments

Featured Reading Standard R4: Author's word choice

Featured Writing Format: Informative/Explanatory writing

See the Unit Curriculum Map for Close Reading for where these assessments might fit into your study of the author. Also, for more information about the rationale behind these two assessments and how they differ, as well as guidance for using the provided rubrics, refer to Step 9 on page 43 and Step 10 on page 50. Also, for evaluating students' performance, see page 45 for the Rubric for Content-Based Assessment (Task 1) and Standards-Based Assessment (Task 2). Turn to page 293, The End of the Story: Reflecting on Student Work, for some sample student work from this unit and commentary.

Task 1: Content Assessment

In this unit, you have studied four picture books all written by Robert Burleigh:

- *Home Run: The Story of Babe Ruth*

- *Flight: The Journey of Charles Lindbergh*

- *Look Up! Henrietta Leavitt, Pioneering Woman Astronomer*

- *Tiger of the Snows: Tenzing Norgay: The Boy Whose Dream Was Everest*

On a separate piece of paper, please answer these questions using what you have learned in these books:

1. What kinds of topics does Robert Burleigh write about? How does he seem to narrow his topics?

2. Name three elements of Robert Burleigh's craft that are present in all or most of his books. Give some specific examples of these crafts from at least two books.

3. Give an example of a powerful image from one of Robert Burleigh's books. What does the author do to create this image?

4. Read the sentences shown below. Then, rewrite them as a free verse poem in the style of Robert Burleigh including at least three crafts that you often see in his books. These could include similes, strong verbs that show tone, repeated lines or phrases, line breaks to emphasize meaning, or any other craft of your choice that you have noticed in Burleigh's writing. You do not have to keep the original words in the sentences, but you have to keep the basic meaning.

"The birds flew through the sky. It was a sunny day with a little breeze. The birds noticed a garden below them. It was a pretty garden and they decided to rest there a while. Maybe they would find some food."

5. When you have rewritten these sentences, explain which crafts you used to make your writing sound like the writing of Robert Burleigh.

Task 2: Learning Pathway and Standard Assessment

Access at least four of these poems* by Robert Louis Stevenson from his book *A Child's Garden of Verses* retrieved from The Project Gutenberg, an archive of public domain texts that may be used without cost or permission: http://www.gutenberg.org/files/25609/25609 -h/25609-h.htm

- *Bed in Summer*

- *My Shadow*

- *The Wind*

- *A Good Boy*

- *The Moon*

- *The Swing*

*Your teacher may select some other poems for you from this site if he or she thinks these poems are too difficult or too easy.

1. What kinds of topics does Robert Louis Stevenson write about? How does he seem to narrow his topics?

2. Name three elements of Robert Louis Stevenson's craft that are present in all or most of his poems. Give some specific examples of these crafts from at least two poems.

3. Give an example of a powerful image from one of Robert Louis Stevenson's poems. What does the author do to create this image?

4. Choose one of the topics below that has something to do with childhood. Write a poem in the style of Robert Louis Stevenson, including at least three crafts that you noticed in his other poems. Your poem does not have to rhyme.

- Going to bed

- The first day of school

- Riding your bike

- Going to the beach

- Celebrating your birthday

- Eating ice cream

5. When you have written your poem, explain which crafts you used to make your writing sound like the writing of Robert Louis Stevenson.

Unit Curriculum Map for Close Reading

How Does Robert Burleigh Write Such Interesting Informational Books?

TEXT	MONDAY	TUESDAY	WEDNESDAY	THURSDAY	FRIDAY
				Unit Preview	Kickoff Lesson
				See Unit Preview Questions and Discussion Points	Read and discuss the article "Robert Burleigh Talks About His Writing." Discussion questions are provided at the end of this document
Home Run: The Story of Babe Ruth by Robert Burleigh	Objective: R1 Close Reading	Objective: SL1; R2 Close Reading Follow-Up	Objective: R4; R5 Word Choice; Genre and Structure	Objective: R2 Theme/ Main Idea: Summarizing	Objective: R7 Nontraditional: Interpreting Nonprint Texts
	Read closely to answer text-dependent questions	Complete the After Reading tasks including a collaborative task for providing a gist statement	Reread selected pages to note elements of author's craft	Students work in pairs to read "baseball cards" containing additional information about Babe Ruth	View video clip of Babe Ruth's sixtieth homerun. How does this add to your understanding?
Flight: The Journey of Charles Lindbergh by Robert Burleigh	Objective: R1 Close Reading	Objective: SL1; R3 Close Reading Follow-Up	Objective: R7 Nontraditional: Interpreting Nonprint Texts	Objective: R4; R5; R6 Author's Word Choice; Genre and Structure; Author's Purpose or Point of View	Objective: W2 Explanatory Writing
	Read closely to answer text-dependent questions	Complete the After Reading tasks including a collaborative task focusing on textual details	View and respond to video of Lindbergh's historic flight	Reread selected pages to identify specific crafts and structural elements in this book	Write a newspaper headline and article for Lindbergh's historic flight in 1927

TEXT	MONDAY	TUESDAY	WEDNESDAY	THURSDAY	FRIDAY
Look Up! Henrietta Leavitt, Pioneering Woman Astronomer by Robert Burleigh	Objective: R1 Close Reading	Objective: SL1; R3 Close Reading Follow-Up	Objective: R3 Story Elements: Setting	Objective: R9 Text-to-Text Connections	Objective: R5 Genre and Structure
	Read closely to answer text-dependent questions	Complete the After Reading tasks including a collaborative task related to character traits	Reread selected pages to consider challenges faced by Leavitt as a female scientist in the early part of the 20th century	Investigate one of the sources identified at the end of this book. How does it add to your understanding?	Compare the narrative structure of this book to the free verse format of *Flight* and *Home Run*
Tiger of the Snows: Tenzing Norgay: The Boy Whose Dream Was Everest by Robert Burleigh	Objective: R1 Close Reading	Objective: SL1; R2 Close Reading Follow-Up	Objective: R4 Word Choice	Objective: R9 Text-to-Text Connections	Objective: R5 Genre and Structure
	Read closely to answer text-dependent questions	Complete the After Reading tasks including a collaborative task focusing on the gist of the text	Reread to identify words in the text that contribute to tone	Read the *Afterword* at the end of this book. What additional information does it provide?	Reread selected pages to examine the line breaks in this free verse format; students write their own free verse image
	Culminating Discussion	Content Assessment	Standards-Based Assessment		
	Respond orally to text-to-text connections for studying this topic. (See Questions for End-of-Unit Discussion Integrating All Texts)	Students complete the content-assessment task integrating all texts in this study	Students complete the standards-based assessment task using cold reads		

AUTHOR

ROBERT BURLEIGH TALKS ABOUT HIS WRITING

I'm going to use the story behind my book *Home Run* to describe my writing process. It's typical of how I often work (or try to).

I wanted to do a book about baseball and my thoughts went to Mr. Big himself, Babe Ruth. I usually begin working on a book by doing a lot of research/reading about the subject. I enjoy musing over the big picture, but what I'm looking for, in most cases, is a significant or dramatic moment that I can blow up into a picture book.

In looking into Ruth, I discovered an incident that I thought would work, namely a moment in September 1927 when Babe hit a home run, at which moment a young teen fan ran out on to the field. (It was true, I checked out the game in the *NY Times*.) Instead of shooing him off, Babe picked the boy up and carried him around the bases on his shoulders!

A cool subject, so I thought. But in fiddling with it, looking for a *whole* story, I found myself stymied because I didn't quite know where to go from there. I felt a certain possible complication (who was the boy, what happened next, etc.) that I didn't particularly want to deal with. In fact, it seemed so odd, that I wasn't sure it had the drama I like. So as I often do, I played a kind of waiting game, thinking that something else might turn up.

One morning I was recalling my own baseball days, and somehow remembered the good feeling one gets when the bat meets the ball at dead center. Bam! Then I realized that Ruth, of course, often had that feeling, or at least waited for it while batting. I decided to try to make a story out of one at-bat. I liked the challenge of that. So that's what *Home Run* became. I try to catch the "You are there" realness of a moment when I can. That's probably why the language gets a bit drawn out (an attempt at poetry, let's say) in places.

I've used that method in related ways in several books—*Flight, Langston's Train Ride, Night Flight, Black Whiteness.*

I don't mean to suggest that the broader historical picture isn't important to me. I try to work that in, at least in the back matter, although the "baseball cards" in *Home Run* are doing just that, too: a kind of quickhand way to overview Ruth's life and career.

What I want more than anything in my writing is to create feeling in the reader. My taking some small incident or moment and blowing it up is one way, to do that.

Source: Written by Robert Burleigh regarding his craft.

Think About

Robert Burleigh wrote this piece especially for students. In it, he talks about the thinking behind his writing. Use the questions below to help reflect on what you learned in the piece. They will also help you prepare for this author study.

- All writers research their topic before beginning to write. What kind of research does Robert Burleigh say he does, and what is he looking for?

- Why did Robert Burleigh say he didn't continue working on the story about Babe Ruth carrying the boy around the bases? What lesson can we learn from this for our own writing?

- What is Robert Burleigh's main goal in his writing? Based on this, what might you expect to see in this author's books?

- What details do you think are especially important in this article? Why?

- How might this article guide you as you read Robert Burleigh's books?

Close Reading Lessons for Home Run: The Story of Babe Ruth

Initial Close Reading Lesson

Text: *Home Run*

Author: Robert Burleigh

Purpose: R1: Close reading for deep understanding of the text

Before Reading

Clues Based on Cover Illustration

- Notice the baseball player, how big he looks compared to the stadium in the background; notice the pinstripes; notice the colors: yellow/gold and blue

Clues Based on Title, Author

- Notice that the title is very short: *Home Run*

Probable Text Type (Literary or Informational); Possible Genre

- It looks like it will be a story

Vocabulary That May Need Pre-Teaching for ELLs or Low Language Students

- Home run, Yankees, baseball, Babe Ruth, bat, pop-up, stadium, pitch, baseball card, infield

---

During Reading

Questions Students Should Ask Themselves for Each Chunk of Text

- What is the author telling me?
- Any hard or important words?
- What does the author want me to understand?
- How does the author play with language to add to meaning?

Follow-Up Text-Dependent Questions for the Teacher to Ask About Each Chunk of Text

Pages 1–2

- What do you know already? (story is about Babe Ruth)
- Why do you think there is only one sentence on this page? (author wants this information to stand out)
- What else do you notice? (extra information in the form of a baseball card [Don't read these "cards" now; come back to them after reading—See *Collaborative Oral Task* at the end of this lesson])

Pages 3–4

- What do you notice here about the author's craft (his style of writing)? (very short sentences)

- Why are some lines just one or two words when they are not even sentences? (for effect: *This baseball; Forever*)

- How does the author make us curious on this page? (says he changed baseball forever—makes you wonder *how*)

- How do the illustrations add to the meaning? (adds to the intensity; shows Babe's fondness for the ball, even as a child; the beige tones remind you of long ago)

Pages 5–6

- What do you think the most important word is on this page? How does the author let you know it's important? (*swing* is important; it is said three times)

- What is the author trying to show you about this swing? (makes it seem beautiful by the words he uses: *easy, upthrusting; pretty*)

- How else does the author make this swing seem special? (makes it seem almost magic: "One day the Babe just swung— / and it was there.")

Pages 7–8

- What is different about the illustration here? (It is in color). Why? (Now Babe is an adult)

- What strategy does the author want us to use here? (visualizing) What do you picture in your mind? (swishing of the bat; twisting round and round; getting dizzy)

Pages 9–10

- Notice where the author creates line breaks. Why does he do this? (emphasizes particular words like *skyward*; creates a sense of rhythm for phrasing: "Even his pop-ups / rise higher than anyone else's. / Skyward. / Higher than the top / of the great stadium")

- Practice reading this page attending to line breaks

Pages 11–12

- Paraphrase the sentence on this page so it is in your own words. (Something like, Babe's body, the ball, and the bat all seemed connected)

- How does the author create this sense of connection? (the use of *and* to tie thoughts together)

- What do the beautiful sky colors seem to represent? (maybe Heaven; everything is perfect)

- Why does the illustrator show Babe as so oversized? (he was sort of "larger than life")

Pages 13–14

- Even without reading the words on this page, what do you predict it will be about? Why? (the ball—based on the picture)

- What craft does the author use here? (similes—three times)

- Why does the author use each simile: *smooth as silk; easy as air on the face; right as falling water*? (shows how "natural" Babe and the ball fit together)

- What is the author doing here: *nothing-quite-like-it-sound*? Why? (making up his own word—because there isn't another one that is just right)

- What words paint a positive picture? (*soft, fat, center*)

Pages 15–16

- How does the author create a sense of time going on and on? (The rhythm: "He waits for it. / He wants it. / Again / and again." Also, it's in the line breaks and the repetition of the words *again and again*)

- What else stands out on these pages? (illustration focusing on one leg—shows power, strength)

Pages 17–18

- What strategy does the author want us to use here? (visualize)

- What does it mean to "stride into the pitch"? (move into the ball with big steps)

- Why does the author describe the ball as "whirling whiteness"? (can visualize it more than if he'd said "the ball."

- Why does "whirling whiteness" sound so nice? (alliteration—words that start the same way; sounds poetic)

- What does the author mean by *this time*? And why is it in italics? (must be important—stands alone; different font; raises suspense)

Pages 19–20

- What is the author doing here? (building suspense)

- How does he do this? (almost like slow motion)

- What does the author mean by "through the ball"—and why does he repeat it? (shows the power, and that this happened over and over)

Pages 21–22

- What does the author mean by "The feeling that is like no feeling at all!" (the thrill of success)

- What words does the author choose to show the glory of success? (*cracks, soars, going, going*)

Pages 23–24

- How does the author show us that success is within reach? (*perfectness, boy-fire*)

- What does the author mean by "The boy-fire inside the body of a man"? (while Babe might have been an adult, he had all of the enthusiasm of a young person)

- How does the illustration add to the magic? (note expression on people's faces)

Pages 25–26

- How does the author slow the action here? (slowly, squints, watches the ball disappear)

- How else does the author add to the effect? (repeats the words *home run, home run*)

Pages 27–28

- What has changed here? (Babe slows down) How does the author show this? (*trots, short steps*)

- What words show that this was a journey? (*over, under, beneath, across*)

- Why does the author use this simile: "Under the roar of cheering voices / that falls on him like warm rain" (comforting, soothing)

- What about the picture? How would you interpret this? (now Babe looks smaller—next to the big leg and foot; might show how he feels about himself—that he's not really that big and powerful)

Pages 29–30

- How does the author show connection here? (He is theirs. They are his.)

- How has the Babe changed baseball forever? (the home run king)
- What word shows how important this was? (Forever)

After Reading (Complete These Tasks on Day 2 of the Lesson Sequence)

Important Words to Talk About the Text

- Babe Ruth, home run, baseball, change, stadium, fans

Theme, Lesson, or Message (if Appropriate)

- Something like, Some people truly have a gift

Summary or Gist Statement

- This is not a problem/solution story or even a neatly designed sequential text, so it might be difficult to summarize it. But students could provide a simple gist statement getting at the idea that Babe Ruth changed baseball forever by making so many home runs and setting so many records. See *Collaborative Oral Task* below.

Review of Text Type (Literary/Information) and Genre

- Fictionalized biography

Collaborative Oral Task

- Ask pairs or small groups of students to create a gist statement of twenty words or less describing the life and accomplishments of Babe Ruth

Follow-Up Lessons: Digging Deeper Through Rereading

Follow-up lessons can be taught in a different order.

Day	Focus Standard	Content for Whole-Class Lessons and Guided Student Practice
2	Close reading follow-up discussion including focus on a gist statement SL1; R2	As a whole group, discuss the important words in the text, the story's theme, and the genre. Then, ask students to work with a partner or small group to create a gist statement of twenty words or less describing the life of Babe Ruth. See *Collaborative Oral Task* above.
3	Word choice; Genre and structure R4; R5	Reread various pages to identify the writer's crafts in this text. Students could work in partnerships or small groups. Or you could reread the pages with the whole class and create a class chart of crafts.
4	Theme/Main ideas: Summarizing R2	Working as a whole class, or in small groups, read one or more of the "baseball cards" from the text, clarifying the meaning of any unknown words or phrases. (Four of these cards have been included at the end of this lesson.) Then, ask pairs or small groups of students to briefly summarize the information. More advanced students can be tasked with creating a summary for a card the class has not discussed.
5	Nontraditional: Interpreting nonprint texts R7	Watch this YouTube clip of Babe Ruth hitting his sixtieth home run. How does this add to your understanding of this person as a remarkable baseball player? See https://www.youtube.com/watch?v=z7Ab8HmUmR0

Close Reading Lessons for Flight: The Journey of Charles Lindbergh

Initial Close Reading Lesson

Text: *Flight: The Journey of Charles Lindbergh*   **Author:** Robert Burleigh

Purpose: R1: Close reading for deep understanding of the text

Before Reading

Clues Based on Cover Illustration

- Notice the old fashioned airplane

Clues Based on Title, Author

- Notice that the title on the front cover contains only one word: *Flight*; notice that the back cover adds the subtitle: *The Journey of Charles Lindbergh*

Probable Text Type (Literary or Informational); Possible Genre

- It appears to be narrative nonfiction

Vocabulary That May Need Pre-Teaching for ELLs or Low Language Students

- Airplane, fly, flight

During Reading

Questions Students Should Ask Themselves for Each Chunk of Text

- What is the author telling me?
- Any hard or important words?
- What does the author want me to understand?
- How does the author play with language to add to meaning?

Follow-Up Text-Dependent Questions for the Teacher to Ask About Each Chunk of Text

---

Pages 1–2

- What important information is the author giving us on the first page? (The year is 1927; the pilot's name is Charles Lindbergh; his nicknames will be Lone Eagle and Lucky Lindy)

- What do you notice about the illustration—the size of the person compared to the plane? What do you think the illustrator is trying to show here? (The man is much larger than anything else on the page; it might symbolize the larger-than-life accomplishment he will achieve in the future.)

Pages 3–4

- Why was Lindbergh's flight considered such a big deal? (No one had ever flown across the Atlantic before; he was going alone.)

- Why did Lindbergh's friends seem so far off as he said good bye? (He would soon be separated from them by many miles in the air.)

Pages 5–6

- How does the author create a sense of the danger that lies ahead for the pilot? (the telephone wire that could entangle the plane, the extra fuel tank that makes it impossible for him to see, the difficulty getting off the ground, leaving behind his radio and parachute)

- What words does the author use that show the tone of Lindbergh's departure, both positive and negative? (negative: *plunge, soggy ground, bumps*; positive: *soars, aloft, rises*)

- What do you notice about the way the sentences are written on this page? How does that affect the tone? (Sentences are short—which makes the writing sound more suspenseful.)

Pages 7–8

- What thoughts were going through Lindbergh's mind as he flew? (Paris seemed a long way off; he wanted to follow the coastline; he wanted to stay close to the water to glide more smoothly; he needed to stay on course in order to have enough fuel; he wanted to keep a diary, so he wouldn't forget the details of this experience.)

- What simile and metaphor does the author use on these pages, and how do they help you picture what Lindbergh was seeing? (Simile: "The land's edge looked like green fingers, pointing at the dark sea"; icebergs were "white pyramids . . . / sentries of the Arctic")

Pages 9–10

- Why was the sun setting "behind the plane"? (Lindbergh was traveling east; the Sun sets in the west)

- What important detail does the author keep repeating? Why is this so important? (the importance of staying on course—or else there won't be enough fuel)

- Why does Lindbergh say, "Now I must cross not one, but two oceans: / One of night and one of water." (Just like an ocean, the night is a vast stretch of darkness.)

- What detail does the author include that might foreshadow trouble ahead? ("As long as the sky is clear he is safe." Perhaps the sky will not remain clear.)

Pages 11–12

- What details add to the tension of this moment? (It is foggy and stormy and ice is forming on the wings.)

- What words contribute to this tense tone? (*curling fog, ghostly white; blackness; stinging pinpricks; quiver; turbulent air*)

Pages 13–14

- What is "the other side of midnight"? (after midnight)

- What is the main idea of these pages? What line shows this the most clearly? (the importance of staying awake; "To sleep is to die!")

- What do you notice about Lindbergh's list of ways to stay awake? (These are the kinds of special memories that anyone might think about.)

Pages 15–16

- Before even reading this page, you might feel more hopeful for Lindbergh. What creates this sense of hope? (The illustration shows that daylight is approaching.)

- Why does Lindbergh feel like he is "flying through all eternity"? (He is on this mission completely alone—and it seems never to end.)

- Why does the ocean seem like "a great blue shaft, with gray walls"? (The water is blue, but the huge waves look like gray walls.)

Pages 17–18

- These pages show contrasting tones—from hopeless to hopeful. What details show these contrasts? (negative: "water, water, water"—repeating these words shows the endlessness of the ocean; "There's no alternative but death and failure." positive: he spies a seagull; he sees fishing boats; he calls out to people—showing he must be nearing land)

- What is ". . . a warmer welcome back to the fellowship of men"? (He longs for human contact.)

Pages 19–20

- Do you think Lindbergh feels relieved at this point? Explain. (accept all reasonable responses)

- Do you think Lindbergh made the right decision to continue on to Paris rather than landing in Ireland? (Accept all reasonable answers, but responses should include mention of achieving his dream.)

Pages 21–22

- Although the author doesn't exactly say so on this page, what can you tell about the way this trip will end? What clues lead you to this conclusion? (Lindbergh will succeed; He says, "*I am here, I am here.*")

- But now he says he does not want this flight to ever end. Why not? (Now that success is within reach, he realizes how he is making history. What a great feeling!)

Pages 23–26

- What does Lindbergh mean: "the sod coming up to meet me." (He has succeeded in flying; now he needs to succeed in landing.)

- What happens as Lindbergh emerges from his plane? Would you expect this? (People go wild cheering; some try to take pieces of his plane.)

- Why do you think people try to tear off pieces of the plane? (proves that they, too, were part of history; this plane just became very valuable)

Pages 27–29

- What details show that Lindbergh is now incredibly famous? (newspaper headlines; talking to reporters; parades, medals, speeches)

- What might those headlines have said? (Accept all reasonable responses that capture the wonder of Lindbergh's achievement.)

After Reading (Complete These Tasks on Day 2 of the Lesson Sequence)

Important Words to Talk About the Text

- Charles Lindbergh, New York, Paris, cockpit, fly, thirty-three and a half hours

Theme, Lesson, or Message (if Appropriate)

- Something like, Determination helps you to achieve dreams that may at first seem unreachable

Summary or Gist Statement

- Although this is a nonfiction text, it is really a problem/solution story and could be summarized based on story parts

Review of Text Type (Literary/Information) and Genre

- This is a personal narrative describing one important moment in Lindbergh's life

Collaborative Oral Task

- Ask students to work in pairs or small groups to locate some of the personal details in this book that make it a personal narrative: What are some details that add interest to this story that might *not* be included in a basic biography about Babe Ruth?

Follow-Up Lessons: Digging Deeper Through Rereading

Follow-up lessons can be taught in a different order.

Day	Focus Standard	Content for Whole-Class Lessons and Guided Student Practice
2	Close reading follow-up discussion including an emphasis on textual details SL1; R3	As a class, discuss the important words to talk about the text, the story's message, and possibly devise a brief oral summary. For a collaborative task, ask students to work in pairs or small groups to identify some of the personal details of this book that make it a personal narrative. Students should be able to identify at least three personal details. See *Collaborative Oral Task* above.
3	Nontraditional: Interpreting nonprint texts R7	Watch the video: *Charles Lindbergh: From New York to Paris 1927*: https://www.youtube.com/watch?v=_R3fGL67mas. How does this video add to your understanding of Charles Lindbergh and his historic flight?
4	Word choice; Genre and structure; Author's purpose or point of view: Identifying author's craft R4; R5; R6	Robert Burleigh uses many of the same crafts in all of his books. As a whole class, examine a few pages that show several crafts (such as strong tone words, sentence fragments, short sentences or sentences that follow a similar pattern, and building suspense). Then, provide pairs of students or small groups with pages of their own to identify Burleigh's crafts.
5	Explanatory writing: Write a newspaper headline and article W2	Ask students to complete this writing task: The year is 1927, right after Lindbergh's historic flight. You are a newspaper reporter assigned to write about Lindbergh's great accomplishment. Create a catchy headline and then write a news article that answers *who, what, when, where, why,* and *how.*

Close Reading Lessons for Look Up! Henrietta Leavitt, Pioneering Woman Astronomer

Initial Close Reading Lesson

Text: *Look Up! Henrietta Leavitt, Pioneering Woman Astronomer*　　**Author:** Robert Burleigh

Purpose: R1: Close reading for deep understanding of the text

Before Reading

Clues Based on Cover Illustration
• Notice the girl looking at the stars; notice that the girl looks a little old fashioned
Clues Based on Title, Author
• Notice the exclamation mark in the title; notice the important words in the subtitle: *Henrietta Leavitt, pioneering, astronomer*
Probable Text Type (Literary or Informational); Possible Genre
• Looks like it could be the story of someone's life (a biography)
Vocabulary That May Need Pre-Teaching for ELLs or Low Language Students
• Sky, stars, astronomer, telescope

During Reading

Questions Students Should Ask Themselves for Each Chunk of Text
• What is the author telling me?
• Any hard or important words?
• What does the author want me to understand?
• How does the author play with language to add to meaning?
Follow-Up Text-Dependent Questions for the Teacher to Ask About Each Chunk of Text
Pages 1–2
• How does the author introduce this story to let you know what it is going to be about? (Henrietta gazed up at the stars; wondered about the sky and the stars; you can tell what she is interested in)

Pages 3–4

- What impressed Henrietta about the sky? (its bigness; it seemed endless)
- Think about this sentence on page 3: "Sometimes she felt the stars were trying to speak, to tell her what they knew": How might this *foreshadow* what is to come in Henrietta's life? (maybe the stars *will* lead her to some important discoveries)

Pages 5–6

- What challenge did Henrietta face concerning her interest in astronomy? (most astronomy teachers and students were men)
- What does the author mean: *vast* distances? (*huge* distances)
- In your own words, explain what a light year is. (the distance light can travel in a year—about six trillion miles)
- How does this help you understand how far away some stars are? (Lots of stars are many light years away.)

Pages 7–10

- Why didn't Henrietta get to use the telescope in her work? (had to do "woman's work"—measuring, recording, calculating)
- What words on this page show you the discrimination against women? (Women were expected to "work, not think.")
- How does the last sentence on this page *relate* to what will probably come next? (Henrietta "had other ideas"; she would find a way to be a *real* astronomer.)

Pages 11–14

- When Henrietta studied the stars she wondered, "What could these tiny dots tell her? What were they saying?" How does this relate to something we read previously in this book? (p. 3: "She felt the stars were trying to speak to her.")
- What were some of Henrietta's favorite sky words? (*asteroids, cosmic dust, eclipse*)
- Why do you think the author included pictures of Copernicus and Galileo on pages 13–14? (famous astronomers)

Pages 15–18

- How does the author show how hard Henrietta worked? (worked until her eyes blurred; could even see the star dots when she closed her eyes; looked, and looked, and looked)

Pages 19–20

- What was Henrietta's big discovery here? (bright stars blinked more slowly than less bright stars)
- What did Henrietta need to figure out now? (*why* these stars blinked more slowly)

Pages 21–22

- Why is it important to know the brightness of a star? (It can show how far the star is from the Earth.)
- What did Henrietta's discovery show? (Even a tiny discovery can lead to something really important.)

Pages 23–24

- What were astronomers able to discover next due to Henrietta's discovery? (The Milky Way is larger than once thought; there are other galaxies.)
- What line keeps coming back? ("The stars had spoken to Henrietta," p. 23)

- As Henrietta grew older, why did she think the sky was so much bigger? (Her discoveries had shown that there were many galaxies, and even our Milky Way is much bigger than she originally thought.)

- This book has a "circular ending." What does that mean? (It ends with some of the same words as we saw at the beginning of the story.)

After Reading (Complete These Tasks on Day 2 of the Lesson Sequence)

Important Words to Talk About the Text

- Henrietta Leavitt, astronomer, observatory, galaxy, brightness, distance, pattern

Theme, Lesson, or Message (if Appropriate)

- You should follow your passion regardless of the challenges that may stand in your way

Summary or Gist Statement

- This wouldn't be a good story to summarize because it doesn't follow a traditional story/solution format and doesn't even offer a clear sequence of events. However, students could produce a gist statement.

Review of Text Type (Literary/Information) and Genre

- This is a biography; it chronicles Henrietta's life from her childhood through adulthood, highlighting her life-long interest in astronomy and featuring the discoveries that made her life memorable

Collaborative Oral Task

- Ask students to work in pairs or small groups to name three character traits that helped to make Henrietta Leavitt a success. Cite evidence from the text to support each choice

Follow-Up Lessons: Digging Deeper Through Rereading

Follow-up lessons can be taught in a different order.

Day	Focus Standard	Content for Whole-Class Lessons and Guided Student Practice
2	Close reading follow-up discussion including an emphasis on character traits SL1; R3	With the whole class, identify important words in the text, discuss the theme/central idea, and briefly discuss the genre including characteristics of a biography. Also, create a gist statement showing the reason we should remember Henrietta Leavitt. For a collaborative task, ask students to work with a partner or small group to identify three character traits that they think contributed to Henrietta's success.
3	Story elements: Setting R3	How might Henrietta's life have been different if she were a female "pioneer" today exploring astronomy? Reread pages that show her challenges as a female scientist during this time in history. What kinds of discrimination did she face? How might people respond to her today? Students could create a T-chart showing "Then and Now."
4	Text-to-text connections R9	The last page of this book identifies several other resources related to astronomy. Ask students to investigate one of these sources or another source. What did they learn? How does it connect to the information in this book about Henrietta Leavitt?
5	Genre and structure R5	In what ways is the craft of this book different from other Robert Burleigh books? Discuss that this text is more of a "narrative," not written as a free verse poem like other Burleigh books in this study. There is not as much imagery or figurative language. Ask students to choose a page and rewrite it as free verse, choosing line breaks carefully to emphasize meaning. They may also add some imagery and figurative language to add to meaning. Rewrite one page together as a class to model the process.

Close Reading Lessons for *Tiger of the Snows: Tenzing Norgay: The Boy Whose Dream Was Everest*

Initial Close Reading Lesson

Text: *Tiger of the Snows: Tenzing Norgay: The Boy Whose Dream Was Everest*

Author: Robert Burleigh

Purpose: R1: Close reading for deep understanding of the text

Before Reading

Clues Based on Cover Illustration
• Notice the shepherd boy with his staff looking toward a mountain covered with snow
Clues Based on Title, Author
• Notice the important words: *Tiger, Snows, Everest*
Probable Text Type (Literary or Informational); Possible Genre
• Probably an informational story (literary nonfiction)
Vocabulary That May Need Pre-Teaching for ELLs or Low Language Students
• Climb, Everest, mountain
Other
• Because this book does not clarify where Mount Everest is located, it would be wise to show this on a map. Some graphics of the geography of the region would also make this book more meaningful. Related words: Nepal, Himalaya Mountains, Sherpa

During Reading

Questions Students Should Ask Themselves for Each Chunk of Text
• What is the author telling me?
• Any hard or important words?
• What does the author want me to understand?
• How does the author play with language to add to meaning?

Follow-Up Text-Dependent Questions for the Teacher to Ask About Each Chunk of Text

Pages 1–2

- What do you notice right away about the illustrations in this book? Why do you think the illustrator made this choice? (Illustrations are in black and white; everything looks lonely and cold; it gives sort of an eerie feeling.)

- What is a "Sherpa"? (You will need to define this since the author doesn't do so: a community of people living on the border of Tibet and Nepal, known for their mountain climbing skills.)

- Why might someone be called "Tiger of the snows"? (strong and brave)

- What words show you that climbing Everest is an incredible challenge? (*Goddess of the Earth; sharpest tooth in the jaw of the great dragon, so tall no bird can fly over it; five miles high*)

- Which image (above) gives you the strongest image? Why? (accept all reasonable responses)

Pages 3–4

- Do you notice a pattern here? (This page also starts with "A song for Tenzing, / Tenzing Norgay.")

- What is being compared here? (Tenzing as a child and Tenzing as an adult)

- What details of Tenzing's childhood showed his early interest in mountain climbing? (*born to heights, child of the Himalayas, looking up*)

Pages 5–6

- Why do you think the author calls the mountain "sky's partner"? (it reaches so high into the air)

- Draw a quick sketch of this mountain. What details from this page should be included? Be able to explain your drawing. (details should include *snow-dotted black-rock peak; sky's partner; crown of whiteness swirling into the air*)

Pages 7–8

- Now how is Tenzing described? (as a pathfinder)

- How did Tenzing prepare to climb this mountain? (desired "the taste of clouds," got to know rocks, learned about climbing ropes, may have gone to Katmandu to study [will need to explain that Katmandu is the capital city of Nepal])

- What does the author mean: "apprenticed himself to death and danger"? (studied how to be a climber even though it is very dangerous work)

Pages 9–10

- What were some of the dangers of climbing this mountain? (crevasses, ice falls, blizzards, glaciers, cascading snow, getting buried in an avalanche)

Pages 11–12

- What important information is the author giving us here? (Tenzing climbed the mountain May 29, 1953.)

- Explain in your own words: "Carver of steps to the impossible." (No one had ever done this before.)

Pages 13–14

- What do you picture in your mind here? (Tenzing standing on a ledge looking over the land below, praying for the people that failed at this climb before.)

- What important details does the author provide here? (He was climbing with Edmund Hillary; it was seventeen degrees below zero.)

Pages 15–16

- Why would someone need to be "deep lunged" in order to climb Everest? (The air is very thin at high altitudes, which makes it harder to breathe.)
- How does the author show contrast on this page? ("agile as a cat / Into the Zone of Death")

Pages 17–20

- What is the author doing on this page? (giving us a sense of the difficulties involved in climbing this mountain)
- Which images stand out to you as the scariest? Why? (accept all reasonable responses)
- Why are there no words on pages 19–20? (author wants readers to see what Tenzing saw: just massive whiteness reaching up into the sky)

Pages 21–22

- What is the author telling us here? (Tenzing Norgay and Edmund Hillary have reached the top.)
- What words express this achievement? (*The rise above them falls away; see an unbelievable vastness on every side*)
- Why does the author call this "the top of the world"? (It is the highest mountain peak on Earth.)

Pages 23–26

- Why do you suppose Tenzing laughed? (relief and joy)
- What mementos did Tenzing leave at the top of the mountain? Why? (four flags, his good luck pencil)
- What does the author mean: "This moment—now— / will not come again"? (No one else will ever be "first" to climb Everest.)

Pages 27–28

- Why is this moment both joyful and sad? (Tenzing has waited for this moment for so long—and now it is over.)
- What does the author mean: "Yet something in Tenzing remains above, / Will never leave"? (this moment will stay in his heart forever)

After Reading (Complete These Tasks on Day 2 of the Lesson Sequence)

Important Words to Talk About the Text

- Tenzing Norgay, Edmund Hillary, Everest, mountain, danger, Sherpa, summit, bravery

Theme, Lesson, or Message (if Appropriate)

- With skill and persistence, you can often accomplish even very difficult dreams

Summary or Gist Statement

- This would be a better text for a gist statement rather than a summary because it does not define a clear sequence of events, but rather a sequence of images

Review of Text Type (Literary/Information) and Genre

- Literary nonfiction: Although the author is presenting *information* here, it is presented in story form, actually as a free verse poem

Collaborative Oral Task

- Ask students to work together in pairs or small groups to devise a gist statement of twenty words or less for this story, using the identified important words from the text

Follow-Up Lessons: Digging Deeper Through Rereading

Follow-up lessons can be taught in a different order.

Day	Focus Standard	Content for Whole-Class Lessons and Guided Student Practice
2	Close reading follow-up discussion including a focus on gist statement SL1; R2	With the whole class, identify important words in the text, discuss the theme/central idea, and briefly discuss the genre. (You will come back to the crafting of this text as a follow-up lesson later in the week.) Then, ask students to work in pairs or small groups to complete the *Collaborative Oral Task* above: devising a gist statement.
3	Word choice R4	In this book, the author creates a sense of danger with the words he chooses. Reread this text to find these powerful images. What words contribute to this sense of danger?
4	Text-to-text connections R9	At the end of this book, there is an *Afterword*. Read this with students. What additional information does this provide to clarify some of the details of Tenzing Norgay's life? Where would it fit with the information learned from the text itself?
5	Genre and structure R5	How does the structure of this text as a free verse poem contribute to its message? Examine selected pages with students and pay particular attention to line breaks, repetition of words and phrases, and sentence fragments. Ask students to create their own (brief) free verse image of Everest using this same style.

AUTHOR

Learning Pathway

How to Study a Time in History

What Choices Would You Make if You Were a Slave Child?

Unit Focus: Slavery

Photo courtesy of Library of Congress, Prints and Photographs Division

Let's begin the unit! This is one of eight units in this book that delivers just the "goods"—the questions, prompts, assessment tasks, and student reproducibles you'll need to implement robust close reading instruction within an inquiry unit. Just about all you need to do a few weeks in advance of starting is to look at the anchor texts on pages 212 to 214 and order those books. From there, the materials provided are all explained clearly in terms of when and how to use them. If you need clarification, look back at the ten steps that begin on page 15.

Introduction to the Unit

The Rationale

The picture books available to children to make history come alive are as varied as they are vast. From these books, students can learn facts, locations, and dates of important battles; names and biographical background; and critical moments forever marked with historic pride or regret. But many of the authors of these books also attend to the human dimension of history, exploring such questions as, What did it feel like to be a person living during these times, experiencing these events? What was gained and what was lost for all those involved? If one peeks behind the curtain of events, whose story still isn't fully told? That is what this unit aims to uncover: the human side of our American past.

I chose as my focus slavery in America in the pre-Civil War South. I chose this period for a couple of reasons. First, it provides an opportunity for young students to put a human face on a situation that cannot be understood with facts and figures alone. It is an era of American History significant in its own right, but important, too, for understanding civil rights issues that followed a century later and, in fact, the racial tensions that exist today. Although discussing the atrocities of slavery may make us uncomfortable as educators, it is important for students to understand that this ugly treatment of fellow Americans is as much a part of our heritage as the moments of pride that we celebrate: the Declaration of Independence in 1776, Charles Lindbergh's flight across the Atlantic in 1927, and the first moon landing in 1969—to name just a few. Each generation needs to learn hard truths about the past in order to address the hard truths that face us now, all over the world.

The four picture books I chose are stories and are fictionalized to some extent, though two are about real people, Harriet Tubman and Sojourner Truth. The other two books are about characters who *could* have been real, so compelling are their stories. These tales are all the more powerful because they each focus on a slave *child*. Our students get a glimpse of the hard road traveled by youngsters no older than themselves who searched for a shred of dignity amid the tight grip of slavery.

With the study of slavery in America as the focus of the unit, let's think about the ultimate goal of any unit teaching: helping students learn how to learn. I call it the learning pathway. With this unit, the pathway is How to Study a Time in History. To that end, during your introductory lesson (and throughout the unit), you can share with students the talking points in the following chart, Learning Pathway: How to Study a Time in History.

Learning Pathway

How to Study a Time in History

- A "time in history" has to do with the important events that happened in a particular place at a particular time: For the time in history you are studying, what were the approximate years? What part of the world or part of the country did this mostly involve?

- When we study history we often have to know special words. We need to know people's names and dates. Sometimes, we need to know the names of laws or places where important events took place. What words are important to understanding this time in history?

- A time in history usually has a few major events. Often one event causes another event to happen. What particular events would be important to remember about this time in history?

- A time in history usually has a strong effect on the people living in this time and place: How did it feel for people to live in this place during this time? Were different people treated differently? How?

- We can often learn lessons from different times in history: Can we learn any lessons from this time in history? What are the lessons?

- A time in history grows out of the events that came before it: What events came before this time in history that led to what happened in this time and place?

- A time in history leads to the events that come after it: What events came after this time in history? How were they connected to what happened in this time and place?

- Studying a time in history often leads us to want to know more about this particular historical period: What else would you like to know about this time in history?

- If you were a researcher studying a time in history, where would you look for information: Are there any museums near where you live that would be helpful? Who could you interview who would have knowledge to share? What websites could you investigate? Where could you find some photographs or video clips of this time period?

The Inquiry Question and Discussion Points

The main question students will answer throughout this unit is **What choices would *you* make if you were a slave child?** From the safe distance of their 21st century world, many students today initially assert, "Well I'd run away, of course." But after closely reading the books in this unit, you'll find many students revising their course of action. There were no easy decisions here for the enslaved people, and they all came with strings attached. Begin this unit with Unit Preview Questions and Discussion Points: for Studying a Time in History: Slavery.

Next, because we want to know from the outset where we ultimately want to take students, I list questions in Questions for End-of-Unit Discussion About a Time in History (Slavery) Integrating All Texts. These are questions you might pose at the end of this unit. That is, with any unit teaching, after completing all of the anchor books, we need to circle back to the inquiry question itself, to consider the books together. The questions help students synthesize their thinking across texts and wrap up the study in a thoughtful way.

Questions for End-of-Unit Discussion About a Time in History (Slavery) Integrating All Texts

- Do you now think you can answer our inquiry question: What decisions would you make if you were a slave child? Briefly summarize your response to this question.

- Which questions for studying a time in history can you answer after reading these books?

- For which questions do you still need more information? Where could you look to find this additional information?

- Thinking about all of the books that we have read in this study, what were the greatest indignities of slavery? (Identify at least three). Which characters/people experienced them?

- Which characters or people in the books we read seemed the most similar? Why? Choose two characters/people and explain using evidence from all the texts.

- Think about the entry from the slave holder's diary that we read at the beginning of this unit: Which slave child that we read about would probably have gotten along best with the slave holder, Keziah Brevard? Which one would have had the most trouble? Explain using textual evidence.

- Each of these characters/people made difficult choices. Discuss one choice that you think was especially difficult for that person to make. Would you have made the same choice? Why or why not?

- What kinds of issues did a slave child have to consider when deciding whether or not to run away? Give examples from the texts we read. What lessons can you learn from the lives of these slave children?

Unit Preview Questions and Discussion Points

for Studying a Time in History: Slavery

- *Define what you mean by a "time in history" or a "historical period." (You can use the simple explanation in Learning Pathway: How to Study a Time in History.)*

- *Ask students to provide some examples of different times in history. (They may suggest the Revolutionary War, civil rights era, or another historical period.)*

- *Discuss how to study a time in history, referring to the points and questions in How to Study a Time in History. Customize these points and questions according to the developmental level of your students. Make a chart of the questions you will try to address through the unit. Make another chart of research tools and sources that come up in the discussion.*

- Introduce the time in history you will study in this unit: slavery in the pre-Civil War South: Ask students what they know about this time in American history.

- Introduce the inquiry question: What choices would **you** make if you were a slave child? (**Students may have some initial responses to this question—which is fine. But don't get too far into this until they've acquired textual evidence.**)

- Introduce the four books selected for close reading. Show the cover and perhaps an illustration inside to pique students' interest. Do not explain the full story.

The Focus Standard

Examining a time in history provides a great opportunity for examining CCRA R3: "Analyze how and why individuals, events, or ideas develop and interact over the course of a text" (http://www.corestandards.org/ELA-Literacy/CCRA/R/, Key Ideas section, para. 3). This unit seems especially well suited to this standard because a time in history is a setting, a context where multiple factors intersect to produce particular outcomes. But because of this unit's emphasis on the "human dimension" of this time in history, children caught in the clutches of slavery, an even deeper application of this standard is the development of character in these texts. Each of these books was selected not just for its depiction of the pre-Civil War South and the day-to-day challenges faced by slaves, but also for the robust characters that come to life on these pages.

The Anchor Texts

The first text listed below is an adapted diary entry intended to be read by the students themselves and discussed during a unit kickoff lesson (discussion questions are provided on page 218). The remaining four texts are picture books, one of which will be read closely and studied during each week of the unit.

"Slave Holder's Diary" adapted from *A Plantation Mistress on the Eve of the Civil War: The Diary of Keziah Goodwyn Hopkins Brevard, 1860–1861,* edited by John Hammond Moore (provided on page 218)

The diary entry is a shorter and somewhat easier to read version of the original text (cited in the bibliography in case you want to go for the "real deal.") I love that this selection gives kids access to a primary source (adapted) showing the true sentiments of someone who was a slave owner. There's some powerful language here and personal thoughts that students will find despicable. This piece is short, but the ideas are so far outside students' frame of reference that you will want to allow plenty of time for them to digest and discuss the material.

Minty: A Story of Young Harriet Tubman by Alan Schroeder

I've had this book in my professional library for a long time. I knew it would be a good fit for this time in history, but I had forgotten all of the wonderful aspects that would make it just right for *this* study. First, it is about a person most students are familiar with, at least to some degree. I liked the idea of beginning this study with a real person, building on a bit of prior knowledge. The strength of this book, however, is not its recounting of information students may have already known about Harriet Tubman (her role in the Underground Railroad) but her life as a young child, both her spunkiness and the fearfulness that kept her from trying to escape from slavery at an early age. The complexity of this book is primarily its multiple themes: weighing the cost and benefits of taking a risk, the indignities of slavery, and parents' love for their children—among other possibilities. There is also some language in dialect. Lexile: 560; Grade level equivalent: 3.9.

Sojourner Truth's Step-Stomp Stride by Andrea Davis Pinkney

This is a happy book. Yes, the content relates to a woman who spent her early years bound by the shackles of slavery. But her passion for her life's work of fighting against slavery and for women's rights virtually dances off the pages. Her infamous line, "And ain't I a woman?" is repeated at key moments. The illustrations add even more vigor to the message. Here is an American who well deserves her hero status. Sojourner Truth is referenced in the next book in this study, hence, the placement of this book as second in the text sequence. Complexities include numerous sophisticated lines from Sojourner Truth's speeches. There's an energy and a poetic quality to the writing in this book that convey the high spirit of Sojourner Truth. Structurally, this story is told as if from a storyteller who knew Sojourner Truth personally. Lexile: 650; No grade level equivalent available.

Now Let Me Fly: The True Story of a Slave Family by Dolores Johnson

This story exudes a much more somber tone than that of Sojourner Truth described above. Although entirely fictional, you will *think* that this is real. The story is told by Minna who as a young child is kidnapped from her African village and sold into slavery. She endures the horrific journey to America, the brutal treatment by her master, the grief of losing her husband who is sold to a different plantation, and the agony of encouraging three of her four children to run away to a better life. An epilogue speculates about the fate of the children: Were they able to secure better lives for themselves? Complexities include a large number of characters, which students need to keep straight, and a great deal of content to absorb. There is also continual reference to a spiritual with which students will not be familiar. Lexile: 860; Grade level equivalent: 5.1.

Up the Learning Tree by Marcia Vaughan

This is not the most complex text in the set according to Lexile. However, this fictional story seems to me the most emotionally sophisticated. A young slave boy wants to learn to read so badly that he risks the wrath of his master and listens in on the lessons of the rich plantation children from high up in the branches of a sycamore tree. He is discovered by the teacher, Miss Hattie, who willingly helps him despite laws prohibiting the teaching of reading to slaves. And then she's caught! Miss Hattie tells the truth when she might easily have lied to save her job. Then, she lies about Henry when she could have told the truth. Students will have much to think about as they sort out these ethical dilemmas. Lexile: 660. Grade level equivalent: 4.2.

Other Texts Useful for Studying Slavery

There are many, many texts from which to choose for studying slavery. Some books focus on the Underground Railroad while others look more directly at the life of a slave. Consider the developmental level of your students as you select books to extend this unit or to substitute texts for those suggested above.

- *Unspoken* by Henry Cole
- *Night Boat to Freedom* by Margot Theis Raven
- *Under the Quilt of Night* by Deborah Hopkinson
- *Dave the Potter: Artist, Poet, Slave* by Laban CarrickHill
- *The Escape of Oney Judge: Martha Washington's Slave Finds Freedom* by Emily McCully

The Unit's Two Assessments

Featured Reading Standard 3: Development of character; significance of setting

Featured Writing Format: Narrative writing

See the Unit Curriculum Map for Close Reading for where these assessments might fit into your study of history. Also, for more information about the rationale behind these two assessments and how they differ, as well as guidance for using the provided rubrics, refer to Step 9 on page 43 and Step 10 on page 50. Also, for evaluating students' performance, see page 45 for the Rubric for Content-Based Assessment (Task 1) and Standards-Based Assessment (Task 2). Turn to page 293, The End of the Story: Reflecting on Student Work, for some sample student work and commentary.

Task 1: Content Assessment

You have studied four books and other texts that show the horrors of slavery in America before the start of the Civil War. Pretend you are *one* of the slaves you read about: Harriet Tubman, Sojourner Truth, Minna, or Henry. Many years have now gone by, and you are writing an entry in your journal about what it was like to be a slave and how it affected your whole life. Please write three paragraphs addressing these things:

- In paragraph 1: Identify three injustices you faced as a slave child using examples from the book about this person.

- In paragraph 2: Explain the choices you have made throughout your life: Were these good choices or bad choices? Why?

- In paragraph 3: Explain how you showed great strength and accomplished something important—even in the face of many hardships.

Task 2: Learning Pathway and Standard Assessment

Read this article about the slave Phillis Wheatley, which you can find at this website: http://gardenofpraise.com/ibdwheatley.htm. Pretend you are Phillis Wheatley and write an entry she might have written in her journal as an adult.* Please do the following in three paragraphs:

- In paragraph 1: You are Phillis Wheatley. Explain three differences between your life as slave and the lives of the other slaves we read about in this unit. Is your life easier? Harder?

- In paragraph 2: You are Phillis Wheatley. Explain *why* your life has been so different from the other slaves we studied: What opportunities have you had that other slaves would not have had?

- In paragraph 3: You are Phillis Wheatley. Explain whether you have made good choices for yourself based on your opportunities: How have your opportunities allowed you to make the best use of your talents?

*If writing three paragraphs and addressing all of these bullet points are too complex for your students (or some of your students), modify the task by requiring fewer paragraphs or points to cover.

HISTORY

Unit Curriculum Map for Close Reading

What Choices Would You Make If You Were a Slave Child?

TEXT	MONDAY	TUESDAY	WEDNESDAY	THURSDAY	FRIDAY
				Unit Preview	Kickoff Lesson
				See Unit Preview Questions and Discussion Points	Read and discuss *Slave Holder's Diary*. Discussion questions are provided at the end of this document
Minty: A Story of Young Harriet Tubman by Alan Schroeder	Objective: R1 Close Reading	Objective: SL1; R5 Close Reading Follow-Up	Objective: R3 Story Elements: Setting (Context)	Objective: R9 Text-to-Text Connections	Objective: W1 Opinion Writing
	Read closely to answer text-dependent questions	Complete the After Reading tasks including a collaborative task for identifying genre features	Examine selected pages to identify elements of the way of life in the South during this time	Read the poem *Harriet Tubman* by Eloise Greenfield. Compare to *Minty*	Write an opinion about a choice Harriet made in her life: good choice or bad choice?
Sojourner Truth's Step-Stomp Stride by Andrea Davis Pinkney	Objective: R1 Close Reading	Objective: SL1; R2 Close Reading Follow-Up	Objective: W4 Word Choice	Objective: R9 Text-to-Text Connections	Objective: R3; SL4 Author's Purpose or Point of View; Give a Speech
	Read closely to answer text-dependent questions	Complete the After Reading tasks including a collaborative task related to summarizing	Reread portions of the text to determine how tone is created by both the author and illustrator	Read the Afterword at the end of the book: "More About Sojourner Truth." What new information does this add to what you already know about Sojourner Truth?	Prepare and give a speech from Sojourner Truth's point of view that shows you understand what was important to her. Use strong words as she would have used

TEXT	MONDAY	TUESDAY	WEDNESDAY	THURSDAY	FRIDAY
Now Let Me Fly: The Story of a Slave Family by Dolores Johnson	Objective: R1 Close Reading	Objective: SL1; R5 Close Reading Follow-Up	Objective: R7; R9 Nontraditional: Text Formats; Text-to-Text Connections	Objective: R3; SL1 Story Elements; Discussion	Objective: W3 Narrative Writing
	Read closely to answer text-dependent questions	Complete the After Reading tasks including a collaborative task for identifying genre features	Listen to the spiritual *Now Let Me Fly*; read lyrics and connect to this anchor text	Students work in small groups to respond to higher level text-dependent questions about text components	Write a letter to Minna as if you were one of her children many years later
Up the Learning Tree by Marcia Vaughan	Objective: R1 Close Reading	Objective: SL1; R2 Close Reading Follow-Up	Objective: R3 Story Elements: Character Analysis	Objective: R9 Text-to-Text Connections	Objective: W3 Narrative Writing
	Read closely to answer text-dependent questions	Complete the After Reading tasks including a collaborative task related to summarizing	Reread selected pages finding quotes that reveal Henry's character	Compare a character from another book in this study to Henry: What are the similarities and differences?	Write a letter to Miss Hattie as if you are Henry—twenty years later: How is your life different now?
	Culminating Discussion	Content Assessment	Standards-Based Assessment		
	Respond orally to text-to-text connections for studying this topic. (See Questions for End-of-Unit Discussion Integrating All Texts)	Students complete the content-assessment task integrating all texts in this study	Students complete the standards-based assessment task using cold reads		

HISTORY

SLAVE HOLDER'S DIARY

by Keziah Goodwyn Hopkins Brevard

Adapted by Nancy Boyles

The journal entry below is adapted from The Diary of Keziah Goodwyn Hopkins Brevard, *a plantation mistress. The year is 1860, right before the start of the Civil War. Keziah has just learned that Abraham Lincoln has won the election to become the next president of the United States. Pay careful attention to her point of view and the language she uses to describe her feelings.*

Nov. 12, 1860

I am devastated that Abraham Lincoln has won the election to be president of my country. I prayed that he would lose this election, but my prayers were not answered. It's not that I don't believe in justice, but the thought of living alongside free blacks is horrid! I have never been opposed to giving up slavery if we could just send them all out of our country. If the North had left us alone, we wouldn't be having this problem. The Master and the servant were content with the way things were, with the Master in charge. But those vile Northerners had to stir things up. They made our Negroes restless with ideas about freedom. I am never angry with my servants unless there is cause, and then, the women are much worse than the men with their sassy back talk. We will likely have to fight to keep our Negroes in their place. We should all be willing to die rather than allow uncivilized slaves to go free.

Source: The diary is published in *A Plantation Mistress on the Eve of the Civil War: The Diary of Keziah Goodwyn Hopkins Brevard, 1860–1861*, edited by John Hammond Moore (Columbia: University of South Carolina Press, 1993).

Think About

Think about the questions below as you reflect on the diary excerpt. These questions can help you as you begin this unit on slavery.

- What is a "slave holder"?

- In what part of the country does Keziah Brevard live? What clues in the text help you to make this inference?

- What is Keziah Brevard's point of view about slavery and slaves? What strong words does she use to make her point of view clear?

- Which statements in this diary entry are especially horrifying to you? Why?

- Keziah Brevard says, "I am never angry with my servants unless there is cause." Do you believe her? Why or why not? What evidence in the text leads you to your conclusion?

Close Reading Lessons for Minty: A Story of Young Harriet Tubman

Initial Close Reading Lesson

Text: *Minty: A Story of Young Harriet Tubman*　　　　　　　　**Author:** Alan Schroeder

Purpose: R1: Close reading for deep understanding of the text

Before Reading

Clues Based on Cover Illustration

- Notice the young black child dressed in rags, bare feet, holding some kind of stick, surrounded by woods

Clues Based on Title, Author

- Notice this is a story about Harriet Tubman; notice that her nickname might have been Minty

Probable Text Type (Literary or Informational); Possible Genre

- Appears to be a *story* about a real person (the author indicates this is a *fictionalized* account)

Vocabulary That May Need Pre-Teaching for ELLs or Low Language Students

- Barn, South, master, big house, haystack, whipping, slave, rag doll, run away, bandanna, courage, muskrat, cabin

---

During Reading

Questions Students Should Ask Themselves for Each Chunk of Text

- What is the author telling me?
- Any hard or important words?
- What does the author want me to understand?
- How does the author play with language to add to meaning?

Follow-Up Text-Dependent Questions for the Teacher to Ask About Each Chunk of Text

Pages 1–2

- What can we *infer* from the information the author gives us on the first page? (Minty was a slave—worked for a mean mistress; Minty was kind of spunky, but didn't talk back for fear of a whipping)
- Why do you think the author began the book with this scene? (shows us a bit about Minty's character and the mistreatment of slaves by their masters and mistresses)

Pages 3–4

- Why do you think the author provides the detail about the doll? (shows slave children were happy with very little)

- What does the story about the shepherd boy show about Minty's feelings? (wanted a better life for herself)

Pages 5–6

- How do the details on this page add to what you already knew about Minty and Mrs. Brodas? (Minty was willing to lie to avoid her mistress; Mrs. Brodas was really mean.)

- What else are you learning about Minty here? (she was clumsy)

- According to the information on this page, was it better to be a house slave or a field slave? Why? (better to be a house slave—the work wasn't as hard)

- What do you think Mrs. Brodas is taking out of the cupboard? (accept all reasonable answers)

Pages 7–8

- Why do you think Mrs. Brodas destroyed Minty's doll? (wanted to punish her by taking something important to her)

- How do you think this will affect Minty? (accept all reasonable answers)

Pages 9–10

- What was Minty's dad afraid would happen to her? (she'd be sold to another plantation owner)

- What does it mean, "If your head is in the lion's mouth, it's best to pat him a little"? (if someone is just about to harm you, it's best to be nice to him)

- What did Minty's mom mean when she said, "Your head's in his mouth, Minty, but you sure ain't doin' no pattin'"? (you're in trouble, but you're not doing anything to fix it)

- What does Minty say that may be important later in the story? (she's going to run away)

Pages 11–12

- What else are you learning on this page about what it's like to be a slave? (it was miserable to work in the fields; you needed a bandanna to keep the heat off; you would be punished if you tried to escape)

- On this page and others, why does the author use words like *ain't, fixin' 'un* (for one)? (showed the way slaves talked, didn't have access to education)

Pages 13–14

- Why might this job that Minty has been given be difficult for her to fulfill? (she wants living creatures to be FREE)

Pages 15–16

- Were you surprised when Minty let the muskrat go free? Why or why not? (not surprised due to her thinking about freedom for all creatures)

Pages 17–18

- What effect do you think the whipping will have on Minty? Why? (accept all reasonable answers)

- Why is the author providing so many of these awful details? (to show the misery that slaves faced)

- Why do you think Minty's mother didn't try to stop the whipping? (this was common practice; she knew it would only make the situation worse)

Pages 19–26

- What is Minty's dad doing on these pages? (teaching her how to survive when she runs away)
- What are some things that Minty learned? (accept text-based examples)
- Do you think this was a good idea or a bad idea? Why? (accept all reasonable responses)

Pages 27–28

- Any predictions? (Students may predict that Minty will use this chance to escape; make sure they explain this inference with details such as she was not ready to survive on her own.)

Pages 29–30

- What made this a good night to escape? (there was a horse that wasn't too big; she saw the North Star)

Pages 31–32

- Why do you think Minty had tears in her eyes? (she wouldn't be able to escape tonight; she was disappointed in herself)

Pages 33–35 (including Author's Note*)

- What does the end of the story leave you wanting to know? (if, when, how Minty escaped)

*The next questions relate to Author's note:

- About how old was Minty when she finally escaped? (She was about 29.)
- What did Minty (Harriet) say she had a right to? (liberty or death)
- Why do we remember Harriet Tubman? (her role in helping so many slaves to escape via the Underground Railroad)
- What important words here should you know to understand this time in history? (abolitionist, Underground Railroad, fugitives)
- What does Harriet mean when she says, "I never ran my train off the track. I never lost a passenger."?

After Reading (Complete These Tasks on Day 2 of the Lesson Sequence)

Important Words to Talk About the Text

- Minty, Harriet Tubman, slave, slavery, Underground Railroad, escape, abuse

Theme, Lesson, or Message (if Appropriate)

- The importance of perseverance and a strong belief in freedom for everyone

Summary or Gist Statement

- Something like, Minty was a young slave girl with spunk who had a burning desire to be free. In the end, she found freedom for herself and helped many other slaves get to freedom, too

Review of Text Type (Literary/Information) and Genre

- This is a *partial* biography because it just describes Harriet Tubman's childhood. Also, it is not entirely true, but it definitely shows the kind of person Harriet was, the way she was treated as a young slave child, and her desire for freedom

Collaborative Oral Task

- With a partner or small group, make a list of details in this book that were almost certainly *true* and those that may have been *made up*. Be able to explain why you placed each item in each column

Follow-Up Lessons: Digging Deeper Through Rereading

Follow-up lessons can be taught in a different order.

Day	Focus Standard	Content for Whole-Class Lessons and Guided Student Practice
2	Close reading follow-up discussion including an emphasis on genre features SL1; R5	As a whole group, discuss briefly: important words from the text, theme(s), and summary. Then, ask students to work in pairs or small groups to think about which events were probably true and which may have been fictitious. See *Collaborative Oral Task* (page 221).
3	Story elements: Understanding the context (setting) R3	Examine selected pages, including photographs, to identify elements of the way of life in the South during the time of slavery. Pairs of students could work together on pages identified by the teacher.
4	Text-to-text connections R9	Read and discuss the poem *Harriet Tubman* by Eloise Greenfield, retrieved from http://www.poets.org/viewmedia.php/prmMID/16485. How does this poem add to your understanding of Harriet Tubman? Students may write about this or respond orally. They can work individually or in pairs.
5	Opinion writing W1	Think about the choices Harriet (Minty) made at different points in her life. Choose one of these choices and explain in one paragraph why in your opinion this was or was not a good choice. Choices could include when Minty pretended she didn't hear her mistress when she called to her; when Minty let the muskrat go free; when Minty almost ran away one night, but lost her courage. Be sure to state your opinion clearly and provide evidence from the text that supports your thinking.

Close Reading Lessons for Sojourner Truth's Step-Stomp Stride

Initial Close Reading Lesson

Text: *Sojourner Truth's Step-Stomp Stride*   **Author:** Andrea Davis Pinkney

Purpose: R1: Close reading for deep understanding of the text

Before Reading

Clues Based on Cover Illustration

- Notice that there's an African American woman; she looks big and powerful; it looks like she's moving quickly or in a rush

Clues Based on Title, Author

- Notice the name (Sojourner Truth); notice other important words: *step-stomp, stride* (If students aren't familiar with these words, let them discover their meaning through the text.)

Probable Text Type (Literary or Informational); Possible Genre

- Probably a story; can't tell if it's true or made-up; look for story parts

Vocabulary That May Need Pre-Teaching for ELLs or Low Language Students

- Preaching, master, valuable, property, speak her mind

During Reading

Questions Students Should Ask Themselves for Each Chunk of Text

- What is the author telling me?

- Any hard or important words?

- What does the author want me to understand?

- How does the author play with language to add to meaning?

Follow-Up Text-Dependent Questions for the Teacher to Ask About Each Chunk of Text

Pages 1–2

- What important information is the author providing on the first page? (Sojourner was large, a black woman meant for great things like speaking, preaching truth about freedom.)

- What can you tell about the time in history that this book is about? (in the time of slavery)

Pages 3–4

- Why was Belle a good name for Sojourner? (*ringing* in good news)

- What can you already tell about the kind of person Sojourner will become? (good news: she will accomplish something important; nothing quiet: she will speak out)

Pages 5–6

- What strategy do you think the author wants you to use here? (picturing)

- What does the author mean by "hands like hams"? (large)

- What does the author mean by "pick a bone" with Belle? (no one would disagree with her)

- Now can you tell what "stomp" means? (step on)

- What is the author trying to show you about Sojourner? (She was powerful from the time she was a child.)

Pages 7–8

- How did Sojourner's strength lead to problems for her? (she was valuable and sold away from her parents to other slave owners)

- What words does the author use to show how bad slavery was? (property, ugly)

Pages 9–10

- What motivated Sojourner to work so hard? (the promise of freedom)

- What do you predict? Will Sojourner be freed? Why do you make this prediction? (Maybe she won't be freed—based on slave holders' reputation for unfairness)

Pages 11–12

- Was Sojourner freed? How did this become a turning point in her life? (not freed, decided to run away)

- What does the author mean, "She fled like tomorrow wasn't ever gonna come"? (ran immediately)

- What does the author mean, "She refused to stop until she saw hope"? (saw the opportunity for freedom)

- What do you notice about the narrator? (speaks in dialect, might be someone who could really relate to Sojourner)

Pages 13–14

- What does the author mean: "hope's front door"? (These people were Quakers. Quakers helped slaves escape to freedom.)

- What is *shelter*? (someplace to stay)

- How was Isaac different from John Dumont? (He really did want to free Sojourner.)

Pages 15–18

- In your own words, explain how Sojourner's life was better now? (She moved to New York and got a real job as a maid.)

- What did freedom mean to Sojourner? (traveling around to speak about freedom)

- Why was Sojourner Truth a good name for this woman? (she traveled; she expressed the truth)

Pages 19–20

- What is an abolitionist? (someone who wanted slaves to be freed)

- Why do you think it was important for Sojourner to meet abolitionists? (they could help her free other slaves)

Pages 21–22

- Do you think Sojourner was smart? What was the evidence? (she could recite every word in the Bible)

- Why do we know so much about Sojourner now? (someone who could read and write recorded her story)

Pages 23–24

- Can you picture Sojourner speaking to a crowd? Based on the information on this page, what do you see? (ex.: someone all fired up, hollering, waving her hands around)

- Explain what the author means by, "Freedom is not a place. Freedom is the fire that burns inside." (a desire deep within you)

Pages 25–26

- Besides supporting black people, who else did Sojourner support? (women)

- Now do you have more insight into the title of this story? Why did the author choose this title? (it got at the heart of Sojourner's big goal)

Pages 27–28

- What were some of the reasons that men gave for saying men were better than women? (many examples on these pages)

- How do you predict Sojourner will answer these men? (She will NOT agree.)

Pages 29–30

- What words does the author use to show you that Sojourner strongly disagreed with these men? (*stormed past the stupidity of the men who had spoken, stomped on the floorboards of ignorance*)

- Why did Sojourner want to "stop-stomp-stomp" all over the men's arguments? (they were keeping women from the freedom they deserved)

Pages 31–34

- What words show the power of Sojourner's feelings? (*slammed, iron fist, BAM, smash, lies*)

- Note: Due to religious differences among students, I would not focus too much on the Biblical references on these pages.

Pages 35–36

- What do you think Sojourner was feeling as she walked off? What evidence from the rest of the book led you to think this? (probably felt angry, but also like she had stood up for what was right)

- Why do you think the author ends this story with the words—as individual sentences: "Big. Black. Beautiful. True"? (Each word carries an entire idea about Sojourner.)

After Reading (Complete These Tasks on Day 2 of the Lesson Sequence)

Important Words to Talk About the Text

- Sojourner, Truth, step-stomp stride, slavery, freedom

Theme, Lesson, or Message (if Appropriate)

- It is important to stand up for what you believe and to take action against discrimination

Summary or Gist Statement

- Encourage a *sequential* summary that identifies four or five key moments in Sojourner's life

Review of Text Type (Literary/Information) and Genre

- Biography (be sure to discuss the voice of the narrator-storyteller: some evidence of dialect)

Collaborative Oral Task

- With a partner or small group, create a sequential summary including four or five key moments in Sojourner Truth's life

Follow-Up Lessons: Digging Deeper Through Rereading

Follow-up lessons can be taught in a different order.

Day	Focus Standard	Content for Whole-Class Lessons and Guided Student Practice
2	Close reading follow-up discussion including an emphasis on summarizing SL1; R2	As a whole group, discuss the important words in the text, the story's theme, and the genre. Then, ask students to work with a partner or small group to create a sequential summary of Sojourner's life including four or five key moments. See *Collaborative Oral Task* above.
3	Word choice R4	How is *tone* created in this text by both the author and illustrator? Reread selected pages with strong tone words, dialect, and direct addresses to readers: What do these show? (informal voice, really connects to Sojourner's life, shows the strength of her feelings about equal rights) Look at selected illustrations: How do these show the tone? (shows strength, shows that Sojourner is active, even hurrying)
4	Text-to-text connections R9	Read with students, "More About Sojourner Truth" at the end of this book: Make a list of new details and how they add to students' understanding of this person.
5	Story elements; Give a speech from Sojourner Truth's point of view R3; SL4	Reread portions of the text that show things that were important to Sojourner. Prepare and deliver a speech that she might have given including some of these important beliefs. In their speech, students could consider using her famous quote, "And ain't I a woman?"

Close Reading Lessons for Now Let Me Fly: The True Story of a Slave Family

Initial Close Reading Lesson

Text: *Now Let Me Fly: The Story of a Slave Family*   **Author:** Dolores Johnson

Purpose: R1: Close reading for deep understanding of the text

Before Reading

Clues Based on Cover Illustration

- Notice that the mom has her arm around two of the children; everyone looks sad or worried; no one is wearing shoes

Clues Based on Title, Author

- Notice the most important words: *fly, slave family*

Probable Text Type (Literary or Informational); Possible Genre

- Probably a story—look for story parts

Vocabulary That May Need Pre-Teaching for ELLs or Low Language Students

- Africa, kidnap, prisoner, chains

During Reading

Questions Students Should Ask Themselves for Each Chunk of Text

- What is the author telling me?
- Any hard or important words?
- What does the author want me to understand?
- How does the author play with language to add to meaning?

Follow-Up Text-Dependent Questions for the Teacher to Ask About Each Chunk of Text

---

Pages 1–2

- Who is telling this story? (Minna, the older daughter)
- What other information do you have about the setting of this story? (Africa, 1815)
- Why do you think the author provides the detail about the caged bird? (it may foreshadow events that will follow)

- Which word in the last sentence seems the most important? (confined). What does this word mean? (can't get out)

- Look back at the cover: Can you make any predictions about how this word might be important to the rest of the story? (family will be enslaved; some will want to fly to freedom like the bird)

Pages 3–4

- On this page, you learn many things about this African culture. What have you learned? (drumbeats sometimes signify a party, but can also mean trouble; there is a "council of elders" that make the decisions; someone sold people of the village as slaves; people were banished as a punishment)

Pages 5–8

- In your own words, explain what has happened to Minna here? (Minna went to the edge of her settlement to follow the free bird and was kidnapped by Dongo. Then she was bound and taken to the western shore of Africa.)

Pages 9–10

- Explain the phrase: "no more than a whisper and a prayer between us." (terribly crowded)

- Explain what life was like for people on the ship? (crowded, sickness, hunger)

- What other important detail is the author giving us here? (Minna made a friend named Amadi, and they comforted each other)

- What was Amadi's advice to Minna, and how might that be important as this story continues? (Be proud of your African heritage; it's important because new life may be so different/horrible)

Pages 11–12

- What word describes what was happening here? (slave auction)

- In your own words, explain how this slave auction worked. (people stood in front of white men/women who bid on the black person or adult they wanted to buy)

- What thoughts were probably going through Minna's head at this point? (fear, anger that she was sold for less than $100)

Pages 13–14

- What does the author describe on these pages? (the horrible conditions of being a slave—students can provide details)

Pages 15–16

- Look again at the cover. Who is shown here? What accounts for the sadness? (This is Minna and her four children after her husband was sold away.)

- What strong words on this page show Minna's feelings? (*tiny shack, meager rations, rags, misery, the cage of slavery*)

- What one word could you choose to sum up Minna's feelings here? (distraught, panicked—something like that)

Pages 17–18

- What words show the great difference between Minna and her Master? (Master: *profit, chains, tear family apart; pushed me aside; the boy is more mine than yours; yelled.* Minna: *special gift; pleaded*)

- How does the illustration on page 18 add to your understanding of this scene? (accept reasonable responses)

Pages 19–20

- In your own words, explain Joshua's new life. (learning to be a blacksmith—who makes shoes for horses; he sent word that he would save his money to buy freedom for his family)

- How has the tone changed on this page? (now a little bit of hope—for freedom)

Pages 21–22

- Describe Sally. (smart, taught herself to read, proud and strong)

- Why did Minna fear for Sally? (slaves were supposed to quietly obey)

- Why do you think Minna let Sally go—even though she wanted to keep her family together? (a chance for freedom; Sally had the strength to take care of herself)

Pages 23–24

- How had Sally gotten to freedom? What is the word for this? (used the *Underground Railroad* to travel north with the help of free black people and white people who were against slavery—abolitionists)

- What words on this page are the most important to understand the Underground Railroad? (night, North Star, hid, slave catchers, refuge, Mason-Dixon Line, free)

Pages 25–26

- Tell Mason's story. (gifted musician; taken from cruel master, but sent to Florida, not up North)

- Do you think this improved Mason's life? Explain. (yes, living with Seminoles he would not be a slave)

Pages 27–28

- Tell Katie's story. (works in the Big House caring for the Master's daughter; neither she nor Minna will be sold if Katie is a good servant)

- What is Minna doing to help Katie know about her heritage? (how to make quilts and pottery, tells stories of her ancestors)

- What does Minna mean when she says, "Katie and I will somehow find comfort in our lives"? (they have each other; they have accepted their way of life to some extent because they believe they will have a better life after this)

- Now you know where the author got the title. Explain. (It is the name of a hymn and means that there will be freedom in Heaven)

Pages 29–30

- What is an *epilogue*? (part that comes *after* the story)

- What became of each of Minna's children? (students provide details identified on this page)

- What events in history made a difference to Minna and her children? (The Seminoles were forced to move to Oklahoma; the Civil War and the 13th Amendment freed the slaves.)

After Reading (Complete These Tasks on Day 2 of the Lesson Sequence)

Important Words to Talk About the Text

- Possible words: Minna, Sally, Mason, Joshua, Katie, slavery, plantation, Underground Railroad, caged, prison

Theme, Lesson, or Message (if Appropriate)

- Something like, The time of slavery was a horrible time in American history because of the way slaves were treated and their lack of freedom

Follow-Up Lessons: Digging Deeper Through Rereading

Follow-up lessons can be taught in a different order.

Day	Focus Standard	Content for Whole-Class Lessons and Guided Student Practice
2	Close reading follow-up discussion including an emphasis on genre features SL1; R5	Discuss briefly: important words from the text, theme(s), and summary. Then, ask students to work in pairs or small groups to think about what makes this historical fiction so realistic. See *Collaborative Oral Task* above.
3	Nontraditional: Text formats; Text-to-text connections R7; R9	Listen to the spiritual *Now Let Me Fly* then look at the lyrics (both retrieved from sites below): Do a close reading of the song lyrics and then discuss why this was a good title for this book. YouTube video clip of third graders singing *Let Me Fly*: https://www.youtube.com/watch?v=45751TOYXBg Song lyrics for *Let Me Fly*: http://www.negrospirituals.com/news-song/now_let_me_fly.htm
4	Story elements; Discussion R3; SL1	Using questions such as those below about various story components, characters, setting, and problem, have students work in small groups to respond orally to *one* question. (More than one group can discuss each question.) Then share responses with the whole class: What event in this story had the strongest effect on you? Why? What do you consider the worst horrors of slavery? Why? (Identify at least three things). The bird in this story is a *symbol*. What does it stand for? Where does the bird show up in this book, and how does it tie the story together? Think about each of Minna's children and their strengths. How did slavery keep each child down?
5	Narrative Writing W3	Choose *one* of Minna's children (Sally, Joshua, Mason, Katie): Think about the life they went on to experience as described in the book. Write a letter they may have sent to their mother many years later describing their new life. Before you write, *research* what life would be like for - Sally as a freed slave speaking out against slavery - Joshua as a slave sold for his skills with horses - Mason as he lived with a Seminole Indian family - Katie as a house slave

Close Reading Lessons for *Up the Learning Tree*

Initial Close Reading Lesson

Text: *Up the Learning Tree*   **Author:** Marcia Vaughan

Purpose: R1: Close reading for deep understanding of the text

Before Reading

> **Clues Based on Cover Illustration**
>
> - Notice the African American child sitting in a tree, ragged clothes
>
> **Clues Based on Title, Author**
>
> - Notice the most important word: learning tree
>
> **Probable Text Type (Literary or Informational); Possible Genre**
>
> - Probably a story. Look for story parts
>
> **Vocabulary That May Need Pre-Teaching for ELLs or Low Language Students**
>
> - Book learning, dull-minded, fever, punished, ancestors, heart desires

During Reading

> **Questions Students Should Ask Themselves for Each Chunk of Text**
>
> - What is the author telling me?
> - Any hard or important words?
> - What does the author want me to understand?
> - How does the author play with language to add to meaning?

> **Follow-Up Text-Dependent Questions for the Teacher to Ask About Each Chunk of Text**

> **Pages 1–2**
>
> - What do you know so far? (Henry is telling the story; Henry was a field slave; slaves were severely punished for learning to read.)
> - How does the author "transition" to what the rest of the book will be about? (last sentence shows that this will be about *learning*)

> **Pages 3–4**
>
> - Why did the mistress's words "sting"? (she thought Henry wasn't good enough to learn to read)
> - Why weren't slaves allowed to learn to read? (it would help them know how to escape)

Pages 5–6

- Now can you figure out why the title is "*Up the Learning Tree*"? (Henry hid in the tree to learn from the teacher)

- Why was Henry so amazed by the teacher's reading? (could find out about faraway and imaginary things like dragons and castles)

- What can you tell about Henry from the last sentence on this page? (he is determined)

Pages 7–8

- What does *lickety-split* mean? (very quickly). Why does Henry want to get his work done "lickety-split"? (so he can get to school and learn)

- What surprising detail does the author include on this page? (Henry carved letters into the bark of the tree to help himself learn.)

- What words show Henry's feelings about his accomplishment? ("Glory be, I got a letter of my own.")

Pages 9–10

- In your own words, explain what Henry figured out on this page. (Henry figured out how letters and sounds could be combined into words.)

- Why did Henry feel "sparks dancing round inside me like a fire that's been fanned by the wind"? (kind of "on fire" with this chance to read)

- Would you have made the same choice as Henry—not telling anyone about your learning? Explain. (accept all reasonable responses that are backed up by evidence from the text)

Pages 11–12

- How did Henry solve his problem when winter came, and he couldn't hide in the tree? (tricked Simon into showing him new words)

- How did Henry keep track of his learning? (carved the words into the tree)

Pages 13–16

- On these pages, what does Henry do now to help himself as a reader? (studies Master Simon's books on the way home, takes a torn book out of the trash)

- What does Henry mean: "Hugging that book's like hugging hope"? (hoping to get free—hoping the book will help)

- What does the shadow help you to predict? (Henry has been caught)

Pages 17–18

- Before reading the words, look at the illustration: Do you think the teacher, Miss Hattie, is going to be angry with Henry? Why do you think she feels this way? (does not look angry, probably believes that *all* children should be able to learn)

- What is Miss Hattie concerned about? (Henry getting caught, herself getting caught)

- How is Miss Hattie extra kind to Henry? (secretly offers to help him—"If Simon has any questions")

Pages 19–22

- Why do you think Miss Hattie shows Henry the map? (wants him to have a better understanding of where he came from)

- Why do you think Henry shows Miss Hattie his tree? (he trusts her)

- Why do you think Miss Hattie is so impressed with Henry's tree? (shows his extreme determination to learn)

Pages 23–24

- Three different points of view are evident on this page. What are they? What words show these points of view? (Henry: shocked that he's been given a new book; "my heart leaps like a wild horse." Miss Hattie: kindness and concern: "It's about Africa"; "you remember now, be careful." Ginny: nasty toward Henry: "scowls"; "What's that slave boy doing here?")

- What is Miss Hattie worried about? (they've been discovered; Ginny will tell her parents)

Pages 25–26

- Why do you think Miss Hattie told the truth about teaching Henry when she could have lied? (she believed that all children should be allowed to learn; she's willing to stand up for her beliefs)

- Why do you think Miss Hattie lied and said she'd been teaching Wilfred, not Henry? (Wilfred couldn't be punished because he had died; she didn't want Henry to be punished)

- What happened to Miss Hattie because of teaching Henry? (she got fired; the men threatened her)

Pages 27–28

- What feelings do the author and illustrator create for readers on this page—for Miss Hattie? For Henry? How do they create these feelings? (illustration shows how they both respect each other; Miss Hattie's words to Henry: "I'll never forget you." Henry's gift to Miss Hattie: tree branch)

Page 29 and inside back cover (author's note)

- In what ways might Henry's life be different if he learns to read? In what ways might his life *not* be different? (there is dignity in knowledge, but he still may not have been *free*)

- Read the author's note: How did this author come to write this book? (inspired by what she'd read about slaves who wanted to learn to read)

- What kind of research did this author have to do to write this book? (read slave diaries; read about what life was like for slaves living on Southern plantations)

After Reading (Complete These Tasks on Day 2 of the Lesson Sequence)

Important Words to Talk About the Text

- Learning, tree, books, Miss Hattie, Henry, slave, forbidden, punish

Theme, Lesson, or Message (if Appropriate)

- Something like, Learning (and reading) set you free—at least in your mind

Summary or Gist Statement

- This is a good text for a sequential summary; it could be summarized in four or five main events

Review of Text Type (Literary/Information) and Genre

- Historical fiction: Discuss elements of historical fiction and how the author makes this story seem so real

Collaborative Oral Task

- With a partner or small group, identify four or five main events in this story. Show how the events are linked together

Follow-Up Lessons: Digging Deeper Through Rereading

Follow-up lessons can be taught in a different order.

Day	Focus Standard	Content for Whole-Class Lessons and Guided Student Practice
2	Close reading follow-up discussion including an emphasis on summarizing SL1; R2	Discuss briefly: important words from the text, theme(s), and genre. Then, ask students to work in pairs or small groups to identify a sequence of four or five main events, showing how the events are connected to each other. See *Collaborative Oral Task* (page 233).
3	Story elements: Character analysis R3	Reread selected pages from this book that show Henry's character. Choose *three quotes* from these pages and explain what they show you about Henry. (The same activity could be repeated for Miss Hattie).
4	Text-to-text connection R9	In the other books we have read about slavery, characters and people took risks to become free (or free in their mind). Choose one other character we have read about (Harriet Tubman, Sojourner Truth, Minna, Sally, Mason, Joshua, Katie) and explain how the character/person is similar to and different from Henry in the risks they took. You might want to use a Venn diagram to show your thinking.
5	Narrative Writing W3	At the end of this story, Henry says he is going to keep learning. Fast forward ten years until Henry is about twenty years old. Pretend you are Henry and write a letter to Miss Hattie, telling about your life since you last saw her: What else have you learned? How has this changed your life? Are you free or still a slave? Be sure to show how your experience "up the learning tree" has made a difference to your life.

Learning Pathway

How to Study a Theme

What Makes Home So Special?

Unit Focus: A Home Is Special for Many Reasons

© Olivierl/Dreamstime.com

Let's begin the unit! This is one of eight units in this book that delivers just the "goods"—the questions, prompts, assessment tasks, and student reproducibles you'll need to implement robust close reading instruction within an inquiry unit. Just about all you need to do a few weeks in advance of starting is to look at the anchor texts on pages 240 and 241 and order those books. From there, the materials provided are all explained clearly in terms of when and how to use them. If you need clarification, look back at the ten steps that begin on page 15.

Introduction to the Unit

The Rationale

I chose *home* as a unit focus because home is a concept to which most children can relate. But before beginning, consider that there are some students who are not fortunate enough to have a permanent home to return to each afternoon after school. And for other children, home may not be as sweet as that adage would have us believe. So proceed with compassion.

A unit of study could simply look at the *concept* of home. That would leave the study wide open where virtually any book on the subject could be integrated in some way. This unit, however, has a sharper *thematic* focus, where we will look at the concept of home in one specific way: A home is special for many reasons. The challenge will be to define that "specialness" through all of the texts on this subject that we read with students, in particular, the article and the four anchor texts.

With the unit focus established, let's think about the ultimate goal of any unit teaching: helping students learn how to learn. I call it the learning pathway. With this unit, the pathway is How to Study a Theme. Students will have the opportunity to think more seriously about the meaning of *theme* and how to find and interpret themes in a text. To get started on this journey, during your introductory lesson, you'll share with your students the talking points in the following chart, Learning Pathway: How to Study a Theme.

The Inquiry Question and Discussion Points

Through this unit, students will answer the question: **What makes home so special?** Although I anticipate that many students will view this in terms of their own home, I thought it best to make the focus more generic (and perhaps even wishful) in case students' personal reality doesn't measure up to the images they will encounter on the pages of these books. The neat thing about this unit is that home is a concept that runs through many books. Once they've learned to explore it here, students can find this theme (A Home Is Special for Many Reasons) in other texts that they read as well. Begin this unit with the Unit Preview Questions and Discussion Points: for Studying a Theme: A Home Is Special for Many Reasons.

Next, because we want to know from the outset where we ultimately want to take students, I list questions under Questions for End-of-Unit Discussion About a Theme (Home Is Special for Many Reasons) Integrating All Texts. These are questions you might pose at the end of this unit. That is, with any unit teaching, after completing all the anchor books, we need to circle back to the initial inquiry question. The questions help students to synthesize their thinking across texts and wrap up the study in a thoughtful way.

Learning Pathway

How to Study a Theme

Share these prompts with students.

- *There are many very common themes that you find in lots of stories: What well-known themes seem to appear in many of the stories you read? Can you think of a story that goes with each of these themes?*

- *A theme is the central idea of a story, the message that the author wants you to take away from what you read: What seems to be the central idea or message of this story?*

- *Sometimes, especially in complex text, a story has more than one theme: How many themes can you find in this text? What are they?*

- *An author begins to develop the theme right from the beginning of the story: Where do you find your first clues about the theme of this story? What details show the development of the theme throughout the story?*

- *A theme is often revealed through the turning point in a story: What did the main character think before the turning point? What changes occurred after the turning point?*

- *Sometimes the title of a story gives a hint about the theme: Can you find any clues to theme in the title of this story?*

- *A theme often gives readers important ideas to think about for their own life: How can you connect personally to the theme of this story?*

- *When you study a theme, consider all of the kinds of texts where this theme could be found: Can you find poems with this theme? How about paintings by famous artists? What about photographs or even music?*

THEME

Unit Preview Questions and Discussion Points

for Studying a Theme: A Home Is Special for Many Reasons

- *Define what you mean by a theme. Make sure students understand that a theme is not a single word (like home), but something about that word—like a home is special for many reasons.*

- *Ask students to provide some examples of different themes that would go with the study of home. (They might suggest homes are different in different parts of the world; all people should have a home; home is where the heart is—or something else related to this concept.)*

- *Discuss how to study a time in theme, referring to the points and questions in How to Study a Theme. Customize these points and questions according to the developmental level of your students. Chart the questions you will try to address through the unit.*

- Introduce the theme you will study in this unit: A Home Is Special for Many Reasons.

- Introduce the inquiry question: What makes home so special? (*Students may have some initial responses to this question—which is fine. But don't get too far into this until they've acquired textual evidence.*)

- Introduce the four books selected for close reading. Show the cover and perhaps an illustration inside to pique students' interest. Do not explain the full story.

Questions for End-of-Unit Discussion About a Theme (A Home Is Special for Many Reasons) Integrating All Texts

- After reading the four anchor texts in this unit and the story *My Home* by Sierra, do you now feel you can answer the inquiry question: *What makes home so special?* Make a list of points compiled from all of these texts.

- Which questions for Learning Pathway: How to Study a Theme can you answer after reading these books?

- Every author develops his or her theme differently. For the texts in this unit, how did each author develop the theme? Which way of developing the theme seemed the most effective to you? Why?

- Remember that an author begins to develop the theme right from the beginning of the story. Choose one of the books we read and show how the author started to develop the theme early in the text.

- Did any of these texts have more than one theme? What other themes did you find?

- Which of these texts had a *turning point*? How did the turning point make the theme clearer?

- Did any of these texts change your thinking in some way? What book had the biggest effect on your thinking? What did you think before? What do you think now?

- After this study of a theme, what do you understand better now about what a theme is? How would you explain theme to another student in this grade who didn't understand the meaning of theme?

The Focus Standard

On the surface, deciding on the focus standard for this unit looks like a no-brainer; it's a perfect match for CCRA R2: "Determine central ideas or themes of a text and analyze their development; summarize the key supporting details and ideas" (http://www.corestandards.org/ELA-Literacy/CCRA/R/, Key Ideas section, para. 2). That certainly works, and I did choose this standard for this unit's primary focus. But I think the meaning of *theme* becomes even clearer when you look at texts with a common theme side by side to consider how an author develops a theme. For that reason we have a supporting standard for this unit, CCRA R9: "Analyze how two or more texts address similar themes or topics in order to build knowledge or to compare the approaches the authors take" (http://www.corestandards.org/ELA-Literacy/CCRA/R/, Integration of Knowledge section, para. 3). One important difference between this unit on theme and the focus on theme in other books students read is that here the theme is identified, and students then need to dig

THEME

deep to discover its nuances in individual texts and across texts. Frequently, in other reading students do, they will be tasked with figuring out the theme themselves. This is why it is so important to make this a unit on *theme* in general, and not just a study of the particular theme, *A Home Is Special for Many Reasons*. Be sure to take this important next step as you study the texts that are part of this unit.

The Anchor Texts

The first text listed below is a short personal narrative that is to be read by the students themselves and discussed during a unit kickoff lesson (discussion questions are provided on page 246). The remaining four texts are picture books, one of which will be read closely and studied during each week of the unit.

My Home by Sierra (provided on page 246)

Every home and the family inside it shares some things that are common to many homes and families—and other features that are unique—just to them. The special features of Sierra's home include her adoption at the age of two. Students will enjoy reading and thinking about Sierra's home life and the way it compares to their own.

Let's Go Home: The Wonderful Things About a House by Cynthia Rylant

You can never go wrong with Cynthia Rylant—and this book is Rylant at her best: warm and fuzzy images about different rooms in a house. This is a nice introductory anchor text because it examines the physical characteristics of a home and promotes a careful look at the word choice that makes mood come alive. It also presents a simple format (brief descriptions based on small details) that students can imitate in their own writing. Complexities include the highly detailed illustrations and the lyrical, descriptive language. No Lexile or grade level equivalent available.

Going Home by Eve Bunting

Eve Bunting is another author who always delivers, and this text moves students to think beyond "the house" itself to a personal experience where visions of "home" collide. This book asks students to examine the sacrifices parents make, giving up their own home to make a better life for their children. In my experience, using this anchor text, some intermediate grade students truly have a difficult time relating to the concept of "sacrifice." All the more reason to read this book closely! Complexities include possible lack of background knowledge about rural Mexican culture and this book's multiple themes. Lexile: 480; Grade level equivalent: 5.4.

A Thirst for Home: A Story of Water Across the World by Christine Ieronimo

Is this a story about the importance of home, or is it a story about the importance of water? It is both—and more. In this book, young Alemitu and her emaye (mother) live in a poor village in Ethiopia where there is neither sufficient food nor adequate clean water. To give her daughter a chance for a better life, Emaye makes the difficult decision to make an adoption plan for Alemitu. The girl is adopted by an American family and is now called Eva. She adjusts well to the love of her new parents and siblings, though she still misses her homeland, even the parts that were not so desirable. In the end, she realizes her "home" straddles both worlds, and she is both Eva and Alemitu. Complexities include lack of understanding about the poverty and disease rampant in Ethiopia, the concept of relinquishing a child to a new home to make her life better, the symbolism present within the story, and the language that leads to visual images. No Lexile or grade equivalent is available.

On This Spot: An Expedition Back Through Time by Susan E. Goodman

This text presents an entirely different vision of home—not as an emotional investment or a space but as a "spot" in the world. And that spot is New York City. This book, through a simple, but highly engaging format, shows readers that "on this spot" now home to millions of people, lived just 160,000 people 175 years ago with peddlers selling corn on Fifth Avenue and pigs running through the streets. On this spot, 350 years ago, fewer than fifteen hundred people lived in New Amsterdam. On this spot even earlier, lived Lenape Indians, woolly mammoths and dinosaurs, and before that, way, way back, this spot was only rock. Yes, our home changes over time, just as we change. "In a hundred years, who knows?" Complexities include the large quantity of information conveyed and the sequential informational structure. Lexile: 790.

Other Texts Useful for Studying the Theme

If you'd like to use additional texts to extend this unit, or texts other than the ones for which lessons have been provided, consider the books below.

- *An Angel for Solomon Singer* by Cynthia Rylant
- *Home* by Thomas Locker
- *If You Lived Here: Houses of the World* by Giles Laroche
- *Four Feet, Two Sandals* by Karen Lynn Williams
- *When Jessie Came Across the Sea* by Amy Hest

The Unit's Two Assessments

Featured Reading Standard: 2: Development of theme

Featured Writing Format: Narrative

See the Unit Curriculum Map for Close Reading for where these assessments might fit into your study of Home. And for more information about the rationale behind these two assessments and how they differ, as well as guidance for using the rubrics, refer to Step 9 on page 43 and Step 10 on page 50. Also, to evaluate students' performance, see page 45 for the Rubric for Content-Based Assessment (Task 1) and Standards-Based Assessment (Task 2). Turn to page 293, The End of the Story: Reflecting on Student Work, for some sample student work from this unit and commentary.

Task I: Content Assessment

In this unit, we read books that helped us understand the theme: "A Home Is Special for Many Reasons." We answered the inquiry question: *"What makes home so special?"* A few points we discussed related to this theme and question were that home is special because of

- The people and pets we live with and who love us

- Traditions or special activities that are part of our lives

- The friends and relatives who come to visit

- A favorite room that contains some favorite things

- Special memories

- The symbols: sights and smells and sounds that say, "This is home"

Write a *story* about what makes your home special as if you are living in New York City *now*. Your story should include a description of a special *room* in your house like the way Cynthia Rylant wrote about rooms in her book, *Let's Go Home*. You should include some *family members* and *traditions* like the way Eve Bunting did in her book *Going home*. You should include some special symbols that you associate with your home such as those we read about in *A Thirst for Home* by Christine Ieronimo. Your story could include something about adoption, if you choose to do that.

Task 2: Learning Pathway and Standard Assessment

In this unit, we read books that helped us understand the theme: "A Home Is Special for Many Reasons." We answered the inquiry question: *"What makes home so special?"* A few points we discussed related to this theme and question were that home is special because of

- The people and pets we live with—and who love us
- Traditions or special activities that are part of our lives
- The friends and relatives who come to visit
- A favorite room that contains some favorite things
- Special memories
- The symbols: sights and smells and sounds that say, "This is home"

You should be able to find evidence for this same theme and inquiry question in texts that you read yourself. Read about the *cultures* below (Your teacher may tell you which of these articles to read.). Choose one culture and write a *story* about what makes your home special as if you were a child in this culture. Be sure to use the facts from the article and include at least three of the bullet points above in your story.

- Mayan culture: http://www.readworks.org/passages/secrets-past
- Inuit culture: http://www.readworks.org/passages/north-america-dear-pen-pal
- Apache culture: http://www.readworks.org/passages/they-call-them-apaches

Unit Curriculum Map for Close Reading

What Makes Home So Special?

TEXT	MONDAY	TUESDAY	WEDNESDAY	THURSDAY	FRIDAY
				Unit Preview	Kickoff Lesson
				See Unit Preview Questions and Discussion Points	Read and discuss *My Home* by Sierra. Discussion questions are provided at the end of the article
Let's Go Home: The Wonderful Things About a House by Cynthia Rylant	Objective: R1 Close Reading	Objective: SL1; R4 Close Reading Follow-Up	Objective: R2 Theme/Main Ideas	Objective: R7; R4 Nontraditional: Examining the Illustrations; Word Choice	Objective: R9; W3 Text-to-Text Connections; Narrative Writing
	Read closely to answer text-dependent questions	Complete the After Reading tasks including a collaborative task for focusing on description	Identify the central idea (the feeling) for each room	Identify objects in the illustrations not described by the author and create strong visual images	Reread Sierra's story and create a written description of a bedroom that would be just right for her—using Rylant's style
Going Home by Eve Bunting	Objective: R1 Close Reading	Objective: SL1; R2 Close Reading Follow-Up	Objective: R3; W1 Story Elements; Opinion Writing	Objective: R2 Theme/Main Ideas	Objective: R7; R9 Nontraditional; Text-to-Text Connections
	Read closely to answer text-dependent questions	Complete the After Reading tasks including a collaborative task for a four-sentence summary	Reread portions of the text to determine the turning point; write an opinion piece about what you believe the turning point in the story to be—and why	Revisit the text to identify opportunities in America and Mexico. Discuss why the parents made the choice to come to America	View and discuss YouTube video about migrant farm workers; connect to Going Home

TEXT	MONDAY	TUESDAY	WEDNESDAY	THURSDAY	FRIDAY
A Thirst for Home: A Story of Water Across the World by Christine Ieronimo	Objective: R1 Close Reading	Objective: SL1 Close Reading Follow-Up	Objective: R2 Theme/Main Ideas: Symbols and Images	Objective: R9 Text-to-Text Connections	Objective: R7 Nontraditional: Examining Illustrations
	Read closely to answer text-dependent questions	Complete the After Reading tasks including a collaborative task for explaining the title	Theme/Main ideas: Reread to identify and analyze key symbols and images in this story	Read and discuss the Author's Note at the end of this book; make specific connections to aspects of this book	Analyze the meaning of individual illustrations and make comparisons between pairs of illustrations
On this Spot: An Expedition Back Through Time by Susan Goodman	Objective: R1 Close Reading	Objective: SL1; R2 Close Reading Follow-Up	Objective: R3 Story Events: How Events Fit Together	Objective: R9 Text-to-Text Connections	Objective: W2 Explanatory Writing
	Read closely to answer text-dependent questions	Complete the After Reading tasks including a collaborative task for a summary with main idea/details	Reread to find details: What would New Yorkers today be astonished to find out about their city long ago?	Examine a current photo of New York City alongside one taken long ago. What are the differences?	Compare New York City today to New York City 175 years ago: What are the differences?
	Culminating Discussion	Content Assessment	Standards-Based Assessment		
	Respond orally to text-to-text connections for studying this topic. (See Questions for End-of-Unit Discussion Integrating All Texts)	Students complete the content-assessment task integrating all texts in this study	Students complete the standards-based assessment task using cold reads		

THEME

MY HOME

by Sierra

My name is Sierra and I am nine. I like to rock climb, swim, play tennis and have play dates. I live in a college town in Massachusetts because my dad is a computer science professor. We have lived here four years. The other people in my family are Mom, Emma and Silas.

My family is special because we like to play sports together outside. My sister and I play soccer in the yard with Silas. Silas likes to make a goal and say, "Goal!!!!" It is really funny for me and Emma.

I was the first kid in our family. When I was two, my parents adopted me. I had been living with a foster

family. My foster parents were wonderful. When my parents adopted me, my foster parents became my god parents. They have a pool and a hot tub—I love to swim in them when we visit.

On my first day with my parents, they took me to an aquarium. I felt nervous because it was my first day of living with my mom and dad. Pretty soon I got used to living with my parents.

When I was three and a half years old, Emma was born. It felt to me like we were twins because she was born so soon after I joined the family. We love each other. Then two years ago, Silas was born. He is so cute.

I love my family, but sometimes I wish I had white skin like the rest of my family or that they all had brown skin like me. Sometimes I wonder about my biological mom and wonder where she is. Is she alive? Is she ok? When I think about her I take deep breaths and talk to my therapist or my mom or my dad to feel better.

My best friend, Sofia, and I love dogs. My family does not have any pets, but I hope we will get a dog when Silas is older.

I am so glad that I have a wonderful family and a wonderful home.

Think About

Think about Sierra and why her home is special to her:

1. Sierra's home is special for some of the same reasons that many families are special. Talk about some of the things Sierra has in common with many families.

2. In what ways is Sierra a "typical" nine year old as far as her needs and wants?

3. Talk about some of the things that make Sierra's home life a little different from other children's family and home.

4. No matter who we are or where we live, we all face challenges in our home and family life. What are some of Sierra's challenges? How does she approach her challenges in a positive way?

5. What are "foster parents"? How might Sierra's foster parents have played an important part in her life?

6. Think about your own family and home: What special features make them unique in some way? What do you have in common with Sierra? What is different?

Close Reading Lessons for Let's Go Home: The Wonderful Things About a House

Initial Close Reading Lesson

Title of text: *Let's Go Home: The Wonderful Things About a House*　　　**Author:** Cynthia Rylant

Purpose: Close reading for deep understanding of the text

Before Reading

Clues Based on Cover Illustration

- Notice what is featured most prominently on the cover (house); notice other details; think about the feeling you get from this picture

Clues Based on Title, Author

- Notice key word in title (home); notice key word in subtitle (wonderful); think about whether you expect this book to be happy or sad

- Notice the author: What kinds of stories does Cynthia Rylant write? (books that show lots of feelings of characters, books about places familiar to her)

Probable Text Type (Literary or Informational); Possible Genre

- Looks more like literary text than informational text

Vocabulary That May Need Pre-Teaching for ELLs or Low Language Students

- Words for various rooms in the house: kitchen, porch, living room, bedroom, bathroom, attic

During Reading

Questions Students Should Ask Themselves for Each Chunk of Text

- What is the author telling me?

- Any hard or important words?

- What does the author want me to understand?

- How does the author play with language to add to meaning?

Follow-Up Text-Dependent Questions for the Teacher to Ask About Each Chunk of Text

Pages 1–2

- In what ways is this page an introduction to the text? (there are many kinds of houses; this book will tell what's wonderful about a house)

- Look at the way the illustration is designed. Describe it (lots of little squares). Does this remind you of anything? (possibly a quilt) How might this help us predict the way this book will be set up? (lots of individual sections)

Pages 3–6 (Porch)

- What are some of the details that help us picture the porch? (too many to list)
- What kind of mood do you think the author is trying to create with these details? (peaceful but active)
- What are some of the words that help to create this mood? (crickets *singing*, cats *love*, *curious* eyes, lights *curl* up the posts, *shine like a jewel*)
- How does the author let you know she is moving on to the next part? ("let's step inside . . .")

Pages 7–10 (Living room)

- How does the author make the living room seem friendly? (many details)
- What details really stand out to you? Why? (accept any text-based answers)
- Choose another word (other than *friendly*) based on these details to describe what a living room is like. (accept all reasonable answers)

Pages 11–16 (Kitchen)

- What details does the author provide that make a kitchen seem *delicious*? (numerous)
- What details show that a kitchen is a caring room? (numerous)
- Has the tone of this text stayed the same or changed since the beginning of the story? (same)
- What message do you think the author wants us to understand about a home? (a happy, active, warm, inviting place)

Pages 17–20 (Bathroom)

- Why was it surprising that the author included the bathroom in this book? (usually think this is something we shouldn't talk about)
- How does the author convince you that a bathroom is a lovely place? (providing positive images to which we can relate)
- What are some of the small details included here that show how lovely a bathroom can really be? (numerous)
- What room do you think might come next? Why? (accept any reasonable prediction)

Pages 21–24 (Bedroom)

- What details does the author include to make a bedroom seem like a *peaceful, quiet place*? (numerous)
- Which one of these images stands out to you? Why? (accept all reasonable responses)
- What senses does the author use to help this image stand out? (touch, sound, see)

Pages 25–28 (Attic)

- We often think of attics as creepy and dirty. How does the author create a different image in your mind? (chooses positive images—see the sky, squirrel's nest, collections—rather than junk)
- What does the author mean: "Attics are filled with the past"? (things that had special meaning to us in the past are often stored away in an attic)
- How does the author link an attic to both the past and the future? (*look out the window, think about what you want to do*)

- How does the author tie everything together at the end? (transition—come down from the attic; includes images from several different rooms)
- Does this conclusion work? Explain. (should include reference to using details shared previously)

After Reading (Complete These Tasks on Day 2 of the Lesson Sequence)

Important Words to Talk About the Text

- Names of different rooms; words that describe feelings in these rooms or words that help you picture the rooms

Review of Text Type (Literary/Information) and Genre

- Descriptive narrative

Retell/Summarize (if Appropriate)

- This isn't a good book to summarize

Theme, Lesson, or Message (if Appropriate)

- Something like, Home is a place where each room makes us feel warm and cozy in its own way. (Save the discussion of theme until Day 3 in the lesson sequence.)

Collaborative Oral Task

- Think about which is your favorite room based on the details Cynthia Rylant has included. Join a small group that shares your opinion and together list the images that led you to this conclusion. Be able to explain why these images were so powerful

Follow-Up Lessons: Digging Deeper Through Rereading

Follow-up lessons can be taught in a different order.

Day	Focus Standard	Content for Whole-Class Lessons and Guided Student Practice
2	Close reading follow-up discussion including details from the text SL1; R4	As a whole group, discuss briefly: important words from the text and the genre (a descriptive narrative). Explain that a descriptive narrative doesn't really tell a story but describes something in a personal way with lots of details. Then, ask students to work in pairs or small groups to think about which room is their favorite based on the author's description. See *Collaborative Oral Task* above.
3	Theme/Main ideas R2	The author creates a different feeling about different rooms in this house. Reread the part of this book about the front porch and ask students to name the central idea. (For the porch, they may say that a porch is welcoming.) What details support this central idea? Then, ask students to work in pairs or small groups to identify the central idea for another room along with supporting details.
4	Nontraditional: Examining the illustrations; Word choice R7; R4	With the whole class, examine one of the rooms in the house for details the author has not mentioned. Describe these objects with words that create strong visual images. Consider extending this lesson by having students work in pairs or independently to create images for objects on other pages not described by the author.
5	Text-to-text connections; Narrative writing R9; W3	Reread Sierra's story to identify some of the things she likes and what is important to her. Ask students to create a written description of a bedroom that would be just right for her, using Rylant's style—creating a warm tone with strong visual images.

Close Reading Lessons for *Going Home*

Initial Close Reading Lesson

Text: *Going Home*   **Author:** Eve Bunting

Purpose: R1: Close reading for deep understanding of the text

Before Reading

Clues Based on Cover Illustration

- Details to notice: collage of images. Pay attention to how the author works these into the story

Clues Based on Title, Author

- Key word in the title: home. Pay attention to *where* home is and *why* people are going home

- Author: Eve Bunting: What kind of stories does this author write? (often writes about issues children should understand)

Probable Text Type (Literary or Informational); Possible Genre

- Appears to be a story: Look for story parts, such as characters, setting, problem, events, solution

Vocabulary That May Need Pre-Teaching for ELLs or Low Language Students

- Mexico, station wagon, Spanish, village, opportunity, burro

---

During Reading

Questions Students Should Ask Themselves for Each Chunk of Text

- What is the author telling me?

- Any hard or important words?

- What does the author want me to understand?

- How does the author play with language to add to meaning?

Follow-Up Text-Dependent Questions for the Teacher to Ask About Each Chunk of Text

---

Pages 1–2

- The author provides a lot of information on this page. What do you know already? (family is going to Mexico; Mexico is home; "here" is home too; Mama and Papa are happy; children are skeptical; narrator is one of the children)

Pages 3–4

- What strategy does the author want you to use in the first paragraph? (picturing)

- Paragraph 2: What do you now understand about the work this family does? (migrant farm work)

- What is the additional evidence the author provides at the end of this page? (children are sad)

- Why do you think the author provided additional details about the children being sad? (may foreshadow something—a change?)

Pages 5–6

- Explain the line: "We are legal farm workers. We have our papeles." (we have our legal papers)

- What do you know about this family now that you didn't know before? (parents speak only Spanish)

- Mexico doesn't *look* different—so why is Mama so happy? (her homeland—in her heart)

Pages 7–8

- In your own words, describe what life is like for this family where they live now. (hard work, long hours in the fields, even children work)

- Why did they leave La Perla? (no work, no opportunities)

- What is the big sister's attitude toward the "opportunities"? Why? (doesn't agree there are many opportunities)

- What kind of "opportunities" might Papa mean? (take any response at this point—not clear yet in text)

Pages 9–14

- What are we learning on these pages? (life in rural Mexico)

- Why do you think the author provides this information? (most children don't know about rural Mexico; it helps us better understand these parents' home)

Pages 15–16

- Why does the author give us the detail about Papa honking the horn? (Papa's excitement)

- Do you think the older sister (Dolores) will feel the same way? Why? What details support your answer? (probably impressed—this looks like a very ordinary little town—paper lanterns, store)

Pages 17–18

- What details seem important on this page? (Mexican relatives think the children have beautiful clothes; American family bought the plow)

- What do these details show? (although the family who moved to America doesn't have much money, they have more than their Mexican relatives)

Pages 19–20

- Why does the author include the detail about speaking English? (shows the opportunities children get in America)

- What detail is repeated here? (opportunities)

- What does the author mean by "But where are the opportunities for our children after"? (no good jobs available, or college)

- Look at the last line: What is the child beginning to *understand*? (why his parents love their home in Mexico)

Pages 21–22

- What is surprising about the details on this page? (children sleep in the car; cow pokes its head in window)

- Why is the narrator (Carlos) confused about La Perla? (doesn't seem special)

Pages 23–26

- Why do the parents start to dance and appear so young? (very happy)
- How does the picture on pp. 25–26 add to your understanding? (shows the mood)

Pages 27–28

- In your own words, explain what Dolores and Carlos are beginning to understand. (Mama and Papa would love to live in Mexico with their family, but for now they will stay in America because they want a better life for their children)

Pages 29–30

- Why do you think the author ends the story with this sentence? (it shows a different attitude from beginning of the story; it shows compassion and understanding)

After Reading (Complete These Tasks on Day 2 of the Lesson Sequence)

Important Words to Talk About the Text

- America, Mexico, opportunities, education, English, Spanish

Theme, Lesson, or Message (if Appropriate)

- Parents often give up the things that are important to them to make their children's life better
- People's attitudes can change when they have an open mind

Retell/Summarize (if Appropriate)

- Students could create a *sequential* summary; they should show that the character changes

Review of Text Type (Literary/Information) and Genre

- Realistic fiction

Collaborative Oral Task

- With a partner or small group, create a *four-sentence summary*. Make sure your summary shows how the children's *attitude changes* from the beginning to the end of the story

Follow-Up Lessons: Digging Deeper Through Rereading

Follow-up lessons can be taught in a different order.

Day	Focus Standard	Content for Whole-Class Lessons and Guided Student Practice
2	Close reading follow-up discussion including details from the text SL1; R2	With the whole class, complete the After Reading tasks: important words and genre. In pairs or small groups, have students complete the Collaborative Oral Task (page 252), a four-sentence summary. (Save the discussion of theme to Day 4 of the lesson sequence.)
3	Story element: Finding the turning point; Writing an opinion R3; W1	Discuss the meaning of the term turning point. Reread portions of the text that could be viewed as the turning point of the story. (There could be multiple answers.) With a partner or small group, ask students to determine what they think is the turning point in the story (when the children begin to understand their parents' feelings about Mexico and why they moved to America). Be sure to use details from the text as support and explain why you think this part is the "real" turning point—instead of a different part of the story. Write a paragraph about this and then share.
4	Theme/Main ideas: Opportunities R2	Revisit the text to examine its themes, especially the idea of opportunities: opportunities in America and opportunities in Mexico. Ask students to work in pairs or small groups to make a T-chart showing opportunities in both places. As a whole class, discuss whether they would have made the same decision as Carlos's parents about coming to America. Why?
5	Nontraditional: Nonprint text; Text-to-text connections R7; R9	Watch YouTube video (2 minutes) about migrant farm workers picking strawberries: http://www.youtube.com/watch?v=d8_JWuWSSLQ Discuss the challenges of this kind of work and how this video adds to understanding of the sacrifices parents in this week's text (Going Home) made for the benefit of their children.

Close Reading Lessons for A Thirst for Home: A Story of Water Across the World

Initial Close Reading Lesson

Text: *A Thirst for Home: A Story of Water Across the World*   **Author:** Christine Ieronimo

Purpose: R1: Close reading for deep understanding of the text

Before Reading

Clues Based on Cover Illustration

- Notice that the girl is in the forefront and she is the biggest image on the cover. Notice that the expression on her face is sort of mysterious—not really happy, not really sad. Notice that the tree in the background doesn't look like the kind of trees we have in this country

Clues Based on Title, Author

- Notice the important words: thirst, home

Probable Text Type (Literary or Informational); Possible Genre

- It is probably a story, but we can't tell yet if it is a true story or fiction

Vocabulary That May Need Pre-Teaching for ELLs or Low Language Students

- Village, watering hole, lion, orphanage, butterfly

Other

- Show students the location on a map of Ethiopia

During Reading

Questions Students Should Ask Themselves for Each Chunk of Text

- What is the author telling me?
- Any hard or important words?
- What does the author want me to understand?
- How does the author play with language to add to meaning?

Follow-Up Text-Dependent Questions for the Teacher to Ask About Each Chunk of Text

Pages 1–2

- What do we know from the first page? (girl's name *used to be* Alemitu; she lived with her mom in Ethiopia; word for mommy in language of Ethiopia is Emaye—pronounced Eh-MY-yay; it is sunny and hot there)

- What words does the author use to describe the sun? (smiling down, whispered, hot, sticky breath)

- What tone is the author trying to create by choosing these words? (two points of view: positive—smiling, whispering; negative—hot sticky breath)

- What do you call it when an author gives words human qualities like "hot, sticky breath"? (personification)

Pages 3–4

- On this page, the author lets us know in various ways how important water was to Alemitu and Emaye. What is this evidence? (walked many miles to watering hole in blazing sun; water is more precious than gold—couldn't live a day without it; water is life)

- What other detail about water is important on this page? (water connects all people on Earth)

- What is this story starting to be about? (the importance of water)

Pages 5–6

- What mysteries does Alemitu encounter at the watering hole? (can't see the bottom, wonders how deep it is and the mysteries hidden beneath, imagined a secret passage)

- Why do you think the author made this page so mysterious? (accept all reasonable answers)

- What sentence on this page may *foreshadow* something unknown in Alemitu's life? (Maybe someday I would find out what was on the other side.)

Pages 7–8

- Why do you think the author includes the detail about the brown grass and cracked earth? (to show there isn't enough water)

- In your own words, what is Alemitu saying about her feet? (she's proud of her feet; they've carried her far)

- What does the author mean by "the fierce lion in my belly"? (hunger)

- Why is this a good metaphor for Alemitu's hunger? (it's huge and strong as a lion)

- What does the author mean: "in the darkness the lion roared his loudest"? (at night she was hungrier than ever)

- How does the picture of Emaye on this page snuggling with Alemitu add to your understanding of their life? (you can tell by the expression on Emaye's face how worried she is about Alemitu)

Pages 9–10

- In your own words, explain what is happening on these pages. (Emaye is leaving Alemitu for good, so she can go somewhere where she will not go hungry.)

- Where do you think Emaye is leaving Alemitu? (Accept reasonable predictions; there is not a lot of evidence for this yet, but ask the question as the answer will become evident over the next few pages.)

- How does the author show the sadness experienced by both Emaye and Alemitu? (tears were like raindrops so precious, cried a shower of tears, I love you forever)

Pages 11–12

- Now where do you think Alemitu is? (seems to be an orphanage)
- What mystery is Alemitu trying to solve here? (how can she find the secrets of the watering hole in this place)
- What sentence on this page may *foreshadow* events to come? (didn't know this was just the beginning of my journey)

Pages 13–14

- In your own words, explain what is happening on these pages. (A white woman came to adopt Alemitu; she spoke a different language; she made Alemitu feel safe.)
- Why does Alemitu say this woman is "the color of the moon"? (she is white like the moon; she probably hasn't seen a white person before)

Pages 15–16

- How can you tell here that time has passed? (Alemita has a new name: Eva; she looks like she has adjusted to her new family; she wears different clothing.)
- Where do you think Eva lives now? (probably America)
- What kinds of details might have been left out between the time Eva left her homeland and now? (issues related to her adjustment to a new country, family, language, etc.)

Pages 17–20

- What are some of the differences in Eva's life in America? (clean water, backpack, going to school, no more hunger)
- How can you tell that there are parts of her old life that Eva misses? (her thoughts about bare feet)
- What else might Eva be missing from her old life? (her mom, friends, other aspects of life in her old village)

Pages 21–22

- What does the butterfly *symbolize* to Eva? (the orange from the blazing sun of Ethiopia, the dark night, freedom from hunger)

Pages 23–24

- What is the simile that the author uses here? (safe like the smallest twig in my bundle of wood)
- Why is this a good simile to describe how Eva feels? (a twig is small and isn't very strong—sort of the way Eva feels, separated from the security of the life she knew)
- How is Eva getting to feel secure in this new life? (crawls into bed with her parents; she has the dog to comfort her, too)

Pages 25–26

- What detail from the beginning of this book is coming back here? (the watering hole)
- What does Eva realize? (now she understands what her mom meant by being on "the other side")
- What is the big idea that Eva realizes here? (she can be part of both worlds—and that water connects these worlds)
- How does the illustration on this page help you to understand this "big idea" of being part of both worlds? (the reflection in the water of both Eva and Alemitu)

- What does Eva realize at the end of this story? (She is both Eva and Alemitu; she will always be part of two worlds; although her life in America is nice, there were also good things about life in her homeland—even though there was much hunger and not enough water.)

- What detail from the beginning of the story has returned here, painting a positive picture of Eva's homeland? ("knows what it's like to feel the warmth of the sun on my face"; everyone is connected by water)

After Reading (Complete These Tasks on Day 2 of the Lesson Sequence)

Important Words to Talk About the Text

- Water, Emaye, Alemitu, Ethiopia, America, adopt, connected

Theme, Lesson, or Message (if Appropriate)

- There are multiple messages in this story: water is essential for life; water connects us all; when children are adopted, they can love their adopted family *and* parts of their former life, too. Discuss how the title of this book represents its themes

Summary or Gist Statement

- This is a good story to summarize because it has a sequential problem/solution structure: Alemitu and Emaye live in a small village in Ethiopia where there is not enough water and they are hungry. Emaye makes an adoption plan for Alemitu who is adopted by an American family. She adjusts well to her new life, but she misses parts of her old life. In the end, she realizes she is Eva Alemitu, part of both worlds

Review of Text Type (Literary/Information) and Genre

- Realistic fiction based on a true story of a little girl who was adopted from Ethiopia

Collaborative Oral Task

- Ask students to work with a partner or small group to explain why the title of this book is such an appropriate one: Why did the author choose this title? They could also identify an alternate title that would support the content and message of this story

THEME

Follow-Up Lessons: Digging Deeper Through Rereading

Follow-up lessons can be taught in a different order.

Day	Focus Standard	Content for Whole-Class Lessons and Guided Student Practice
2	Close reading follow-up discussion including symbols from the text SL1	With the whole class, complete the After Reading tasks: important words, brief summary, review of genre, and theme. In pairs or small groups, ask students to think about the title and why it was such a good one for this book. They could also identify an alternate title that would support the content and message of this story. See *Collaborative Oral Task* (page 257).
3	Theme/Main ideas: Understanding symbols and images R2	As a whole class, identify some of the key symbols and images from this story such as water, the sun, the butterfly, the scarf, feet, the twig, or anything else students suggest as possible symbols. Reread pages that examine some of the key images and symbols. With a partner or small group, ask students to choose one image or symbol and explain how it connected to a key idea or theme in the story.
4	Text-to-text connections; Author's purpose or point of view R9; R6	Read and discuss the author's note at the end of this book. Identify some of the problems faced by people (especially women and girls) in Ethiopia today. Now consider: What do you think the author's purpose was in writing this story, A Thirst for Home?
5	Nontraditional: Examining illustrations to add to meaning R7	There are many powerful illustrations in this book and connections that can be made between several illustrations. • Some illustrations to study by examining the choice of colors, feelings revealed in the faces of the characters, images of life in Ethiopia, and the symbolism: pp. 1–2 (When I was Alemitu . . .); pp. 3–4 (Emaye and I . . .); pp. 9–10 (One day Emaye . . .) • Some pages to compare: pp. 5–6 (Finally, we . . .) and pp. 25–26 (In the morning . . .); pp. 7–8 (We walked home barefoot . . .) and pp. 19–20 (Today I am going . . .); p. 8 (That night I lay . . .) and p. 23 (That night I hear the raindrops . . .); pp. 11–12 (In this new place . . .) and pp. 27–28 (I am Eva Alemitu . . .)

Close Reading Lessons for On This Spot: An Expedition Back Through Time

Initial Close Reading Lesson

Text: *On This Spot: An Expedition Back Through Time* **Author:** Susan Goodman

Purpose: R1: Close reading for deep understanding of the text

Before Reading

Clues Based on Cover Illustration

- Notice that there are tall buildings, dinosaurs, Native Americans, people dressed in old-fashioned clothes

Clues Based on Title, Author

- Notice important words: *spot, expedition, time*

Probable Text Type (Literary or Informational); Possible Genre

- Hard to tell—could be either literary or informational. Need to wait to read to find out

Vocabulary That May Need Pre-Teaching for ELLs or Low Language Students

- New York City, back through time, on this spot, Broadway, mammoth, glaciers, volcano, mountain

---

During Reading

Questions Students Should Ask Themselves for Each Chunk of Text

- What is the author telling me?
- Any hard or important words?
- What does the author want me to understand?
- How does the author play with language to add to meaning?

Follow-Up Text-Dependent Questions for the Teacher to Ask About Each Chunk of Text

Pages 1–2

- What do you suppose this picture shows—New York City (NYC) now or long ago? Why? (now—tall buildings)
- Why do you suppose the author began the book with an illustration such as this? (most of us can relate to a picture of a big city, even if we haven't been to New York City)

Pages 3–4

- What are some of the sights and sounds that characterize NYC today? (many examples such as subway, Broadway, Fifth Avenue, lots of cars and trucks, 8 million people)

- What thinking strategy does the author want you to use when she tells you about the way 8 milliion people would look? (visualize)

Pages 5–6

- 175 years ago would be about the year _____ (1840)

- Are you already seeing how the author organized this book? (different times in history)

- What might the next page show? (farther back in time)

- How is NYC 175 years ago different from today? (horse-drawn carriages, cobblestone streets, oil lanterns, etc.)

- How many people now—and how far would they stretch? (160,000 people would stretch to Connecticut)

Pages 7–8

- 350 years ago would be about the year _____ (1665)

- What differences do you see here? (city is called *New Amsterdam*, windmills, a "rattle watch" kept the city safe, many different languages)

- How many people now—and how far would they stretch (1,500 people; they'd stretch to the Statue of Liberty)

- What do you predict NYC was like before this? (might be able to predict Native Americans)

Pages 9–10

- 400 years ago would be about the year _____ (1610)

- Now what did NYC look like? (forest, large trees, elk, bears, blackberries, cougars)

- What kinds of things did people do in NYC? (Lenapes tribe hunted for deer and turkeys; they lived in campsites; they followed a trail that became Broadway.)

- What might have come before this? (accept any reasonable prediction)

Pages 11–12

- Now how many years ago? (15,000)

- If our years are now in the 2000s, how could it be 15,000 years ago? (BC)

- Now what was this spot like? (no forest, very cold—most plants couldn't grow)

- Why did some animals change in appearance? (to blend in with this cold land that no longer had any plants)

- What other kind of animal existed then that doesn't exist today? (woolly mammoth)

- What might have come before this? (accept any reasonable predictions)

Pages 13–14

- Now how many years ago? (20,000)

- What was this time in history called? (The Ice Age)

- What covered the Earth? (glaciers)

- What do you *not* see? Why not? (Do not see animals—much too cold for even very well protected animals)
- What might have come before this? (accept any reasonable predictions)

Pages 15–16

- Now we've gone back in time _____ (190 million years)
- Hot weather: NYC was like a tropical rain forest
- Could animals exist here? (yes—provide examples stated on page)
- Do you think there was plant and animal life before this? Explain. (accept reasonable hypotheses)

Pages 17–18

- Now we've gone back in time _____ (220 million years)
- What surprising detail does the author tell us about here? (there were lots of volcanoes)
- When the boiling lava cooled, what was formed? (rivers)

Pages 19–20

- Now we've gone back in time _____ (300 million years)
- What surprising detail does the author tell us about here? (there was a mountain on this spot taller than any mountain that is now in America)
- What do you *not* see in this picture? Why not? (no animals, probably too cold)

Pages 21–22

- Now we've gone back in time _____ (370 million years)
- What are you surprised to learn here? (some of the same animals we have today existed 370 million years ago)

Pages 23–24

- Now we've gone back in time _____ (540 million years)
- Now there was only _____ (rock)
- What important difference was there between this spot and the Moon? Why was this important? (this spot had algae, which is a form of *life*)

Pages 25–30

Ask these questions *before* reading these pages:

- What was the author's purpose in writing this book? (Students should suggest that the author wanted to show how things change over time)
- Just as *places* change, what else changes? (people's lives)

After reading these pages:

- What are some ways your home and the way you live your life may change in the future? (accept all reasonable suggestions)

Important Words to Talk About the Text

- New York, spot, thousand, million, change, plants, animals

Theme, Lesson, or Message (if Appropriate)

- Things change over time—this includes the place we call "home"

Summary or Gist Statement

- A main idea/detail summary would probably work best. Something like, New York has changed over time. Now it is a busy city. Hundreds of years ago, there were fewer people and a different way of life. Thousands and millions of years ago, dinosaurs roamed this spot, and at one time, there was only rock

Review of Text Type (Literary/Information) and Genre

- Did this book tell a story or give us information? (information)

- What made this book interesting? (help students see that the way the author *organized* and *presented* the information made all the difference—as a *sequential* text)

Collaborative Oral Task

- Students work in pairs or small groups to identify the main idea of this book along with a few supporting details. They can share their summary aloud. (See above under *Summary* for a suggested response.)

Follow-Up Lessons: Digging Deeper Through Rereading

Follow-up lessons can be taught in a different order.

Day	Focus Standard	Content for Whole-Class Lessons and Guided Student Practice
2	Close reading follow-up discussion including details from the text SL1; R2	Discuss briefly: important words from the text and the genre. Then, ask students to work in pairs or small groups to identify the main idea of this book along with a few supporting details. See the *Collaborative Oral Task* above.
3	Story elements: Sequence—and how things fit together R3	With a partner or small group, choose one of these time periods. List five things that New Yorkers today would have been astonished to see: at that time on this spot. Why would they have been so astonished based on what New York is like today?
4	Nontraditional: Text forms; Text-to-text connections R7; R9	Examine a current photograph of New York City alongside one taken long ago. Compare the photos: What has changed? What has remained the same? Lots of photographs of New York City then and now can be retrieved from https://ephemeralnewyork.wordpress.com/tag/new-york-then-and-now/
5	Explanatory writing W2	Although 175 years ago doesn't seem that long ago when you think about how long this "spot" has existed, there have still been many changes between 175 years ago and now. Compare New York today to New York 175 years ago. Use a Venn diagram to show what is the same and what is different. Then write about these similarities and differences in a paragraph.

Learning Pathway

How to Study a Current Issue

What's the Big Deal About Clean Water?

Unit Focus: Clean Water

© Stockbyte/Thinkstock Photos

Let's begin the unit! This is one of eight units in this book that delivers just the "goods"—the questions, prompts, assessment tasks, and student reproducibles you'll need to implement robust close reading instruction within an inquiry unit. Just about all you need to do a few weeks in advance of starting is to look at the anchor texts on pages 269 to 271 and order those books. From there, the materials provided are all explained clearly in terms of when and how to use them. If you need clarification, look back at the ten steps that begin on page 15.

Introduction to the Unit

The Rationale

I hope all of the units in this book help students to develop not just as closer readers but also as analytical readers who use their knowledge in thoughtful, responsible ways to make their planet a better place. Nowhere will that "take action" step be more important than it is in this unit that explores the need for clean water in so many corners of our world. My most serious complaint about the Common Core is that these standards do not go far enough in asserting the importance of actually *using* the power of reading to make a positive difference in society. So as teachers, we will need to embrace the need for this action ourselves and do what we can to turn *thinking* into *doing* in the classroom based on the complex texts we read with our students.

An entire close reading curriculum could easily be written around any number of current issues: state, national, and international. There's plenty of material from which to choose: the environment, education, safety, sports, and so many more. I decided to focus here on the critical need for clean water because it is a problem that directly affects millions of children. Our intermediate grade students will certainly be able to relate as they look into the eyes of kids just about their age who struggle to have this very basic need met. And while this public health issue impacts people in some parts of our own country, it's particularly dire in developing countries around the world.

With the importance of clean water as the focus of the unit, let's think about the ultimate goal of any unit teaching: helping students learn how to learn. I call it the learning pathway. With this unit, the pathway is How to Study a Current Issue. Use this study about the need for clean water as a model for studying other present-day issues and problems. During your introductory lesson, you'll share with students the talking points in the following chart, Learning Pathway: How to Study a Current Issue.

The Inquiry Question and Discussion Points

Through this unit, students will answer the question: **What's the big deal about clean water?** While most students we teach probably don't face a water crisis themselves, the facts and figures and personal stories about the dangers associated with dirty water or not enough water are so riveting that there will be plenty of student buy-in right from the start. In fact, you might get too *much* emotional response. We want to give kids an honest view of problems and issues and develop a healthy awareness without scaring them (that they're next in line for this particular problem) or weighing them down with too much guilt (how irresponsible of you not to do something about this problem!). Let's instead try to raise awareness to an appropriate level for our population of students. Get your unit off to a positive start with the discussion points in the Unit Preview Questions and Discussion Points for Studying a Current Issue: Clean Water.

Learning Pathway
How to Study a Current Issue

Share these prompts with students.

- *In order to study a current issue, you need to know what the basic issue is: Can you explain the issue you will explore here?*

- *In order to recognize the importance of a current issue it is often helpful to have a little background on it from the television news, the newspaper, or some other source: Have you heard about this issue before? Where? What have you heard?*

- *To really understand a current issue you need to get a lot of trustworthy information on the topic: Where could you learn more about this issue? What makes your sources trustworthy?*

- *Many current issues are controversial, which means people have different points of view about what is causing the problem and how to solve it: Is this issue controversial? What are the different points of view? Who do the spokespeople seem to be?*

- *After researching the issue, you should know lots of specific points and details about it—and where you got this information: What are the most important details related to this issue, and where did you get each piece of information?*

- *After researching the issue, you should know lots of words about this topic, so you can talk about it clearly: What words do you need to understand to talk about this topic in a smart way?*

ISSUE

- *After researching the issue, you should see clearly who it affects and how these people are affected: Who is affected by this issue? How are they affected?*

- *After researching the current issue, you should be ready to take a stand. That means "decide what you think about the issue" and explain why: Where do you stand on this issue? Why?*

- *It's often not enough to just understand a current issue; there needs to be a possible solution: What would be a way (or ways) to solve this particular issue?*

- *The best problem solvers often take action themselves to help to solve the issue: Is there anything you could do personally that would aid in resolving this issue?*

- *A good researcher understands the implications of an issue: If the problem has been around for a long time, why hasn't it been solved yet? Who is affected the most? Has anyone benefited from the problem? What might happen if this problem does not get solved?*

- *Where could you search to learn more about this issue? Are there people you could interview? Are there magazines or journals that focus on this issue? Are there organizations that focus on clean water? Do these organizations have websites that you could visit?*

Unit Preview Questions and Discussion Points

for Studying a Current Issue: Clean Water

- *Define what you mean by a current issue.*

- *Discuss what it means to study a current issue, referencing the questions for How to Study a Current Issue. Customize these points and questions according to the developmental level of your students. Chart the questions you will try to address through the unit.*

- *Ask students to provide some examples of current issues that have been in the news recently. (You could chart these according to issues that are local, state, national, or international—clarifying the meaning of these terms.)*

- *Introduce the issue you will study in this unit: The need for clean water.*

- *Introduce the inquiry question: What's the big deal about clean water? (Students may have some initial responses to this question—which is fine. But don't get too far into this until they've acquired textual evidence.)*

- *Introduce the four books selected for close reading. Show the cover and perhaps an illustration inside to pique students' interest. Do not explain the full story.*

Next, because we want to know from the outset where we ultimately want to take students, I list questions under Questions for End-of-Unit Discussion About a Current Issue (Clean Water) Integrating All Texts. These are questions you might pose at the end of this unit. That is, with any unit teaching, after completing all of the anchor books, we need to circle back to the inquiry question itself, to consider the books together. The questions help students synthesize their thinking across texts and wrap up the study in a thoughtful way.

Questions for End-of-Unit Discussion About a Current Issue (Clean Water) Integrating All Texts

- After reading the four anchor texts in this unit and the nonfiction article, do you now feel you can answer the inquiry question: *What's the big deal about clean water?* Make a list of at least five reasons why clean water is a "big deal."

- Which questions for How to Study a Current Issue can you answer after reading these books?

- Which text that we read was the most convincing to you? Why? What did the author do that made the information so convincing?

- What *specific* problems related to clean water need to be solved?

- Is the issue of clean water controversial in any way? Explain.

- What words would be the most important for talking about the issue of clean water?

- What are the most surprising or alarming statistics about the lack of clean water in the world?

- What do you see as possible solutions to this issue of clean water? What information that you read led you to these solutions?

- What is your position about the importance of clean water—and what should be done to solve this problem?

- Is there anything you could do personally to help to solve this need for clean water?

- How will studying *this* issue (of clean water) help you the next time you study a current issue? What do you need to consider when studying a current issue?

The Focus Standard

As a focus standard, not many units in this book will lend themselves to CCRA R8: "Delineate and evaluate the argument and specific claims in a text, including the validity of the reasoning as well as the relevance and sufficiency of the evidence"(http://www.corestandards.org/ELA-Literacy/CCRA/R/, Integration of Knowledge and Ideas section, para. 2). This unit, however, is well suited to this standard, as it is inherently controversial. In fact any current issue, almost universally, will provide some controversy that requires critical evaluation because the matter has not yet been resolved. Issues like water scarcity, climate change, poverty, and racial equality are not only complex but often connected to other intractable issues as well, so opposing viewpoints abound, providing fertile soil for close reading and debate.

This unit comprises solely informational texts, the only text type specified by the Common Core for the application of this standard. You will find a follow-up close reading lesson for Standard 8 each week with one of the anchor texts. In my view, this is the most difficult standard for young children to handle because it is so abstract, and thinking critically about an issue often demands lots of background on the subject. Remember that at the elementary level, this standard mostly asks students to decide if an author has supplied sufficient evidence to justify a claim. Keep that in mind as you teach your text-based lessons related to Standard 8.

The Anchor Texts

The first text listed below is a personal essay intended to be read by the students themselves and discussed during a unit kickoff lesson (discussion questions are provided on page 277). The remaining four texts are picture books, one of which will be read closely and studied during each week of the unit.

Water, Water Everywhere, but Not a Drop to (Safely) Drink, a personal essay by Stephanie Young (provided on page 276)

I was stewing over what to include in this unit for a nonfiction article when I remembered that a good friend of mine (actually my college roommate from several decades past) had gone to Kenya with an organization, Living Waters for the World, which installs water purification systems to communities in need of clean water. Steph happily agreed to write a short piece for me. And even better, she takes great pictures. This article, intended to be read by the students themselves, contains several details that they will surely remember for a long time, details that the anchor texts will build upon throughout the remainder of this unit.

A River Ran Wild by Lynne Cherry

This is a wonderfully engaging story, factually based on the pollution and then cleansing of the Nashua River, a tributary of the Merrimack River in New Hampshire and Massachusetts. For good measure, there's a little fantasy added, too. A Native American spirit appears to inspire people who live along the river to reconsider the damage done to this once sparkling body of water and clean it up. Complexities include the contradictory ideas of what constitutes "progress" by the Native Americans and later settlers and the detailed margin illustrations that provide many cultural references. Lexile: 670; Grade level equivalent: 5.5.

A Life Like Mine, a DK/Unicef Publication

You may be a little perplexed as to why I'm suggesting this book—for which we will read only a small portion as part of this unit. My hope is that once you have this book in your classroom, you will find many opportunities to use it beyond the boundaries of these close reading lessons and units. This book addresses four "rights of childhood": survival, development, protection, and participation, with many subtopics under each heading. It may do more with its stunning photographs, maps, charts, and personal narratives to build global awareness among the kids in your class than nearly any other book that's on the market today. Tell your principal I said that he or she should buy you a copy. Complexities include the large quantity of information included and the widely diverse cultures represented, many of which will be unfamiliar to students. No Lexile or grade level equivalent is available.

One Well: The Story of Water on Earth by Rochelle Strauss

This book is part of the Citizen Kid series, and it builds awareness of the need for clean water based on the concept that ultimately we all drink from one global well. The book is divided into various subtopics. Not all of them have been incorporated into this week's close reading lesson because it would be more information than students could reasonably absorb at one time. Do consider returning to this book another time, however, to catch up on sections you didn't get to study during the first round. Complexities include quite dense information with fewer, but still engaging, illustrations. Lexile: 960; Grade level equivalent: 5.8.

The Boy Who Harnessed the Wind
by William Kamkwamba and Bryan Mealer

This is the true story of William, a Malawi boy whose perseverance, creativity, and resourcefulness led to his design of a functioning windmill (built out of broken bicycle parts, rusted bottle caps, and the like) that brought power to his small village in Africa and, in turn, irrigated the drought-ravaged crops. William is now a young man and a graduate of Dartmouth College. Students can hear him tell his own story in a YouTube video referenced in one of the follow-up lessons for this book. The story includes some words written in the Malawi language, which may have inflated the Lexile. Other complexities include the book's multiple themes and lack of background knowledge about people's struggles in a rural African village. Lexile: 910; Grade level equivalent: 6.3.

Other Texts Useful to a Study of the Importance of Clean Water

To extend this study or to use texts other than those identified above, you might want to consider the following titles. These books expand the study of water to include information about the water cycle and a poetic look at various bodies of water. This unit could easily integrate science along with a current issue.

- *Water Dance* by Thomas Locker
- *A Drop Around the World* by Barbara McKinney
- *A Drop of Water: A Book of Science and Wonder* by Walter Wick
- *The Snowflake: A Water Cycle Story* by Neil Waldman
- *Did a Dinosaur Drink This Water* by Robert Wells

The Unit's Two Assessments

Featured Reading Standard R8: Critiquing text

Featured Writing Format: Opinion writing

See the Unit Curriculum Map for Close Reading for where these assessments might fit into your study of a current issue. Also, for more information about the rationale behind these two assessments and how they differ, as well as guidance for using the provided rubrics, refer to Step 9 on page 43 and Step 10 on page 50. Also, for evaluating students' performance, see page 45 for the Rubric for Content-Based Assessment (Task 1) and Standards-Based Assessment (Task 2). Turn to page 293, The End of the Story: Reflecting on Student Work, for some sample student work and commentary.

Task 1: Content Assessment

In this unit, we have read several texts about the importance of clean water and the difficulties people face when their water is not clean. On a separate piece of paper, write a letter to the editor in which you address the following:

- In your opinion, what are the three worst problems related to not having enough clean water? Describe each problem giving specific examples from at least two of the texts that we read. What makes these problems so bad?

- Identify at least one solution that you feel would help to solve the problem of unsafe water: How would this solution make a difference?

- Identify at least one point in this article that you would need to know more about to understand it more thoroughly. What else do you need to know?

Task 2: Learning Pathway and Standard Assessment

Read this article: *Ryan's Well*: http://www.readworks.org/passages/ryans-well

Watch the video clip about struggling to get clean water in Ethiopia: http://www.christineieronimo.com/ (When you get to this website, click the tab for Book Trailer. Click Short Film)

On a separate piece of paper, please address the following:

- Name three new insights you gained from this article and video about the struggle for clean water. Explain each of these points in a sentence or two.

- Choose *one* of these struggles that you consider very serious. Identify at least one solution that you feel would help to solve this problem: How would this solution make a difference?

- Identify at least one point in this article or video that you would need to know more about to understand it more thoroughly. What else do you need to know?

Unit Curriculum Map for Close Reading

What's the Big Deal About Clean Water?

TEXT	MONDAY	TUESDAY	WEDNESDAY	THURSDAY	FRIDAY
				Unit Preview	Kickoff Lesson
				See Unit Preview Questions and Discussion Points	Read and discuss the article *Water, Water Everywhere, but Not a Drop to (Safely) Drink.* Discussion questions are provided at the end of this document
A River Ran Wild by Lynne Cherry	Objective: R1 Close Reading	Objective: SL1; R2 Close Reading Follow-Up	Objective: R8; R9 Critiquing Text; Text-to-Text Connections	Objective: R7 Nontraditional: Formats	Objective: W1 Opinion Writing
	Read closely to answer text-dependent questions	Complete the After Reading tasks including a collaborative task related to summarizing	Students identify unanswered questions about this river; read the Author's Note at the beginning to clarify meaning	View and discuss video about river pollution today	Write an editorial about the problems related to river pollution. Use evidence from all texts this week
A Life Like Mine DK/Unicef Publication	Objective: R1 Close Reading	Objective: SL1; R3 Close Reading Follow-Up	Objective: R8; R9 Critiquing Text; Text-to-Text Connections	Objective: W3 Narrative Writing	Objective: R1 Close Reading
	Read closely to answer text-dependent questions	Complete the After Reading tasks including a collaborative task related to finding details to support a main idea	Students identify unanswered questions about clean water. Watch a video clip to clarify meaning	Write a story about a child from a country identified in this section of the book as he or she goes in search of water	To make greater use of this wonderful book, choose another segment to read closely

TEXT	MONDAY	TUESDAY	WEDNESDAY	THURSDAY	FRIDAY
One Well: The Story of Water on Earth by Rochelle Strauss	Objective: R1 Close Reading	Objective: SL1; R2 Close Reading Follow-Up	Objective: R3 Story Elements: Elaborate on the Facts	Objective: R7; R8 Nontraditional: Examine Text Format; Critiquing Text	Objective: W2 Explanatory Writing
	Read closely to answer text-dependent questions	Complete the After Reading tasks including a collaborative task to summarize the information	Choose one interesting fact. Explain its importance, and illustrate	Watch a video on getting water from a well. What do you need to understand more clearly?	Write a letter to the editor explaining why clean water is so important to the world
The Boy Who Harnessed the Wind by William Kamkwamba and Bryan Mealer	Objective: R1 Close Reading	Objective: SL1; R8 Close Reading Follow-Up	Objective: R3 Story Elements: Character Traits	Objective: R7 Nontraditional: Text Formats	Objective: W1 Opinion Writing
	Read closely to answer text-dependent questions	Complete the After Reading tasks including a collaborative task focusing on critiquing the text	Reread the text to identify examples of character traits that led to William's success	Watch and respond to a video clip of someone interviewing William about his windmill	Was William a hero? Why or why not?
	Culminating Discussion	Content Assessment	Standards-Based Assessment		
	Respond orally to text-to-text connections for studying this topic. (See Questions for End-of-Unit Discussion Integrating All Texts)	Students complete the content-assessment task integrating all texts in this study	Students complete the standards-based assessment task using cold reads		

ISSUE

WATER, WATER EVERYWHERE, BUT NOT A DROP TO (SAFELY) DRINK

by Stephanie Young

Photo Courtesy of Stephanie Young

Every morning these two sisters walk forty five minutes to this beautiful mountain stream for their daily supply of water. This morning they are also doing their laundry. But note . . . the woman washing the clothes is downstream from the one collecting the drinking water. She doesn't want her water to taste sudsy! What she can't see, though, is another woman doing HER laundry . . . or the team of oxen who have just gone to the bathroom further upstream! The water may look clear and clean, but it's probably full of all kinds of bacteria and germs that might make them sick.

Cholera and typhoid fever are just a couple of the diseases that are caused by contaminated water. Babies, children, and the elderly are the ones who are most likely to get sick. Many of them will die.

There are a lot of people trying to change this. I was part of a team that went to Katito, a village in western Kenya, to help the community build a simple water purification system. Using swimming pool filters and PVC pipe, we were able to take the existing unclean water, filter it, and make it pure. For the families in the village this was a miracle.

Sadly, the system can't provide an unlimited supply of good, clean, pure water. If you have taken a shower, brushed your teeth, flushed the toilet, and washed your breakfast dishes this morning, you have already used more clean water than these children will have for a whole week. So, through songs and games, we taught them that the CLEAN water is for drinking, for brushing teeth, for cooking, and for caring for babies. The DIRTY (unfiltered) water is used for anything that doesn't go directly into your mouth. Watering the garden, washing the dishes, doing laundry, taking a bath, scrubbing the floors, and giving the farm animals a drink are all good uses for the unfiltered water.

Source: Article and photo by Stephanie Young.

Think about the questions below as you reflect on the essay and begin this unit on the importance of clean water.

- What details in this article really stand out to you? Why?

- What do you think the author's purpose was in writing this article? What did she want you to think about?

- In what ways are the lives of people in Kenya more difficult because they don't have enough clean water?

- In what ways are the lives of people in Kenya unsafe because they don't have enough clean water?

- How does the photograph here give you a greater appreciation for why the people of Kenya need a better supply of clean water?

- This author went to Kenya with an organization called Living Waters for the World. Check out their website or the website of another organization that tries to improve water quality in communities around the world. What did you learn about their efforts?

Close Reading Lessons for A River Ran Wild

Initial Close Reading Lesson

Text: *A River Ran Wild*   **Author:** Lynne Cherry

Purpose: R1: Close reading for deep understanding of the text

Before Reading

Clues Based on Cover Illustration

- Notice the Native Americans and the animals in a beautiful natural world
- Notice the border designs: combination of Native American pictures and pictures of inventions that led to progress

Clues Based on Title, Author

- Notice the important words: river, wild

Probable Text Type (Literary or Informational); Possible Genre

- This looks like a story, though you can't tell yet whether it is fiction or nonfiction

Vocabulary That May Need Pre-Teaching for ELLs or Low Language Students

- Native Americans, progress, river, pollution

During Reading

Questions Students Should Ask Themselves for Each Chunk of Text

- What is the author telling me?
- Any hard or important words?
- What does the author want me to understand?
- How does the author play with language to add to meaning?

Follow-Up Text-Dependent Questions for the Teacher to Ask About Each Chunk of Text

Pages 1–2: Maps

- Examine these pages to learn about where different Native American tribes lived, and especially the location of the Nashua River.
- Read and discuss items included in timeline as appropriate for your class.
- For now, omit the Author's Note on the preceding page; this would be great to use after reading the story for a text-to-text connection.

Pages 3–4

- How do the words on this page connect to the title? What does the author mean by these words? ("A River Ran Wild"—animals made their home in the river valley)

- What strategy does the author want you to use here? (visualizing)

- What words (other than animal names) help you picture this scene? (*towering* forests, *peaceful* valley, *clear* waters)

Pages 5–6

- What is the main idea on this page? (When the Native Americans arrived, the river was clean and beautiful)

- How did the Native Americans use the river? (to quench their thirst)

- How does the illustration add to the main idea here? (shows the beauty of the river)

- How do the margin designs support the main idea? (examples of the many kinds of animals that lived in this area long ago)

Pages 7–8

- What stayed the same and what changed as the Native Americans built their village? (Their respect for the land and nature *didn't* change; they planted crops and built houses.)

- What do you think is the *most important* detail on this page? (They killed only what they needed to survive, nothing more.)

- What does it mean: "The Nashua people saw a rhythm in their lives and in the seasons"? (They lived in harmony with nature.)

- How does the illustration add to your understanding of this way of life? (accept all reasonable responses)

- How do the margin designs help you to understand this culture? (shows what they made)

Pages 9–10

- How does the information on this page fit with what we learned before (previously)? (Now things have changed with the coming of the "pale-skinned traders.")

- Why did the Native Americans think the trader's goods were "treasures" and "like magic"? (These wares seemed like progress; they made their world more modern and fancy.)

- How does the illustration on this page contrast with the margin designs? (illustration shows the natural world; margin designs show the new material inventions that the traders brought)

- Based on the margin designs, what were some of the inventions brought by the settlers? (glass beads, teakettles, pots, scissors, etc.)

Pages 11–12

- What were the signs of "progress" brought by the settlers? (cleared land, hunted to make money, built sawmills and dams, cut down forests to make lumber)

- How did the settlers' point of view about the land differ from the Native Americans' point of view? (Settlers wanted to use the land to help them make money; they thought the forests were full of danger; Native Americans wanted to live in harmony with nature.)

- What words show the settlers' point of view? (*danger, conquer, killing; goods and money*)

- What is the author trying to show us about "progress"? (Making things more modern doesn't always improve our life.)

- How do the illustrations and margin designs support the main idea on this page? (Nature is now being replaced with material things.)

Pages 13–14

- Explain the meaning of *disrupt*. (the old ways were changed)

- In your own words, explain how these American Indians' ways were "disrupted." (American Indians couldn't trespass on the settlers' lands: no more hunting, no more fishing rights)

- What do you think the author thinks about this "progress"? What words show this? (didn't approve of this kind of progress; Important words: trespass, disappeared, vanished, claimed, disrupted, drove from the land)

- What big advantage did the settlers have in fighting the American Indians? (they had guns)

- Why do you think the author includes the last paragraph on this page? (shows that despite the conflicts at this time, the water was still clean)

Pages 15–16

- Just looking at the illustration, how does this page connect to the previous page? (now the water doesn't look clean anymore)

- What years is the author talking about here: "At the start of the new century"? (early 1900s)

- What is an "industrial revolution"? (a time when industries and factories grew in number)

- In some ways, what was happening here was "progress," and in other ways, it wasn't "progress." Explain. (Some of these inventions made people's lives easier and better—like a phonograph and a bicycle, but the waste was dumped into the river and polluted it.)

Pages 17–18

- What was one of the unfortunate outcomes of the dirty river? (fish and wildlife died from the pollution)

- Look at the illustration: What are some of the contrasts you see here? (lots of green land, but a big factory by the river and a river that does not look clean)

Pages 19–20

- What caused most of the pollution in the Nashua River? (making paper)

- What details show the problems caused by paper manufacturing? (pulp clogged the river, and it ran more slowly; bad stench; no fish lived there; no birds came around; couldn't see the pebbles on the river bottom)

Pages 21–22

- In your own words, explain this legend. (A Native American Indian descendant dreamed about the river and cried when he saw the dirty water. His tears cleansed the river and made it clean.)

- What is the point of this legend? (We can clean up this river if we try.)

- Why do you think the author added this fantasy to a story that is informational? (shows the transition between the polluting of the river and cleaning up the river; *someone* has to get a project like this started)

Pages 23–24

- What was Marion's "vision"? (a clean river once again where you could see the pebbles on the bottom)

- How did Marion and others support this cause? (signed petitions and sent letters, protested to politicians, convinced paper mills to build a waste processing plant, persuaded factories to stop dumping, passed new laws)

- What do you think the author is trying to show with these examples? (regular people can make a difference if they fight for a cause in a positive way)

Pages 25–26

- What details show that Marion's efforts were successful? (waters now flow freely, paper no longer clogs river, no more chemicals, waters are fragrant)

- Compare the illustration with the margin designs here: What are the similarities? (Both past and present, people are enjoying the opportunity to spend time on the river—in canoes or kayaks.)

Pages 27–28

- What words from earlier in the book are repeated here? (*river runs wild, pebbles shine up through clear water*)

- Why do you think the author has chosen to end the story in a similar way to the beginning? (In some ways, we've gone back to the "beginning" as now the river has been returned to nature.)

After Reading (Complete These Tasks on Day 2 of the Lesson Sequence)

Important Words to Talk About the Text

- Nashua River, Native Americans, settlers, pollution, industry, progress, clean, pebbles

Theme, Lesson, or Message (if Appropriate)

- Something like, Progress is not an easy thing to define: What is *progress* in some ways may be destructive in other ways

Summary or Gist Statement

- This story would work well for a sequential summary. Students should identify four or five key historic points in the river's past and present

Review of Text Type (Literary/Information) and Genre

- This is a good example of literary nonfiction. Through a story form, it explains the history of the Nashua River. There is some fantasy (the Native American Indian's dream)

Collaborative Oral Task

- Ask students to create a list of key moments in the history of the Nashua River. Explain how one moment led to the next

ISSUE

Follow-Up Lessons: Digging Deeper Through Rereading

Follow-up lessons can be taught in a different order.

Day	Focus Standard	Content for Whole-Class Lessons and Guided Student Practice
2	Close reading follow-up discussion including an emphasis on summarizing SL1; R2	As a class, discuss and list the important words in this story. Review the genre (narrative nonfiction) and genre characteristics. Discuss the themes. Ask students to work in pairs or small groups to list four or five key moments in the history of the Nashua River. They should also be able to explain how one moment led to the next. See *Collaborative Oral Task* (page 281).
3	Critiquing text; Text-to-text connections R8; R9	Discuss with students what the author could have explained more clearly to help them understand the pollution and purification of the Nashua River. What questions do they still have? Then, read and discuss the Author's Note at the beginning of this book. Identify details that add to the understanding of the story. How did this information help to clarify meaning?
4	Nontraditional: Video of river pollution today R7	Use this link about river pollution in Indonesia to help students develop a deeper understanding that river pollution continues today and that it has a serious impact. Discuss the impact and possible solutions. Visit https://www.youtube.com/watch?v=tvYXOW6dXSg
5	Opinion writing: Writing an editorial W1	Ask students to write an editorial in which they explain some of the serious problems created by river pollution. Who is affected by this? Why should people care? What can be done to solve this horrible problem? Use evidence from all sources this week to support your claim.

Close Reading Lessons for A Life Like Mine (excerpt)

Initial Close Reading Lesson

Text: *A Life Like Mine* (pages 10–17)   **Publisher:** DK/Unicef

Purpose: R1: Close reading for deep understanding of the text

Before Reading

> **Clues Based on Cover Illustration**
>
> • Notice that there are children from different countries
>
> **Clues Based on Title, Author**
>
> • Notice "Life *like mine*"—think about what the authors will help us to understand through this book
>
> **Probable Text Type (Literary or Informational); Possible Genre**
>
> • Informational (may need to look through a few pages to make this determination)
>
> **Vocabulary That May Need Pre-Teaching for ELLs or Low Language Students**
>
> • Survive, water, food, home health

During Reading

Questions Students Should Ask Themselves for Each Chunk of Text
• What is the author telling me?
• Any hard or important words?
• What does the author want me to understand?
• How does the author play with language to add to meaning?
Follow-Up Text-Dependent Questions for the Teacher to Ask About Each Chunk of Text
Pages 10–11
• What do you consider some of the most important details about "The Water of Life." (most precious possession, can survive only a few days without water, water is used in different ways, not everyone can get water easily)
• Why do you think the author included these illustrations? (they show the many ways that water is used)

Pages 12–13

- What interesting or surprising details does the author include on this page? (Without faucets you would need to get water from a lake, well, pump, etc.; about 97 percent of water on Earth is salty and can't be used; most fresh water can't be reached; only 1 percent of water is available; more than 70 percent of the Earth's surface is covered with water.)

- In your own words, explain each of the bullet points on page 13. (accept reasonable responses)

- Look at the bucket chart at the bottom of pages 12–13. Discuss each of these pieces of information. Also, think about other activities that require water and estimate the possible number of buckets of water they would represent on the chart.

Pages 14–15

- In your own words, explain what is difficult about obtaining water in Afghanistan, India, The Netherlands, and Jamaica.

- Which means of getting water do you think would be the most challenging? Explain.

Pages 16–17

- Locate Laos on a map. Where is it in relation to where we are in the United States?

- How is life better in Nou's village now that the water is safe? (less risk of illness)

After Reading (Complete These Tasks on Day 2 of the Lesson Sequence)

Important Words to Talk About the Text

- Well, survival, salt water, fresh water

Theme, Lesson, or Message (if Appropriate)

- Something like, Water is one of the most important things that people need to survive

Summary or Gist Statement

- Gist statement: People need water to survive. In many parts of the world, people do not have enough clean water

Review of Text Type (Literary/Information) and Genre

- This is an informational text with both factual information and personal stories about individual children

Collaborative Oral Task

- With a partner or small group, find five facts on these pages that support the gist statement (above)

Follow-Up Lessons: Digging Deeper Through Rereading

Follow-up lessons can be taught in a different order.

Day	Focus Standard	Content for Whole-Class Lessons and Guided Student Practice
2	Close reading follow-up discussion including an emphasis on summarizing SL1; R3	As a whole class, discuss the important words in the text, the story's theme, the gist, and the genre. Then, ask students to work with a partner or small group to find five details that support the gist statement. See *Collaborative Oral Task* (page 284).
3	Nontraditional: Text forms; Critiquing text; Text-to-text connections R7; R8; R9	Ask students what the author could have explained to explain this topic more clearly. What questions do they still have? Then, watch this video clip as a third grader explains nature's role in providing clean water: https://www.youtube .com/watch?v=Dw9p8jEB7m0 (2 min.). How does this clip help you to better understand the importance of clean water? Could you try a similar experiment yourself? What would you need to do?
4	Narrative Writing W3	Choose a country described on page 14 or 15. Write a story about a child from this country who is going to get water. Be sure to use information from the text to make your story authentic. What kind of adventure could this child have while going on this errand?
5	Close reading for deep understanding of the text R1	If you have time this week, do a close reading of another part of this book in the manner described for Day 1. This is such a wonderful resource; try to return to it often to raise students' awareness of issues that affect us all globally.

Close Reading Lessons for One Well: The Story of Water on Earth (excerpt)

Initial Close Reading Lesson

Text: *One Well: The Story of Water on Earth***   **Author:** Rochelle Strauss

Purpose: R1: Close reading for deep understanding of the text

**This book presents its content under several main headings. Since the focus of this unit is access to clean water, I have included parts of the book that feature issues related to that. Rather than engaging in the follow-up lessons specified at the end of this plan, you may want to closely read additional sections of the book not included in this lesson. Note that this book also provides additional "boxed" facts on several pages, which you may or may not want to include in your lesson depending on the needs and interests of your students. It may take more than one day to closely read the pages below indicated for this lesson. Or you may want to read additional pages closely that are not specified for this lesson. In that case, you will do fewer follow-up lessons.

Before Reading

> **Clues Based on Cover Illustration**
>
> - Notice there are lots of different bodies of water: ocean, river, pond, lake
>
> **Clues Based on Title, Author**
>
> - Notice the word *well*. (If students don't know the meaning of this word, you will need to explain as the author doesn't actually define it.)
>
> **Probable Text Type (Literary or Informational); Possible Genre**
>
> - Probably informational
>
> **Vocabulary That May Need Pre-Teaching for ELLs or Low Language Students**
>
> - Well, water, clean, body of water

During Reading

> **Questions Students Should Ask Themselves for Each Chunk of Text**
>
> - What is the author telling me?
>
> - Any hard or important words?
>
> - What does the author want me to understand?
>
> - How does the author play with language to add to meaning?

Follow-Up Text-Dependent Questions for the Teacher to Ask About Each Chunk of Text

Pages 4–5: One Well

- Why should we think of all the water on Earth as "one well"? (all water is really connected)
- In your own words, explain why having one well makes it important for all of us to treat water carefully. (accept all reasonable responses)
- Which fact(s) on page 5 would be especially important to remember? Explain. (accept all reasonable responses)

Pages 6–7: The Water in the Well

- Why do we call Earth a watery planet? (70 percent is water)
- What is ground water? (water beneath the Earth's surface—filling in cracks between rocks; water in soil)
- Where is most of the water on Earth? (oceans)
- Did any of the water facts on this page surprise you? (Students may indicate limited amount of fresh water.)

Page 19: Freshwater in the Well

- How does the author help us to understand how much fresh water is on Earth? (compares it to the water that would fill a large bathtub)
- How does the author help us to understand how much fresh water is available to us? (nine pop/soda cans from a full bathtub)
- Where is most of the fresh water, and why is this a problem? (most fresh water is frozen in ice caps—and so it is not available to us)

Pages 20–21: Access to the Well

- What does the author mean by the "distribution of water across the world"? (Based on the amount of rainfall, sometimes different places in the world have too much water or too little water.)
- What parts of the world would be likely to *not* have enough water? (desert areas)
- What detail on this page shows you that you are very lucky in the way you get drinking water? (Many people have to walk at least fifteen minutes to get to the nearest water supply.)
- Discuss the chart on page 21: Average Daily Water Use Per Person. What stands out? Explain this information in your own words. (Take the time to explain and discuss this chart.)

Pages 22–23: Demands on the Well

- Why is it so important that we find a balance between our demands for water and the amount of water available to us? (We use more water today than ever before; the world's population is continually growing, increasing the demand for water.)
- Why do you think we use more water today than we did one hundred years ago? (more industry, more uses for water)
- What will happen if we don't stop using so much water? (even more people will be without water)

Pages 24–25: Pollution in the Well

- How does water clean itself? (Plants and rocks help to filter water that is dirty.)
- What causes pollution to get into the water? (Sometimes, waste from industry and chemicals like pesticides and detergents are dumped into rivers and other bodies of water.)
- If water can clean itself, why does it become polluted? (Water can't clean itself fast enough for all of the pollutants dumped into it.)
- Why are wetlands so important? (They do a really good job of filtering water.)

- Explain what the author means by "Water has the power to change everything." Discuss each detail that follows in this paragraph. (with clean water, people's lives will be easier, healthier, and safer)

- What are some ways that we can all *conserve* water? (After students identify ways of conserving, read the next two pages in the book: *Becoming Well Aware*.)

After Reading (Complete These Tasks on Day 2 of the Lesson Sequence)

Important Words to Talk About the Text

- Well, conserve, conservation, water supply, fresh water, salt water

Theme, Lesson, or Message (if Appropriate)

- Something like: There is not enough fresh water on Earth to make sure that everyone has enough of it. We all need to do our part to conserve and bring fresh water to everyone in the world

Summary or Gist Statement

- Summarize each section individually rather than summarizing the book as a whole. The format will generally be main idea/details

Review of Text Type (Literary/Information) and Genre

- Informational—expository with headings, key words, facts, charts, and graphs

Collaborative Oral Task

- In pairs or small groups, ask students to summarize the information from *one* part of this book

Follow-Up Lessons: Digging Deeper Through Rereading

Follow-up lessons can be taught in a different order.

Day	Focus Standard	Content for Whole-Class Lessons and Guided Student Practice
2	Close reading follow-up discussion including an emphasis on summarizing SL1; R2	As a whole class or in small groups, identify the important words in the text and discuss the genre (expository). For a collaborative task, have students work in pairs or small groups to summarize the content of *one* section of the text. See *Collaborative Oral Task* above.
3	Story elements: Elaborate on the Facts R3	Ask students to work individually or in pairs to choose one interesting fact from this book; explain what it means and why it is so important. Then illustrate it. All facts could be combined into a class book of "One Well Facts."
4	Nontraditional: Getting Water From a Well; Critiquing text R7; R8	Watch the YouTube video clip: *Getting Water From the Well*: https://www.youtube.com/watch?v=5v7Q2pLJrUs. What challenges are involved in getting water from a well? How does this video help you to appreciate the ease with which you get water? What could this video explain more clearly?
5	Explanatory Writing W2	Ask students to do the following: Write a letter to the editor *explaining* the water situation in the world and why it is so important to conserve water. Be sure to use some of the interesting facts from the book to strengthen your letter.

Close Reading Lessons for *The Boy Who Harnessed the Wind*

Initial Close Reading Lesson

Text: *The Boy Who Harnessed the Wind*   **Authors:** William Kamkwamba and Bryan Mealer

Purpose: R1: Close reading for deep understanding of the text

Before Reading

Clues Based on Cover Illustration

- Notice the boy staring in a dreamy way; notice the windmill

Clues Based on Title, Author

- Notice the words *boy, harnessed, wind*; pay close attention to the story if you're not sure of the meaning of *harnessed*

Probable Text Type (Literary or Informational); Possible Genre

- This looks like a story though it is uncertain whether it is fictional or true

Vocabulary That May Need Pre-Teaching for ELLs or Low Language Students

- Wind, harnessed, determined, windmill

During Reading

Questions Students Should Ask Themselves for Each Chunk of Text

- What is the author telling me?
- Any hard or important words?
- What does the author want me to understand?
- How does the author play with language to add to meaning?

Follow-Up Text-Dependent Questions for the Teacher to Ask About Each Chunk of Text

Pages 1–2

- What do you already know from the author on this first page? (the setting is Malawi; it was a poor village without electricity; the main character is William)
- What do you *not* know? (where Malawi is located—I would show this location to students using a map or globe since the author doesn't really make this clear in the text)

- What do you think the author is going to talk about next, based on the transition at the end of this page? (what William dreamed about)

Pages 3–6

- How did the modern world connect to the world of his ancestors for William? (wondered how mechanical things worked, like radios and truck engines; wondered about the magic of witch planes and ghost dancers and magical creatures in the garden)
- What kind of kid does William seem to be? (creative thinker, interested in science)

Pages 7–8

- What problem does the author identify on this page? (no water—which caused plants not to grow and people to go hungry)
- Does the author paint a positive or negative picture of the sun here? (Negative) What words show this? (the sun rose *angry*; *scorched* the fields, turning maize into *dust*)
- How does the illustration on this page add to this image? (land looks dry, plants are dying, sun looks like a ball of fire)

Pages 9–10

- What further evidence does the author provide about the problems associated with too little rain? (only one meal per day—just a handful; no money; couldn't go to school)
- What does the author mean by "the monster in his belly and the lump in his throat"? (*monster* was hunger; *lump in his throat* was sadness)
- Why do you think William thought about the library as a solution to his problem? (books can provide many answers)

Pages 11–12

- Why did William think that the windmill he saw in the book was "the greatest picture of all"? (a windmill can produce electricity and pump water; it could bring light to his valley)
- What do you think William was dreaming about? (creating a windmill that could produce electricity)

Pages 13–14

- Why is the windmill described as "a weapon to fight hunger"? (having no water was like a war against survival—a windmill could give people a chance to survive)
- Based on the evidence so far in this story, do you think William, who is only a child, can succeed in building a windmill? Explain. (There is lots of evidence that William is interested in machines and understands them; he seems to be really motivated to solve this problem.)

Pages 15–16

- How did William go about solving this problem? (searched through trash for parts to build his windmill)
- Why do you think people responded so negatively? (They didn't have an understanding of engines like William did; they probably didn't think a young child could invent something useful like this.)

Pages 17–20

- Does this look like a good "science laboratory" to you? Explain. (No, he had to deal with squawking chickens and barking dogs and people who criticized him.)

- Why do you think William continued in the face of such poor conditions? (He was determined to solve this problem; some of his friends finally helped him.)
- How does the simile help you picture the windmill: "this strange machine that now leaned and wobbled like a clumsy giraffe"? (accept all reasonable responses)

Pages 21–24

- What words does the author use to create a positive image on this page? ("surged as bright as the sun")
- How has the author shaped print on pages 21–22 to add to your understanding of the windmill? (words are placed like the blades spinning around and around)

Pages 25–28

- Why did William think he had not completely succeeded yet? (He had created light, but he needed another windmill to provide water.)
- Why does the author call this "the strongest magic of all"? (although it was really a machine, not magic, it may have seemed like magic to the people of Malawi who didn't understand machines but were grateful that the land now had enough water to grow food)
- Do you think this story was true or made up? (accept reasonable responses)
- Now that we've finished the book, what do you think *harnessed the wind* means? (*made use of* the wind)

Pages 29–30 (read to provide background information and to clarify that this is a true story)

- How do you feel about William after reading these final two pages? Why? (accept reasonable responses—should mention respect for his perseverance, resourcefulness, commitment to his family and his community, etc.)

After Reading (Complete These Tasks on Day 2 of the Lesson Sequence)

Important Words to Talk About the Text

- William, wind, Malawi, famine, drought, starve, harness, determined, electric wind

Theme, Lesson, or Message (if Appropriate)

- Resourcefulness and perseverance can help you overcome many problems.

Summary or Gist Statement

- A problem/solution summary would work well for this: A young Malawi boy whose family was starving because of a severe drought figured out how to harness the wind by creating a windmill. His family could then have electricity for lights and a way to water their land to make plants grow

Review of Text Type (Literary/Information) and Genre

- Personal narrative—details from a boy's life describing where he lived and how he solved a problem by bringing electricity to his family's farm in Malawi

Collaborative Oral Task

- With a partner or small group, identify evidence for at least three characteristics of a personal narrative

Follow-Up Lessons: Digging Deeper Through Rereading

Follow-up lessons can be taught in a different order.

Day	Focus Standard	Content for Whole-Class Lessons and Guided Student Practice
2	Close reading follow-up discussion including an emphasis on genre characteristics SL1; R8	As a whole class or in small groups, identify the important words in the text, determine the story's theme, provide a brief summary, and identify the genre (personal narrative), reviewing characteristics of a personal narrative. For the *Collaborative Oral Task*, ask students what else the author could have done to help them understand how a windmill produces power.
3	Story elements: Character traits R3	Reread this story to identify character traits that accounted for William's success. Name these traits and locate a detail in the text to support each one.
4	Nontraditional: William's Story (video clip) R7	Access the TED talk from the site below to see William talk about his windmill project. Ask students how this video added to their appreciation for what William accomplished: http://www.ted.com/talks/william_kamkwamba_on_building_a_windmill
5	Opinion writing W1	In your opinion, was William Kamkwamba a hero? Explain your thinking using evidence from the text.

The End of the Story
Reflecting on Student Work

Of course, reflecting on student work is not really the end of the story since literacy instruction (or any instruction) is not linear and has no actual end point. Rather, it is a continuous cycle where, in this case, examining our students' responses to text leads us to a new beginning and a new question: What can we learn from the data about where we need to take them next?

Still, with the examination of student work, we will have come full circle from the planning of robust close reading lessons and units to carefully articulated instruction—and now to that critical point where children show us how well they have learned—and how well we have taught. There are dozens of areas we *could* monitor. The work samples that follow have been selected to represent areas that we especially want to monitor in light of standards-based teaching:

- Identifying important words

- Paraphrasing to demonstrate comprehension

- Summarizing informational text

- Understanding the connection between events

- Recognizing elements of a genre

- Connecting reading and writing through author's craft

- Supporting a generalization with evidence and insights

- Synthesizing multiple texts

These samples were collected from students in Grades 3 through 5 at several school sites throughout New England. Some of the lessons were taught by me, others by a longtime teacher friend, and still others by a pair of teachers I had known for exactly one day. For each sample, I provide a bit of the backstory to supply a context and then examine the student response according to the three criteria I identified on (pages 51–52) for reflecting on individual student performance:

- Successes

- On the verge of understanding

- Next instructional point

The final reflection examines trends for a class of students: What was observed overall from students who performed well and not so well on a particular assignment and where to go next with the instruction for each group.

From New Haven, Connecticut

Identifying important words

The Inside Scoop

I taught the lesson myself that led to this follow-up task. It took place at Clinton Avenue School in New Haven, Connecticut, where I have served as an outside literacy consultant for several years. I love working with this large urban district because over the last decade we've evolved a professional development model that I consider ideal. Here's why: I get to go back. With so much professional development (PD), you go to a school, do the workshop or classroom modeling, and then ride off into the sunset. But in this district, I serve four schools each year. I visit each one for two half days per month, and we work together on data-driven initiatives that the district and school view as critical to teachers' and students' needs. There are grade level seminars, demonstration lessons, and, most important of all, return visits to see teachers implement the strategies they've seen modeled. Then we all debrief: the literacy coach, the teacher, the principal, and I. I know some coaching models frown upon adding administrators to this mix. But in my view, we're a team, and all the players need to be at the table to reflect and take responsibility for moving forward.

On the day of this lesson, I was modeling in a fourth grade classroom while all the Grade 4 teachers observed. I taught a close reading lesson using the book *The Boy Who Harnessed the Wind* by William Kamkwamba and Bryan Mealer that was part of the *Current Issues* unit. I told students up front that this was a true story, which got just the reaction I was looking for: fascination that a kid no older than themselves used his ingenuity to build a windmill, changing the lives of people in his small African community. There was no shortage of enthusiasm for the follow-up task either, identifying important words to talk about the text. I proposed that they work in pairs, which they happily did. The sample here is from Christian and Kenya. Here's my take on what these students produced.

IMPORTANT WORDS IN THE TEXT

My group: Christian   Kenya

This word is important...	...because
Harnessed	They harnessed the wind to make electricity
Scorched	The crops died from the heat
Wind	Helped the windmill spin
Crazy, Misla	William was crazy for digging threw trash
Wind mill	The whole point of the story
William	The most important chracter
Crops	The food that died from the sun
Water	Helped grow the food

Successes

- They selected very appropriate words and easily justified their word choices with accurate, insightful details from the text.

- They remembered the Malawi word for "crazy" *(misla)*, which we discussed during the lesson.

- They saw that the "whole point of the story" was "windmill" and that you couldn't talk about this text without several of these other related words.

- They included the word *scorched*, which was not just a new, cool word, but also an important one to the meaning of the story.

On the Verge of Understanding

- There are no obvious weaknesses here. Some students had a little more difficulty distinguishing between the most important words and just *any* word that they remembered from the text.

Next Instructional Point

- These students and all students who succeeded with this task should now have the opportunity to use these words to summarize this story. This would show how well they could integrate key vocabulary and also their skills in summarizing text.

- Students that produced more of a random word list need support thinking about *how* to decide which words are the most essential. This is a great opportunity for a small group lesson with only the children who demonstrated this need. Make sure they know that the purpose of identifying these important words is to talk meaningfully about the text, not to show their understanding of obscure vocabulary. Model first how *you* determine the important words. Show them that you look for characters' names, places where key events took place, and words that recur over and over (such as words like *wind, windmill,* and *village* in this book). Then let them have a go. Do not be surprised if *many* students need support with this skill as this is not a way we have commonly approached the language of the text. But if we want students to summarize successfully, we will recognize that this is an essential first step in achieving that goal.

From Belfast, Maine

Paraphrasing to demonstrate comprehension

The Inside Scoop

I taught this lesson, too. Technically, I taught it in a school in Belfast, Captain Albert Stevens Elementary, though the teachers who participated in this professional development came from the whole district, Regional School Unit (RSU) 20. I've been working with this district for a few years now, and except for the long drive to get there, it's been great: dedicated, eager teachers; supportive administrators; and a top-notch literacy coordinator who is both an efficient manager and a wonderful example of an instructional leader. Over the years, we've worked on comprehension strategies, writing, and, now, close reading. I visit there a couple of times a year, including a trip in August for some summer PD. Yes, these teachers give up a day of their summer on the Maine coast for an unpaid day at school to continue to build their literacy instruction skills. (And did I mention the bountiful lobster that is available at day's end? My husband even comes along for this trip.)

This May when I visited, we organized half-day sessions for each grade, K–5. I met with teachers first to talk about the close reading lesson they would see. Then, I went into a classroom to teach the lesson accompanied by about a dozen adults—which kids always find sort of amusing (and which I've noticed also serves to reduce behavior problems to practically zero). During the last hour, we debriefed and prepared for our August work, creating close reading lessons together.

I taught this close reading lesson in a fourth grade [class] using the book *Looking at Lincoln* from the Abraham Lincoln unit. We then charted a few key lines, some of which were quotes from Lincoln himself, and students were asked to decide which one was most important to their understanding of Lincoln as a president. This student chose this line: *Lincoln wrote to a friend, "If slavery is not wrong, nothing is wrong."*

Grace Hall

WHICH QUOTE IS MOST IMPORTANT TO UNDERSTANDING LINCOLN? WHY?

1. He was born in a small log cabin in Kentucky on February 12, 1809. The family was poor. Abe was a dreamer. He did not like to do chores. He loved to read.

2. He lived in Springfield, Illinois. And got a reputation as a smart and honest man. They called him Honest Abe.

3. He was thinking about democracy. The Declaration of Independence and the Constitution created by the founders of this country. He was thinking about freedom and doing good for mankind.

4. Lincoln wrote to a friend, "If slavery is not wrong, nothing is wrong."

5. The Southern states (the Confederacy) wanted their own country where slavery was allowed. Lincoln said no. We must stay one country.

6. "...government of the people, by the people, and for te people shall not perish from the earth."

7. But a great man is never really gone.

8. "...With malice toward none, and charity for all."

I think the most important quote for understanding Lincoln is # __4__ because the quote "If slavery is not wrong, nothing is wrong" because this quote means that slavery is like a crime and if slavery isn't a crime then nothing is. This quote really shows you that Aberham Lincoln is very caring and believes in equal rights torwords everyone.

- She is able to provide the meaning of this line in her own words, showing comprehension.

- She compares slavery to a crime, which shows her understanding of the intensity of Lincoln's feelings.

- She infers that Lincoln is caring and mentions "equal rights," which came from our deep reading of the text.

On the Verge of Understanding

- She could have gone back to the text for evidence about Lincoln's care and compassion and examples of his emphasis on equal rights since there were numerous details that could have supported these generalizations.

Next Instructional Point

- This student, like many intermediate grade students, could benefit from continued work on providing supporting evidence. I see this as the number one challenge in the elementary grades. I believe that this student most likely *knew* the evidence or she wouldn't have been able to make the generalization. They assume that if the information is in *their* head, it must be in their teacher's head, too. So what's the point of writing it down? We all need to keep working on this. . . .

- When students are working with a duplicated page that they can annotate, I tell them they may not write anything down for which they have not underlined something in the text. And they must also include that evidence in their response. But of course that strategy won't work with a picture book. So another technique is to ask students to use the phrase "I know this because . . ." (or something similar) for every opinion, claim, or generalization they state in an answer. Here's a final bit of advice: Sometimes I hear teachers tell students that they "must provide two pieces of evidence." This is a slippery slope because there may be only a single strong detail. When kids feel compelled to get "something else" down on their paper, the additional detail may weaken the argument rather than strengthen it.

From Naugatuck, Connecticut

Recognizing elements of a genre

The Inside Scoop

I haven't done too much professional development at Salem School in Naugatuck, but I always find a way to fit them in if they call me because this school is teamwork in action. Both the principal and the literacy coach exude the kind of joy in working with children that I wish was present in every educator. In fact, every adult at this school is viewed as a partner in contributing to students' success. When I mentioned during a recent visit that I was looking for a few intermediate classrooms to try out some close reading lessons, I barely had the sentence out of my mouth when everyone around the table jumped into the fray, carving out the plan to make this happen. The feedback did not disappoint. I received this message from Gina, the literacy coach, after the third grade lessons had been completed:

> Please find attached the reflection for the Grade 3 Minty lesson that Brianne Forcucci and I co-taught. What a wonderful series of lessons. Not only did the students enjoy them, but Brianne and I loved teaching them! I mailed the permission slips and student samples to you a few days ago so they should be arriving any day. Of the samples we provided you, only one student didn't send back his permission slip. We know that the parent would most likely not have an issue with this but we promise to get this note signed right in the beginning of the year and send it off to you. (This young man often struggles with school but was highly engaged from the onset of lessons. We were so extremely proud of his efforts and quality of responses, both orally and written. When we told him we were going to share his work with you he beamed and worked even harder.)
>
> P.S. Thank you again for providing us with this amazing opportunity.

Source: E-mail from Gina Kotsaftis, 6/27/2014.

Just WOW! Who *wouldn't* want to work with a school that is so passionate about good teaching! Their reflection was (of course) thoughtful with observations about teaching and learning worthy of the consideration of any literacy educator. I'd like to include many of those work samples and teacher insights here but, with limited space, have selected only one. It's not one of the most successful tasks or "best" samples in that it shows more student needs than some others. But I believe as teachers that we can learn something important from it.

This task relates to the book *Minty: A Story of Young Harriet Tubman*, an anchor text in the *Slavery* unit. It's a "fictionalized biography," essentially historical fiction.

Students were asked to determine which incidents in the book they thought to be "real" and which ones could have been "fictionalized." Below is a sample from one third grader. And here is what Gina and her co-teacher acknowledged in their reflection:

> Students had a difficult time with this task. They understood the terms "probably true" and "fictitious" but were very unsure of their capability to identify those in the text. They kept asking for reassurance and wanted to know if they were right or wrong. We even questioned ourselves on those true and false details. We began as a whole group and discussed an event that could go on each side. Students talked with a partner. (Gina Kotsaftis, *Reflection on Minty Lessons*, July 2014)

Name: _Aniyah B._ Date: _6-17-14_

Text: _Minty_

Which events in the story were probably true and which may have been fictitious? Be able to explain why you placed each item in each column.

Details that were almost certainly true	Details that were probably fictitious
• minty doll	• Minty sticking her toung out
• getting wipped	• Minty spilling the cider
• preparing to run away	
• having a friend at the feilds	
• Minty becoming a feilds slave	

- The point of this exercise was to recognize that in historical fiction, the big ideas have to be accurate, but authors may invent details to make those events come alive for readers. This student saw that Minty (Harriet) must have prepared to run away. She was a field slave and most likely made friends with other slaves in the field. She recognized that Minty sticking out her tongue and spilling cider may have been invented by the author to illustrate the harsh treatment of slaves by slave masters and mistresses.

On the Verge of Understanding

- Unless there is research evidence to the contrary, I would probably put Minty's "doll incident" in the *Fictitious* column, too. It again may have been devised to illustrate the cruel treatment of slaves.

- This student (and others) according to this literacy coach (as well as the teachers themselves) are on the verge of understanding the characteristics of historical fiction—but are not quite there.

Next Instructional Point

- What this sample and commentary show is that both teachers and students need to tune in more thoroughly to genre characteristics. Although I realize historical fiction is a stretch for third graders, it would be worth investigating whether we would have had similar findings with tasks related to other genres. A next step here would be to explain more about the characteristics of historical fiction, model looking for these traits in grade-appropriate texts, and then letting students practice with a partner or on their own.

More From Naugatuck, Connecticut

Summarizing informational text

The Inside Scoop

I'll skip most of the scoop here since I talked about Salem School for the work sample above. This close reading lesson was taught in a fourth grade at this same school based on the book *Home Run*, part of the author study about the craft of Robert Burleigh. The task was for students to work collaboratively in pairs to extend their knowledge of the text by reading "baseball cards." These were not real baseball cards but factoids about Babe Ruth, the subject of the book, cleverly inserted to add more information to the story. I thought it was a perfect opportunity to work on nonfiction summarizing, which is very different from summarizing a problem/solution story. Two student work samples are provided to better illustrate differences in summary style.

Ella

> **SUMMARY OF *BABE ON BATTING***
>
> This baseball card is mainly about Babe Ruth using his technique when batting. He said that he swings as hard as he can and he just keeps on swinging. Babe says that the y harder you grip the bat the more you can swing it through the ball, the farther the ball will go. When Babe Ruth retired he had over 40 American League hitting records.

Je Waya

> **SUMMARY OF *"THAR SHE BLOWS"***
>
> This baseball card is mainly about how far Babe Ruth hit the ball. Some of his home runs went 500 feet in the air. One of his hits went over the fennce of the stadium, over one of the streets, over the roof of a house, anther house, and two blocks awa. Babe's last game the ball went over the double-deck field. A length that has never been dun before

Successes

- **Student A** (Summary of *Babe on Batting* [baseball card]): This student successfully identifies the main idea of the card and then paraphrases two details to demonstrate the development of the idea. She ends with a final sentence that shows Babe's batting record.

- **Student B** (Summary of *"Thar She Blows"*): This student also begins by stating the main idea, and she also develops this idea through details.

On the Verge of Understanding

- **Student A:** I think this student met the criteria very well. There's not anything substantive I would change about this response.

- **Student B:** This student mostly parrots back details in the exact wording of the text without making the language her own. She also includes too many very specific details: *Over the fence of the stadium, over one of the streets, over the roof of a house, another house, and two blocks away.*

Next Instructional Point

- **Student A:** Move on to a different skill. This student doesn't need to spend too much more time reinforcing nonfiction summarizing.

- **Student B:** Spend some time paraphrasing key ideas so that the message is retained, but in language that belongs to the student, not the author. Also, show how you can capture an idea without using details that are too small. (Instead of all of the details above: *Babe hit those balls way out of the stadium.*)

From Meriden, Connecticut

Understanding the connection between events

The Inside Scoop

My professional development in Meriden kicked into high gear this year when the district decided it wanted to design a close reading curriculum for Grades 3 through 5, and my name made it to the top of the short list. Writing curriculum is never a smooth process, but here's what this district did right that made the job immeasurably easier: There were only four members of the curriculum team. It may sound overwhelming for four people to be tasked with producing units and close reading lessons for three entire grades. But when it comes to writing curriculum—less is more. Too many writers in the mix yields inconsistencies in quality, even when there's a lesson planning template and you think everyone understands *perfectly*. These people even tied their units to social studies and science standards, an additional challenge, but worth the effort.

So when I was looking for a site for obtaining the photographs for this book, I asked if we could use one of Meriden's elementary schools. On a steamy day in June, a professional photographer arrived on the scene at John Barry Elementary School along with the whole curriculum team, several literacy coaches, the district's curriculum director, other assorted administrators, my Corwin editor, Wendy, and me. I wished it had occurred to me before the previous afternoon that it would be nice to lose twenty-five pounds before the camera trained its lens on me. But other than that, everything went well. To get some authentic kid action, I taught a couple of close reading lessons. The work sample here is from a fifth grade lesson on the book *Up the Learning Tree* from the unit on slavery. The follow-up task focused on the sequence of events, not just the events themselves, but also what connected one event to another. This coherence is a major emphasis of the Common Core. Students worked in pairs.

Up the Learning Tree: Making Connections between Events

My group: Jaalah gale   Jamieonna

1. Mistress asked Henry to walk Master Simon to school.

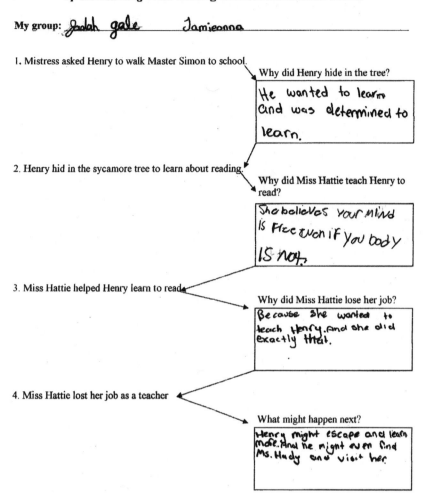

Why did Henry hide in the tree?

He wanted to learn and was determined to learn.

2. Henry hid in the sycamore tree to learn about reading.

Why did Miss Hattie teach Henry to read?

She believes your mind is Free even if you body is not.

3. Miss Hattie helped Henry learn to read.

Why did Miss Hattie lose her job?

Because She wanted to teach Henry. And she did exactly that.

4. Miss Hattie lost her job as a teacher

What might happen next?

Henry might escape and learn more. And he might even find Ms. Hady and visit her.

- These students consistently recognized the connection between events.

- They used concepts we discussed through our close reading: determination, a free mind versus a free body, and living by your principles.

On the Verge of Understanding

- The final prediction here isn't exactly realistic. It's what these students *want* to happen, not what the evidence in the text suggests. Several other students showed this same thinking.

Next Instructional Point

- Work on inferences based on evidence.

- Read a portion of a story and ask students to write an ending that follows logically from the first part of the text.

From Greenland, New Hampshire

What We're Monitoring

Connecting reading and writing through author's craft

The Inside Scoop

These are the two teachers I knew for a single day, but even that might be a bit of an exaggeration. They attended a regional close reading workshop I presented in Bedford, New Hampshire. We talked during one of the breaks. Or more accurately, they talked and I croaked some kind of response. I was on Day Three of a four day/four city professional development blitz and came down with an epic case of laryngitis by noon of my first day. Every utterance was painful and was surely equally stressful for my audience who had to suffer along with me. Somehow, these two teachers were not dissuaded by my pathetic workshop delivery and still liked close reading at the end of the day. We continued our dialogue through e-mail, and before long, I gave them an assignment: could they please teach a couple of close reading lessons for me to their third graders and get me some feedback? (Warning: this is what happens to teachers who send me e-mails after a workshop: I give them work).

The feedback I'm sharing here is from a lesson these teachers taught from the *Home* unit. This task is related to the Cynthia Rylant book *Let's Go Home* and asks students to write about a room of their own or a "dream room" in Rylant's same style. The teacher included the model she had crafted with the class, before they attempted their own writing, in which she wrote about a deck. Clearly, her teaching hit upon all of the salient points of Rylant's word choice, tone, and phrasing, or she would not have gotten back a piece of writing from a third grader that looked like this:

Piper

Your very own
bedroom is

a special place. The warm

and cozy bed becons you

to stay just awile. It

pulls you in and keeps

you there, huddled up in blankets

until you can take

and stuffed animals. , lush

no more
of the
welcoming

pillows comfort you. The

dresser oh my! Wonderful clothes

and glitter.

with sparkles and sequins,

Pretty as a dimond. The toys

flip and flop allaround

the room like a frog on a rainy day!

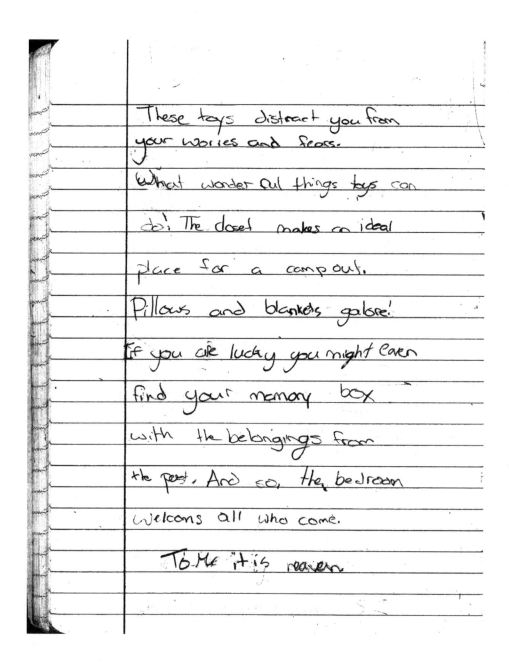

These toys distract you from
your worries and fears.
What wonderful things toys can
do. The closet makes an ideal
place for a campout.
Pillows and blankets galore!
If you are lucky you might even
find your memory box
with the belongings from
the past. And so, the bedroom
welcomes all who come.
To Me it is heaven

Successes

- Check out those verbs: *beckons, pulls you in, huddled, flip and flop, distract.*

- Check out the visual imagery: *huddled up in blankets and stuffed animals, wonderful clothes with sparkles and sequins and glitter,* and *pretty as a diamond.*

- Check out the well-crafted sentence fragments: *The dresser, oh my, pillows and blankets galore,* and *to me it is heaven.*

- Check out the wisdom: *These toys distract you from your worries and fears; if you're lucky you might find your memory box.*

On the Verge of Understanding

- Move over, Cynthia Rylant. You've got a little competition here. This child is on the verge of understanding so many things about author's craft. Is she aware of all of these crafts that she so expertly worked into her writing? Or did she somehow intuit the mood, and the words sort of appeared accidentally?

Next Instructional Point

- There's a better chance this student will be able to produce other great writing like this if she's aware of the author's crafts she is using. Instruction should include opportunities to learn about different writer's craft devices, name them, find them in literature, and apply them in writing of various kinds.

From North Haven, Connecticut

Supporting claims with evidence and insights

The Inside Scoop

The remaining student work samples were obtained from a longtime friend and colleague, Jeanne Savoia. Jeanne and I first connected when she was a student in several of my graduate reading courses at the university where I taught. We've stayed connected because we share so many of the same affinities for quality literacy instruction. Furthermore, she teaches in the district where I taught for many years; talking to her is like going back to my roots.

Lots of teachers taught wonderful lessons in support of this book. Jeanne taught a whole unit. When she agreed to this early in the winter, she may not have factored in the mountain of new initiatives heaped on her teacher-plate this year: new Common Core assessments, new teacher evaluation system, new, new, new. So it was June before I heard back from her: Could I stop by her classroom to hear the kids reflect on the *Leadership* unit they had been exploring? I was traveling at the time, but said I'd be home by June 20th and would be delighted to stop by about noon. "Perfect!" Jeanne replied. "It's the last day of school. We dismiss at 1:00."

An hour before dismissal on the last day of school didn't sound perfect to me, but I couldn't pass up this chance to see what Jeanne's class of fifth graders had done with this study. I was glad I took the time to find out. These students had studied all of the anchor texts and the accompanying nonfiction article. Witnessing their discussion was like stepping into a high school seminar. There were so many cross text connections, insights into the minds of Nelson Mandela, Jackie Robinson, and even some of the individuals specified in the assessment texts that I could barely keep track of the brilliance. I was praying for no hard questions directed at me since the students' command of these texts was much more current than my own. At the end of the session, Jeanne handed me a bundle of their written responses, which I later savored in the quiet of my front porch, iced tea in hand. Below, I provide two work samples that address the critical area of supporting generalizations with evidence and insights.

Nadia Kavgac

Testing the Ice- True Story About Jackie Robinson

By Sharon Robinson

012

What is the theme of the text and what evidence supports that theme?

The theme of the text is to have courage.
I know this because in the text it stated, "Now,
years have passed, and we understand even
more how much courage it took for my
father to step out on the ice." Jackie Robinson
also had courage when he was playing
baseball. I know this because in the text it
stated, "In fact, Dad showed the same
courage on the ice that day as he did when
he broke the color barrier in
baseball."

By: Carly Fresh

Nelson Mandela

By Kadir Nelson

012

What are three characteristics that contributed to Mandela's success? Provide an example of each trait form the text?

Three characteristics that contributed to Mandela's success are sacraficial, smart, and wise.

Nelson was sacratical because he was in prison for 27 1/2 years and didn't get to see his family. I know this by a picture of Nelson Mandela at the window of his jail cell in the Utube "Fly Like an Eagle." He had sorrow on his face, which showed me he sacraficed 27 1/2 hard sad years.

He was wise because, also in the same Utube, there is a picture of his quote "The brave man is not he who does not feel fear but he who conquers that fear." This shoulded both that he was wise but also smart because he tought people that it is okay to be afraid but if you want to be brave you must conquer the

012

After watching and listening to the video- the line "Fly like an eagle for you were born to fly," fear in convey the theme of Nelson Mandela's life?

only a fe powerful words.

The theme of Nelson Mandela's life is sacrific. I think that this is the thene because, as it stated in the text, Nelson Mandela spent 27 1/2 years in prison. This shows he sacraficed 27 1/2 years being away from his family & friends, all he saw cold hard walls. secondly Nelson lost happiness during his long term of jailing. I know that he was un-happy because the picture of him looking out window of his cell with sorrow on his face showed me he felt like he was in a cage, and wanted to break free to help his people. The quote "Fly like an Eagle" represents the fact he had to open his wings an fly to help others to do so too.

Successes

- **Student A:** This student accurately identified a theme, found two examples, and included quotes as evidence.

- **Student B:** This student also correctly identified a theme and included evidence—but took an additional step by offering an insight: "This shows . . ." This is a goal we should set for all students.

On the Verge of Understanding

- **Students A and B:** A complex text often has multiple themes. These students could be encouraged to draw more than one theme from the books they read closely.

- **Student A:** This student is ready to take the next step: using the evidence to formulate an insight.

Next Instructional Point

- **Students A and B:** Phrase questions about theme so students are encouraged to look for multiple themes, not just a single theme. Also ask for an insight: Instead of "What is the theme of the text and what evidence supports that theme?" use language such as, "What themes do you find in this text? Identify at least two themes and support each one with evidence as well as what this evidence means to you."

- **Student A:** Confer with this student about ways she could strengthen her response by adding an insight. Model this and provide some examples. Show possible wording to use: "This evidence shows me that . . ."

More From North Haven, Connecticut

Synthesizing multiple texts

The Inside Scoop

One of the reasons we want to use these picture books within units rather than for stand-alone close reading lessons is that we then have a platform for students to synthesize their thinking across texts. In the question below, Jeanne Savoia asks her students to integrate their learning from three different books.

In your opinion, which individual that we have read about (Jackie Robinson, or Wesley) is most like Nelson Mandela in terms of leadership qualities? Explain using evidence from the text.

In my opinion Jackie Robison is more like Nelson Mandela in terms of leadership qualities than Wesley. I say this for 2 reasons, 1.) Nelson & Jackie were fighting for the same cause 2.) Jackie risked his and his people's dignity while Wesley risked his own.

Jackie and Nelson were both fighting for the equalizum of black people. Jackie fought for his people by paving the way for other black people to come and play baseball. Also fighting for black people in South Africa.

Secondly Jackie Robinson made huge risk for not only his dignity but for the dignity of his many people. Nelson did the same, he risked his dignity, ~~my own~~ 27½ years of his life, and of many other black people's dignity. As they are the same in a risk taking Wesley only risked his dignity, only changing 1 life while Nelson and Jackie changed many.

Successes

- The student clearly stated her opinion and identified two reasons, both of which show excellent inferential thinking about abstract ideas (fighting for the same cause and dignity).

- The student supplied well-aligned evidence, which was paraphrased in her own words.

- This student provided a counterargument to further strengthen her position (Wesley risked only his dignity and only for one person).

On the Verge of Understanding

- Remember to *always* provide evidence. The final part of this response, while specifying a counterclaim, does not actually elaborate on that claim.

Next Instructional Point

- This is not quite an "instructional point" because I'm sure this student is aware of the need to provide evidence. But we can never provide too many reminders about *always* including evidence.

Reflecting on Trends

We could look at individual student work samples in a thousand different ways and still find more to observe and discuss. Continue this process yourself by choosing areas of focus that you want to monitor. Additionally, look for trends that you find while assessing a class set of your students' work. See Reflecting on Class Performance for a Close Reading Follow-Up Task to get a sense of how helpful this kind of analysis can be. What do you see?

Reflecting on Class Performance for a Close Reading Follow-Up Task

Text: *Home Run*

Task: Summarizing baseball cards

Teacher: Mrs. Troccolo and Mrs. Kotsaftis (co-teaching)   **Grade:** 4

What did you see from students who performed well on this task? (Try to be specific: What made their responses strong?)

Response Numbers 1, 2, and 3

- Main Idea is identified in the beginning of each response and supported with direct evidence from the text
- Responses are concise—stay on topic
- Students use their own words ("technique" in response no. 1)
- Quotes from text (student doesn't use " " though—response no. 1)
- Responses are "fluent"—not choppy; one sentence connects to the next

What would be a next step for students who did well on this task? (This could relate to both reading and writing)

Response Numbers 1, 2, and 3

- Independently research more on the topic of their card
- Research other baseball players that made a difference in this game
- Use teacher-provided lessons on how to directly quote from a source (response no. 1) and lessons on how to effectively use direct quotes in order to enhance their summaries
- Read and summarize longer text

What did you see from students who did not perform well on this task? (Try to be specific: In what ways were their responses weak? What were you hoping to see that you did not see?)

Response Numbers 4, 5, and 6

- Responses do not include a main idea statement in the beginning
- Response 4 includes a stream of facts from the text that are strung together

- Response 5 is directly copied from the text
- Response 6 is "choppy" with short sentences

What would be a next step for students who did not do well on this task? (This could relate to both reading and writing)

Response Numbers 4, 5, and 6

- Students could benefit from instruction on identifying the main idea or theme of text
- Students could benefit from instruction on paraphrasing
- Students could benefit from instruction on sentence fluency
- Students could benefit from the use of a summary frame and rubric

Reflecting on Class Performance for a Close Reading Follow-Up Task

Text: *Going Home* by Eve Bunting

Task: T-Chart on opportunities and paragraph

Teacher: Hoppe and Simons   **Grade:** 3

What did you see from students who performed well on this task? (Try to be specific: What made their responses strong?)

Students that performed well were able to infer the opportunities in either country without support. They were able to elaborate on the specific opportunities by giving examples. They were able to retain many details that were discussed during the lesson.

What would be a next step for students who did well on this task? (This could relate to both reading and writing)

These students may benefit from each choosing a specific side (United States and Mexico) and having some sort of oral debate.

What did you see from students who did not perform well on this task? (Try to be specific: In what ways were their responses weak? What were you hoping to see that you did not see?)

Students that did not perform well had a difficult time picking out the opportunities in each country. It was beyond their understanding. I was hoping that these students would at least be able to pick out the opportunities mentioned in the book, but there were some that could not.

What would be a next step for students who did not do well on this task? (This could relate to both reading and writing)

An activity that gives them more background knowledge on Mexico, especially rural villages. They may need to read books about Mexico as well as migrant farmers. Then, just write a paragraph about the opportunities that are in Mexico versus United States.

You may have noted some additional insights derived from these reflections. Here are a few points I discovered that could be helpful to these teachers' future instructional planning:

- They identified very specific things that students were doing well and not so well (such as infer opportunities, staying on topic, stating the main idea in the first sentence, no main idea stated, copied from the text). This will make it easier to choose a subsequent lesson objective.

- They recognized the importance of background knowledge and suggested that students obtain this knowledge through other texts—not from the teacher just handing it to them.

- They had a plan for supporting advanced students in addition to the students who struggled (independent research, debating)

It may seem that taking the time to reflect systematically on student work is too time consuming and that you can support your students just as well by filling out the rubric for one child and moving on to the next kid and the next. Sometimes I think that too—until I take the time to appraise the "why" behind the score for a particular child, or study the trends hidden among student responses for a whole set of papers. Nowhere will this kind of analysis be more important than it is in close reading where the standards are high and the text is complex. Taking this final planning step is your pledge to go the whole distance in achieving the maximum benefit in meeting your students' literacy needs.

References

Works Cited

Blauman, L., & Burke, J. (2014). *The Common Core companion: The standards decoded, Grades 3–5: What they say, what they mean, how to teach them*. Thousand Oaks, CA: Corwin.

Boyles, N. (2012). *That's a GREAT answer! Teaching literature-response strategies to elementary, ELL, and struggling readers* (2nd ed.). Gainesville, FL: Maupin House.

Boyles, N. (2014). *Closer reading, grades 3–6: Better prep, smarter lessons, deeper comprehension*. Thousand Oaks, CA: Corwin.

Bruner, J. (1960). *The process of education*. Cambridge, MA: Harvard Education Press.

Coherence. (n.d.). *The American Heritage dictionary of the English Language* (4th ed.). (2003). Retrieved from http://www.thefreedictionary.com/coherence

Dowson, N. (2011). *North: The amazing story of arctic migration*. Somerville, MA: Candlewick Press.

Guthrie, J. T. (n.d.). Contexts for engagement and motivation in reading. Retrieved from International Reading Association, http://www.readingonline.org/articles/handbook/guthrie/index.html

LaMarche, J. (2002). *The Raft*. New York: HarperCollins.

National Governors Association Center for Best Practices & Council of Chief State School Officers. (2014). *Common Core English language arts standards/anchor standards/college and career ready anchor standards in reading*. Washington, DC: Author. Retrieved from www.corestandards.org/ELA-Literacy/CCRA/R

Pearson, P. D., & Gallagher, M. C. (1983). The instruction of reading comprehension. *Contemporary Educational Psychology, 8*(3), pp. 317–344.

Anchor Texts

Ada, A. F. (2007). *Extra! Extra! Fairy-tale news from Hidden Forest*. New York, NY: Atheneum Books.

Ausch, M., & Ausch, H. (2002). *The princess and the pizza*. New York, NY: Scholastic.

Bruchac, J. (1992). *Thirteen moons on turtle's back: A Native American year of moons* (J. London, Ed.). New York, NY: Philomel Books.

Bunting, E. (1996). *Going home*. New York, NY: HarperCollins.

Burleigh, R. (1991). *Flight: The journey of Charles Lindbergh*. New York, NY: Philomel Books.

Burleigh, R. (1998). *Home run: The story of Babe Ruth*. New York, NY: Harcourt Brace.

Burleigh, R. (2006). *Tiger of the snows: Tenzin Norgay: The boy whose dream was Everest*. New York, NY: Atheneum Books.

Burleigh, R. (2008). *Abraham Lincoln comes home*. New York, NY: Macmillan.

Burleigh, R. (2011). *Night flight: Amelia Earhart crosses the Atlantic*. New York, NY: Simon & Schuster.

Burleigh, R. (2013). *Look up! Henrietta Leavitt, pioneering woman astronomer*. New York, NY: Simon & Schuster.

Cherry, L. (1992). *A river ran wild*. New York, NY: Scholastic.

Crelin, B. (2009). *Faces of the Moon*. Watertown, MA: Charlesbridge.

DK in association with Unicef. (2002). *A life like mine: How children live around the world*. New York, NY: Dorling Kindersley.

Fleischman, P. (1999). *Weslandia*. Somerville, MA: Candlewick Press.

Floca, B. (2009). *Moonshot: The flight of Apollo 11*. New York, NY: Simon & Schuster.

Goodman, S. (2004). *On this spot: An expedition back through time*. New York, NY: HarperCollins.

Ieronimo, C. (2014). *A thirst for home: A story of water across the world*. New York, NY: Bloomsbury.

Johnson, D. (1993). *Now let me fly: The story of a slave family*. New York, NY: Simon & Schuster.

Johnston, T. (1996). *The cowboy and the black-eyed pea*. New York, NY: Putnam & Grosset.

Kalman, M. (2012). *Looking at Lincoln*. New York, NY: Penguin Books.

Joyce, W. (2011). *The man in the moon: The guardians of childhood*. New York: Atheneum Books.

Kamkwamba, W., & Mealer, B. (2012). *The boy who harnessed the wind*. New York, NY: Penguin Books.

Kunhardt, E. (1993). *Honest Abe*. New York, NY: Greenwillow Books.

Nelson, K. (2013). *Nelson Mandela*. New York, NY: HarperCollins.

O'Malley, K. (2005). *Once upon a cool motorcycle dude*. New York, NY: Walker.

Pinkney, A. (2009). *Sojourner Truth's step-stomp stride*. New York, NY: Disney Book Group.

Rappaport, D. (2008). *Abe's honest words: The life of Abraham Lincoln*. New York, NY: Hyperion Books.

Robinson, S. (2009). *Testing the ice: A true story about Jackie Robinson*. New York, NY: Scholastic.

Rylant, C. (2002). *Let's go home: The wonderful things about a house*. New York, NY: Simon & Schuster.

Schroeder, A. (1996). *Minty: A story of young Harriet Tubman*. New York, NY: Penguin Books.

Strauss, R. (2007). *One well: The story of water on Earth*. Tonawanda, NY: Kids Can Press.

Vaughan, M. (2003). *Up the learning tree*. New York, NY: Lee & Low Books.

A SAGE Company

Corwin is committed to improving education for all learners by publishing books and other professional development resources for those serving the field of PreK–12 education. By providing practical, hands-on materials, Corwin continues to carry out the promise of its motto: **"Helping Educators Do Their Work Better."**